INTRODUCTION

Some account of Joseph Mainzer's early musical life in Germany, Belgium and France, his emigration to England, and the circumstances which led to the publication of *Singing for the Million* as a textbook for his London classes, appears in the Introduction to that book published in the present series. Mainzer's *Music and Education* was a treatise of a different sort, written seven years later when he had left London and made Edinburgh the centre of his activities.

Scotland then possessed a well-documented folksong tradition; but at a time when almost the only opportunity for ordinary folk to experience 'art music' was at church, narrow Presbyterianism had effectively destroyed the choral element in worship. Under two and a half centuries of Calvinist influence the organ was rigorously banned in churches, congregational song was limited to a dozen plain psalm tunes, but Genevan example had not been followed to the extent of providing musical instruction for churchgoers. Singing in churches was consistently bad. And though attempts at reform had begun in the second half of the eighteenth century, the people's efforts at psalmody were still described as 'discordant bawling and drawling' early in the century that followed.[1] It was toward remedying the dearth of

1. Millar, Patrick, *Four Centuries of Scottish Psalmody*, London, 1949, pp. 193-5

choral skill in Scotland that Joseph Mainzer had been invited to Edinburgh by the city's Lord Provost in October, 1842.

During eighteen months already spent in England Mainzer soon realised that much wider opportunities existed there for developing singing classes than had been the case in France. Although thirty years had passed since music teaching was formally admitted to the schools of Paris, far from spreading throughout the provinces, it had still 'scarcely reached the suburbs'.[2] In England, on the other hand, the drive to develop music teaching was nationwide and supported by central government. Mainzer thus found it possible to establish singing schools in many provincial towns— attracting enrolments by first making a personal visit, then leaving direction of the classes to his approved deputies. The Lord Provost's invitation afforded an opportunity for him to extend his activities even further afield, across the border into a land where policy was not decided by the English Committee of Council on Education, and where their seal of approval upon Hullah's rival teaching *Manual* presented no serious handicap.

During his first year in Scotland Mainzer travelled widely, setting up provincial centres in his accustomed manner. In response to those dour Scots who opposed his campaign and claimed that musical antipathy was a longstanding and desirable national characteristic Mainzer conducted an investigation of his own into the country's musical past. This revealed the existence, alongside a

2. *infra*, p. 89

CLASSIC TEXTS IN
MUSIC EDUCATION 12

MUSIC AND EDUCATION

CLASSIC TEXTS
IN MUSIC EDUCATION

GENERAL EDITOR of the Series
BERNARR RAINBOW MEd PhD

Joseph Mainzer

MUSIC AND EDUCATION

(1848)

Introduced by
BERNARR RAINBOW

Reproduced under the direction
of Leslie Hewitt for
BOETHIUS PRESS

Additional Material
© 1985 Boethius Press Limited
Clarabricken, Clifden
Co Kilkenny, Ireland

and

Bernarr Rainbow

 British Library Cataloguing in Publication Data

Mainzer, J.
Music and education (1848).—(Classic texts
in music education; 12)
1. Music in Education
I. Title II. Series
780'.7 ML83

ISBN 0-86314-045-9

The publishers would like to thank
Dr Bernarr Rainbow for lending his copy
for reprinting.

Printed by Boethius Press
Clarabricken, Clifden
Co Kilkenny, Ireland

wealth of folksongs, of many hitherto forgotten indigenous psalm tunes which he re-published with an introductory dissertation in two volumes in 1844.[3] And whatever may have been the objections raised by bigotry and prejudice, from the common folk themselves Mainzer received the warmest of welcomes. As a result, in several towns independent committees were formed 'for the promotion of musical instruction in schools and classical institutions'. With the formation of an Association for the Revival of Sacred Music Mainzer was formally appointed its Instructor.

It was at this encouraging stage of Mainzer's Scottish enterprise, in 1847, that a formal submission to the Town Council requesting that singing be taught in the exclusively classical High School, Edinburgh, was unexpectedly rejected by the subcommittee appointed to consider it.[4] Mainzer's response to this arrogant philistine rebuff was to write *Education and Music*, a book in which indignation and erudition make a telling partnership as the author draws upon his own wide reading to reveal to the members of the Town Council of Edinburgh just how close was the connection, imperceptible to them, between Music and Greek. Not content to leave the issue there, Mainzer went on to compile a complete treatise,

3. (a) *Illustrations of Ancient Scottish Psalmody: the Gaelic Psalm Tunes . . . with an Introductory Dissertation*, Edinburgh, 1844
   (b) *Highland Psalmody, the Sacred Melodies of Northern Scotland*, London, 1844. Mainzer also published *Standard Psalmody of Scotland*, London, 1845, which brought back to currency several forgotten tunes from the 1564 Psalter.
4. *infra*, p. viii, quoting *The Scotsman*, 22 September, 1847

unprecedented in Britain at that time and seldom equalled subsequently, defining the nature of Music in relation to its potential as an educational force.

Merely to turn Mainzer's pages consulting the footnotes alone reveals the astonishing breadth of resources upon which he drew. There are excerpts in half a dozen languages including the classical Greek so highly prized by his opponents on the Town Council at Edinburgh—a language in which Mainzer's prowess is revealed as at least equal to their own. A modern reader is left wondering just how Mainzer found the time among all his other commitments to research and compile this treatise. And even discounting such of his arguments as have lost their force in today's changed circumstances *Music and Education* remains a valuable quarry of relevant historical quotation for use today.

MUSIC AND EDUCATION

MUSIC

AND

EDUCATION.

BY

Dr. MAINZER.

LONDON:

LONGMAN, BROWN, GREEN, AND LONGMANS,

PATERNOSTER-ROW.

EDINBURGH: ADAM & CHARLES BLACK.

MDCCCXLVIII.

DEDICATED

MEMBERS OF THE

EDUCATIONAL INSTITUTE OF SCOTLAND.

CONTENTS.

INTRODUCTORY REMARKS.

At the conclusion of the Annual Report of the High School of Edinburgh, (1847,) we read the following lines by Dr. Schmitz, its Rector :—

" In regard to singing, no one in our days will venture to deny the salutary, refining, and moral influence which the practice of the art of music in general, and especially the music of the human voice, exercises upon youthful minds ; and it is confidently hoped, that both the patrons of the High School and the public at large, will heartily welcome and sanction the introduction of so powerful an agent, in inspiring our youthful pupils with a love of what is noble and beautiful. Singing once was the glory of Scotland ; and may it again become an ornament to the country, and serve in our churches to enhance our best feelings of piety and devotion."

This question of the introduction of singing into the High School came before the Town Council on the 21st September. Bailie Duncan, who had, with some others, been appointed as member of a committee to examine this subject, made his report, advising :[1] *that singing should not be taught; that the Scottish mind was not prepared for it; and that he could not see what connection Music had with Greek.* (A laugh.)

At the same time that the Town Council of Edinburgh was carrying such resolutions, committees were forming in several towns of Scotland for the promotion of musical instruction in schools and classical institutions; and from some of these towns we received letters, in which the writers, as by common consent, protested against the opinion of the City Magistrates in regard to the ripeness of Scotland for music. A teacher of the Canongate passed a more severe sentence on this decision, in saying, that he hoped the Town Council had only meant Edinburgh, and not the Canongate, as there the mind was quite prepared, and singing had been taught a long time. We fear, when we examine the question more closely, that it is not the Scottish mind, but the mind of the Town Council of Edinburgh, that is unprepared.

Since the Town-Council is not yet prepared to make mathematics, history, and the physical sciences, indispensable branches of a curriculum in a High School, can we expect it should be more so for the

[1] See *Scotsman* of 22d September 1847.

cultivation of the fine arts ?   Let us suppose that Latin and Greek had never been taught, and that their
introduction had been proposed instead of music; we
should have read in the *Scotsman* of the 22d, that the
College Bailie had moved, and that the Council had
unanimously approved of the resolution, that Greek
and Latin should not be taught; that the Scottish
mind was not prepared for it; and that they could not
see what connection these dead languages, the tongues
of heathen philosophers and popish priests, had to do
with the present youth of Scotland, who had a great,
and very pardonable predilection for the language of
their ancestors, and were not at all inclined to ex-
change it !   (Sensation.)

Although much inclined to indulge in a further
analysis of the exposition which the Town-Council
have made of their sentiments in regard to music, yet
we abstain.   We remark only, that we intended to
address a letter to the Lord Provost, Bailies, and
Councillors, on their resolution of the 21st September,
but the letter became a book.   Should they find it
surprising that they occupy a place in it, may they
consider, that since they have spoken of music, music
has a right to speak of them.   They will understand
in what relation music stands to the Town-Council,
although they cannot see what connection it has with
Greek.

At all events, the friends of youth, the friends of
education, those who appreciate music as an educational element, will thank me for having raised this

little public monument in honour of the Magistrates, as a memento of their services and patronage, bestowed with such lustre and enlightened views, upon science, literature, and art, especially that art which has been treated by them with such peculiar favour, and has enjoyed their unanimous recommendation, that it should not be taught: words of oracular importance, and which will mark a glorious epoch, both in the history of music and that of Town-Councils in Scotland.

PREFACE.

Dr. Johnson said, in his *Journey to the Western Islands:* " The character of a schoolmaster is less honourable in Scotland than in England ; it is therefore seldom accepted by men who can adorn it." Scotland seems to have but little felt this stigma thrown on the profession of the teacher, and the want of appreciation of so important a ministry of the public welfare. Almost a century passed, and not a step was taken towards its intellectual and social advancement. The teacher at last, filled with the importance of his mission, and forced by the claims which the progress of time and civilization imposed on him, rose to efface, from his profession and his country, a reproach unworthy of both. He thus called to his brethren : Let us advance in knowledge ! let us study ! let us unite ! if union be strength, study is knowledge !

The call was heard and re-echoed from every hill and every shore ; the light of hope, like the beacon-fire of former days, was seen from every village, and in a moment there stood eighteen hundred teachers, as a phalanx united, ready to defend the rights and claims due to the youth, and to the honour of their country.

The National Schools in Ireland, the Teachers Union of England, and the Educational Institute of Scotland, are heralds of a new era in the history of education in Great Britain. The hour in which the latter was decided, we consider the hour of the emancipation of the teacher in Scotland. From being the neglected, the despised member of society, he will, by his talents, superior accomplishments, and public usefulness, rise and reach that station which he deserves,—he in whose hands are the morality and happiness of the coming generation. This Institute, which placed itself high above all sectarian differences, and has thus shewn a superior spirit quite in conformity with the age, and worthy of the high vocation of the teacher, will become a powerful lever to raise the social and intellectual standing of that profession which cannot but be considered as one of the mightiest pillars of society and nations.

In dedicating the present work to the Educational Institute of Scotland, we do so, not that we deem the teachers particularly learned in music, or that they have bestowed particular attention on it, either as a science or an art; but because the Institute has, despite the national prejudices, acknowledged music as a branch of public instruction, as an element in the education of youth.

Yet there are still some who would rather impede than favour its cultivation in schools, as much from

a disappreciation of it, as from an exaggerated importance of the branches they teach. It can be de-
monstrated, that hitherto the Scottish teachers and
the Scottish clergymen are infinitely behind the
rest of Europe in the knowledge of music. The
stern Covenanter, though he fought at the battle
of Drumclog and Bothwell Bridge, to the tune of
John come kiss me now, or died singing psalms in the
midst of the crowd at the Grassmarket, or on the
heather of his solitary moors ; yet, his fright of a
fiddle, or a dance, in which he always saw the clo-
ven foot behind, has become well nigh the general
feeling of Scotland with regard to music. On the
other hand, singing has been too much associated
with drinking ; many sing only when they are drunk.
Can we wonder, then, that Music is not considered
an agent of mental and moral culture by those who
know it only as an art of debauchery, the priestess of
revels and public-houses ? Can we be surprised that
young men are peculiarly guarded against music,
when it is considered to be to them, what the flame is
to the moth—destruction ? But even this fear is a
new homage of its power, a genuflection before its
throne. The young man who knows music is sought,
is courted, and carried along in the whirlpool of youth.
If he were the rule and not the exception, were there
many such musical phœnixes, the individual would
not be so much thought of. If the family afforded
recreation through music, they would not want to
seek it elsewhere. A country which has allowed the

art to sink to so low an ebb, wears, like the galley-
slave, the chain of its own guilt.   How couldst thou
forget, land of song, home of the bard, " meet nurse
of a poetic child," Caledonia ! that there is also a
holy music, a music that lives, and loves, and suffers
with us, that raises the soul, bent in sorrow, out of the
dust, and bears it beyond the clouds ; a music that,
like an aurora of eternity, penetrates into the night
of life, cheers and illumines our path ! how couldst
thou forget that, like the rainbow, music is a me-
morial of a covenant between the earthly and the
celestial, blending equally, and reflecting all colours !
that she has accents for all nations, all ages ; that
every epoch of our life has its own tones : that to
the boy she appears, with his spring, his plays, his
birds and butterflies ; to the adolescent with his love
for every thing that is beautiful, great and elevating,
for liberty and country ; to the aged a sweet ripe
fruit of life and wisdom, a setting sun that throws a
purple veil over days and recollections of the past, and
brightens the pilgrim's path towards futurity.   He
who thus penetrates and reveres music, to him she is
the virgin of charity, who, with her love, her tears,
and her inspiring breath, is near him in all moments
and trials of life, a sister-soul in whose bosom he con-
fides every silent thought, and every emotion.

Thus has the Scottish Institute looked upon music,
and therefore has it acknowledged it an educational
element; a late and feeble homage paid to the art, but
a distant foreboding of better days to come. As it ap-

pears to us as a pharos of hope in the darkness of the night, we have associated our thought and our work with theirs ; and in exposing our principles, hope to strengthen and support their own, and shew how, in united zeal and activity, they can be realized for a country's welfare, and a nation's glory.

Music will no longer be a destitute child of persecution : it will become a welcome guest under every roof, in every cottage. Soon the youth will cease to be mute ; not a hundred children, but a hundred schools, will unite in love, and harmony, and innocence. In those sublime moments, when simple but graceful strains are carried upon thousands of infant voices, all will feel the power of the multitude, as Haydn did, in tears, when he heard the charity children of St. Paul's ; or, overcome by the majesty of simple grandeur, exclaim with Catalani, when she heard the primitive chants of the Grecian Church : " My song is of this world, but this is a choir of angels."

MUSIC AND EDUCATION.

I.

Origin of Music—Invention of Instruments—The Lyre, the Harp, the Bagpipe, the Organ—Vocal Music—Gradations of Music according to the Mental and Moral Development of a People.

MUSIC originates daily among us, as it originated thousands of years ago, under all climes, among all nations of the earth; for nature follows unchangeable laws. Sound, the first element of music, ere it rises to that degree of charm and power by which our admiration is fixed, presents itself as a very simple physical phenomenon, as the result of vibration communicated by the air. In this, its elemental state, it not only strikes our ear and acts on our nerves, but exercises an influence, more or less sensible, on objects even of inanimate creation. If we proceed from this point, and if we advance from the simple sound, the breath of air, towards the immensity of the ideal world in which it reigns as art, a whole empire lies extended before us, in which the soul feels as in a land of wonder and enchantment.

Every tightened string which vibrates in the air, every hollow tube through which the wind passes, taught man the use of instruments. A thick or long string or tube produces deep sounds; a thin or short, high ones. In this simple discovery lies the principle of all stringed and wind instruments. If the string be stretched upon a piece of wood, the finger which presses upon the board diminishes its length, and, consequently, raises the sound. The same result is obtained by making holes in the iron tube, or the wooden pipe. By covering or uncovering these holes with the fingers, we render the column of air contained in the tube longer or shorter, which, set in motion by the wind, or by the mouth, gives higher or lower notes. The notes which chance seems at first to produce, are, by a little skill and observation, brought into connection, and thus the regular scale of ascending and descending notes is established. When once in possession of an instrument, giving a more or less limited series of sounds, we begin to employ these sounds in a successive or inverted order, and thus produce a tune or melody. We select the notes from the scale, and compose a musical idea, as words and thoughts are expressed, by bringing the letters of the alphabet into a certain connection with each other. Thus music has been taught us by nature; we can witness its origin yet daily. Give to a child a string, and he will soon call you to listen to the music he makes, by fastening it between the finger and the teeth, and then by increasing or diminishing its tension, produce higher or lower sounds. This is the principle upon which stringed instruments are constructed, and it is so simple, that their invention seems almost the first that must occur to men in pastoral life. The strings of different size and length, generally furnished by the bowels of animals, are attached to a piece of wood, a sounding board; and, in this manner, we have an instrument which, in its different forms, has been called, in ancient and modern times, either the lute, the lyre, the cithara, or the harp. Its origin must as little be sought among the Hebrews, the Egyptians, or the inhabitants of the fabulous Atlantides, as among the Scythians, Goths,[1] or Britons, but over all the world, among all people, and in all times. Montfaucon examined 600 different kinds of lyres, citharas, and harps, without being able to discover any peculiar and *national* differences.[2] Those learned treatises, there-

---

[1] See Pinkerton's *Enquiry*, Vol. i., p. 390.
[2] Montfaucon, *Antiq. Expl.*, Tom. iii., lib. v., cap. 3.

fore—those erudite historical researches about the climate,
the people, or the century, which first gave birth and cultivation to music, are researches thrown away.[1] Music is as old
as mankind, and has been invented by every people upon the
globe. Wherever we find a people, however secluded or isolated, separated by sea or mountains from other people, there
we find music and musical instruments. Every shepherd
may be said to be its inventor. The reed on the moors, the
little pipe cut from the tree, are the parents of flute, clarionet,
oboe, and bassoon; the cow-horn is that of the horn, the
trumpet, and the trombone; a hollow tree, pieces of slate, of
iron, that of the instruments of percussion, drums, timbrels,
and cymbals.

If we follow these observations one step further, we shall
find, that, in proportion as musical skill progresses in the
construction of the instrument, musical inspiration rises in
the field of invention. The simple pastoral pipe must soon
have become insufficient. He who possessed one, would feel
that two or three connected together would produce more
effect; for a primitive taste will seek effect in strength. Two
or three pipes of different size were added to it; but there
were only two hands to cover and uncover the holes of the
one which was made to sing; therefore, each pipe would produce only one additional sound. There was, moreover, but
one mouth for the additional pipes, so that a more powerful
originator of wind was invented, in form of a bag; and thus
we find again, among all nations of ancient and modern times,
that pipe which is called the bagpipe. The contempt generally thrown upon this ungraceful child of antiquity, I do not
participate in. This uncouth instrument, low as is its standard among the more perfect and more civilized means of communicating sound, has an interest of a manifold kind, and
holds among popular instruments the first rank, as being one
of the oldest and most universally known. The bagpipe,
moreover, although a humble pastoral instrument in its ori-

[1] Some Scotch historians are puerile enough to say, that James I. of
Scotland, others that Rizzio, were the inventors of the Scotch music.

gin, became a warlike instrument among the Romans,[1] and is still so among the sons of ancient Caledonia. The bag-pipe, limited in its mechanism, poor in its expression, is not, on these accounts, deficient in the accents of joy and grief; and no instrument has been a closer witness of heroic deeds; none has ever found a warmer echo in warmer hearts! Many pipers have died as heroes; the history of pipe-tunes is the history of battles; and these are the bloody records of the history of a country. The pipe deserves more than any other its biographer. The interest it lacks in polite society, it amply compensates for in popular life. Though unfit for the drawing-room, it was not found unfit for the field of battle. The piano and violin, which reign in the former with a glorious and well-deserved supremacy, would, under the thunder of the cannon, but miserably supply its place. The principal merit of this instrument, however, re-mains to be told. Although one of the humblest and coarsest, it is the parent of the grandest, the most magnifi-cent, the most complete—the organ; not without reason call-ed the wonder of art. The bag has grown into the bellows, and two or three pipes into hundreds.[2] The principle upon which the sounds are produced, is in both exactly the same.

Not only is the invention of musical instruments found among all nations, but vocal music also belongs to man by nature. The child even, when building its miniature palaces of cards or erecting mountains and cities of sand, hums me-lodies never heard, never learned before, and invents, like the inhabitant of the groves, unconsciously, its own little

---

[1] Procopius, Lib. ii., cap. 22. It was called *tibia utricularis* or *chorus*, (from *corium,* skin), among the Romans; and ἄσκαυλος (see ἀσκαύλης, the bagpiper, mentioned by Dio Chrysostomus) among the Greeks. From the Italian *cornomusa*, the French call it *cornemuse* or *musette*. The name *Bock* (he-goat), which the Poles give to this instrument, comes from their using for the bag the skin of a he-goat, to which they leave the head, with beard and horns attached.

[2] Upon a medal of Nero, we find a flute of Pan, a *Syrinx*, with a num-ber of pipes growing gradually less, attached to bellows; exactly the di-minutive organ, our organ in its infancy.—See *Dr Burney's History of Music*, Vol. i., p. 501.

warbling tunes. When more advanced in age, the feelings
and emotions which occupy the human breast find relief in
song. We may hear the voice of the young shepherd of the
Pyrenean, the Swiss, or the Tyrolean Alps, expressing in
wild, irregular strains, the actual sentiment of his soul—his
happy or his melancholy mood. What inhabitant of the
South Sea Islands can be more unacquainted with music
than he ? and yet his voice may be heard morning and evening; and his notes are often answered from the distant rock
by another voice; and, it may be, that before the snow
drives the herds from the summer pastures, both singers
have passed the precipices which separated them, and inhabit
the same *Alma*.

Although circumstances and natural scenery change the
manners and habits of life, man is the same every where. He
seeks communication—he seeks sympathy ; and when distance is wide—when precipices and rivers divide him from
his fellow creatures, nature points out the same means: the
modulation of speech will be replaced by the modulation of
song. Even the lifeless voice of the echo, in seclusion and
solitude, has charms ; and where there is an ear to listen,
and even where there is but an echo, there soon will be a
voice to speak or to sing.

The tones of song are carried farther than those of speech.
Ask of those thousand singers, of those men, women, and
children, who, in the streets, sell the commonest objects of
life, why they announce their approach to the inhabitants of
the populous city by a chant instead of a short speech ?
Their voice must reach their customers, whether they be in
kitchens, cellars, or attics ; and, therefore, in all countries,
and under all climes, they sing. Hence those thousand
songsters, those innumerable different melodies, that strike
you first when you enter a large city. Wherever you go, by
day or night, you meet them at every turn. The doleful cry
of the little chimney-sweeper in London—the argentine voice
of the little Savoyard in Paris—penetrate, long before day-
light, into the most hidden recesses of your alcove, and call
you without mercy from your deepest, sweetest dreams, and,

with a cruel monosyllable, destroy the enchanting gardens of Armida, through which you were borne as upon eagles' wings. The same may happen to you at Rome, at Naples, at St Petersburg, or in Rio Janeiro.   Those who sell water in the streets of Paris, as they must be heard beyond the rolling thunder of carriages, and the sound must reach the sixth and seventh floor, have a cry, which much resembles a cry of distress—that of a man who, too late, calls over from one shore to the other for the ferry boat; or of one who, from the midst of the consuming flame, cries for a helping hand.[1] The Sakas in Mecca, who, with water, offer paradise and salvation to the passing pilgrims, sing, on the contrary, in a quiet, sacred strain, their *Sebyl Allah!*" [2] Necessity, the great teacher of man in all other things, is also his teacher in music.   What the desires of the mind, its dispositions and feelings, leave unaccomplished, circumstances bring into being.   The same that we observe daily around us, travellers and historians have told of the people of other hemispheres and other ages.   Sailors in hoisting masts, masons in lifting huge stones, have special tunes to give uniformity to their exertions.   The boatman, to relieve the monotonous movement of the oar, has his song likewise; and the little melodies of this latter are on every coast to be found, as well in Arabia as among the fishermen of the Feroe Islands, or the gondoliers of the Venetian lagunes.   We must all be familiar with those tunes with which mariners facilitate their wearisome labour, and gain regularity of step in dragging their boats against the stream.   The beautiful description which Ovid gives of this, we find still realized, after almost two thousand years, by all those who navigate on canals and inland rivers.[3]   This may lead us to understand why, when

---

[1] See my Work, *Les Cris de Paris.*   Paris: Chez Curmer.
[2] Burckhard's *Travels in Arabia.*
[3]   —— Hoc est cur . . . .
     Cantet et innitens limosae pronus arenae
        Adverso tardam qui trahit amne ratem.
     Quique ferens pariter lentos ad pectora remos,
        In numerum pulsa brachia versat aqua.
                    Ovid.   Lib. Trist. iv. 1.

Lysander destroyed the walls of Athens, he caused all the musicians of his army to play during the operation of the workmen. Chardin, in his Travels in Persia, says, that oriental nations cannot accomplish any work which requires great bodily exertion, without a regular noise of some kind." [1]

Music, therefore, is natural to man. To man, in combat with toil, it is the handmaid of necessity; to man at rest and in abundance, it is a recreation. Among the former, it will always bear a rougher stamp, and will be characterized more by a strongly marked rhythm than by melody; among the latter, melody will predominate; and, as being in closer connection with the sentiments, will come more and more under the dominion of art. It would, therefore, be in vain were we to expect to hear, every where alike, regular and expressive melodies.

The music of a people depends upon their mental and moral development. The first impressions man receives are those communicated by the senses. From them he passes to those which are the result of reflection, and bear the stamp of a higher, a more intellectual nature. The life of a nation is the same as that of an individual; the nearer a man is to the state of nature, the more he is under the dominion of the senses. The advance a people may have made in civilization, may easily be determined by the means they use to awaken their feelings or to gratify them. Drums, and rude pipes, or whistles, are the instruments of a savage people; their songs are cries, shouts, and a sort of monotonous howling. The warrior and the hunter like horns, drums, whistles, bells, and every instrument that conveys sound to a distance, and produces noise, and, through it, excitement; but to the fisherman, the shepherd, music soon ceases to be mere noise;

[1] Burckhard, in his *Travels in Arabia,* makes many similar remarks. The Arabs or Persians, on their pilgrimage to Mecca, especially when navigating in boats, replace the want of instruments, by clapping their hands in a certain rhythmical movement. A French traveller says:—
" Les Arabes ne peuvent pas exécuter le plus léger travail qui exige un peu d'accord et d'ensemble, sans entonner de chants simples et monotons, qui ne laissent pas d'avoir une certaine harmonie. Il est rare qu'on voit passer une barque sur le Nil sans entendre chanter les mariniers."

they have no desire to be heard but from rock to rock, or from grove to grove, like the shepherds of Theocritus and Virgil.

Music extends itself with the circle of feeling, as language does with that of thought. As soon as it was possible to convey a sense, a meaning, a sigh, by a succession of sounds, music gradually became a language—the language of the soul, of its dearest emotions ; music became an Art.

II.

Triple Effect of Music :—1st, Upon the Nerves ; 2d, As Remembrance ; and, 3d, As Art.

THE first effect that music produces is merely physical. Sounds strike the nerves of the ear, and make, according to their power, quality, character, roughness, or sweetness, analogous impressions upon our senses. Too powerful, too sudden strokes might occasion nervous convulsions, destroy the faculty of hearing, or even extinguish life. In the endless variety of organizations, an endless variety of sensations is awakened by one and the same sound. A delicate, sensitive ear is otherwise affected than that of a stronger, rougher nature. The tumult, the whistles, and the shrieks in which the latter delight, would throw the other into the highest state of alarm or discomfort. Hence the curious anecdotes of men who could not tolerate certain sounds, and who, on hearing particular instruments, became the subject of the most unaccountable nervous sensations, of which no other person was conscious. The beating of a drum produces in many persons a corresponding tremulousness in the chest. Some persons cannot refrain from weeping whenever they hear a certain note. J. J. Rousseau says, that he knew a lady who could not hear any kind of music without being seized with involuntary and convulsive laughter. The delicacy of the ear of Mozart was so great, that, without being modified by other instruments, he could not tolerate the sound of a trumpet. His father, who wished him to overcome this sensibility, took him one day by surprise with a violent blast of a trumpet. The boy shrieked, grew pale, and

fell senseless to the ground.[1] The monk of St Gallen tells
us of a woman, who, when she heard an organ for the first
time, was so transported with rapture, that she never reco-
vered from the effect, and died in consequence.[2] Certain
chords act in a peculiar manner upon some constitutions. Instances are known, where the second inversion of the perfect
chord causes feverish excitement; and a distinguished virtuoso
on the violoncello in Germany, cannot hear a composition in
the key of *B min.* without getting positively ill.[3] The effects
music produces upon the deaf born, and to whom the sense
of hearing has been restored, are extraordinary, though not
surprising. Often they feel oppression, short breath, trembling of the limbs, grow pale, or have a quick pulse, a burn-
ing face, headache, giddiness, and at last faint.[4]

Animals, as well as men, are accessible to the effect of
sound. It is generally admitted that the spider delights in
music, and that, like the large green lizard of Italy, it will
draw near and nearer to it. A blind man in Silesia, by
whistling a few notes, drew, as by enchantment, all the crabs
from their hiding-places to a certain spot, and had no trouble
in catching all that came within his hearing.[5] The musical
susceptibility of certain dogs is very remarkable. In the
year 1827, all Rome went to see a dog, who, every day,
marched at the parade, before the military band; in the
evening he was found sitting in the orchestra of the theatre
Della Valle; no one ever knew whence he came, or to whom
he belonged. Some dogs will whine at certain sounds of instruments; they are indifferent to some keys, and extremely
sensitive to others. Experiments have been made upon a
certain dog, in playing in different keys; *A maj.* made him
always uneasy, but a composition *in E maj.*, excited him so
much that, on one occasion, when the cruel experiment was
continued too long, the poor animal became furious, and died

[1] *Biography of Mozart,* by Nissen.
[2] See also, *Vie de Charlemagne,* par Gaillard, Tom. iii., p. 95.
[3] *Encyclopædie der Tonkunst,* Vol. v., p. 71.   Stuttgart.
[4] Magendie's *Physiologie,* Vol. i., from p. 242.
[5] See *Historia Morborum,* p. 567.   Breslau, 1720.

in the most frightful convulsions.[1] Well known is the remarkable effect of music tried in Paris in 1798, upon elephants.

But sounds not only act upon the nerves of man and animals,
but even upon inanimate objects. Glasses, mirrors, china
vases, have been seen to vibrate and break at certain sounds
of the flute, and notes of the human voice.[2] We may witness the latter in cathedrals, where certain pipes of the organ
cause a shaking of the windows, walls, and pillars. A
powerful bass voice in the lower notes, has, in a limited space,
the same effect upon chairs and tables.

Bartolini, in his work *on the flutes of the ancients*, gives
the most curious facts on the variety of musical effect on objects and individuals. It would be a labour of hours to read
only the titles of books communicated in Forkel's *Litera-
tur der Musik*, and Sulzer's *Theorie der Schönen Künste*,
and written by scientific men of all nations, on the effect of
music in bodily and mental disease. It would be necessary
to begin with Aristoxenus and Euclid, and enumerate works
in all languages, down to Rousseau and Buffon.

We see from these simple facts, that the magical power of
music is not always attributed to its right cause. We are
too often inclined to ascribe to the talent, either of the composer or of the performer, the whole merit of the wonderful
effects produced. Undoubtedly, the power of talent and
genius in the melodious and harmonious combinations of
sound should be acknowledged; but it must not be forgotten,
that there is in the nature of sound itself something mysteri-
ously affecting. A simple sound, by whatever physical cause
produced, similar to that which issued from Memnon's statue,[3]
or which is heard from Fingal's Cave at Staffa, excite in us,

---

[1] *Musical Gazette of Leipzig,* viii. Jahrgang, No. 26. Compare
Kausch's *Psychologische Abhandlung* über den Einfluss der Töne, und
insbesondere der Musik auf die Seele.

[2] See Bourdelot *Histoire de la Musique,* T. i., p. 51 ; comp. *Universal
Lexicon,* article *Musik,* Vol. xxii.

[3] The Colosse of Memnon issued, according to tradition, two sounds :
at the first ray of the sun, in the morning, the sound which was heard
was gay ; at the last ray, in the evening, it was plaintive. The sounds

with all their monotonous repetition, a something that either
fills us with melancholy or with awe.   At midnight, the
repeated call of the sailor who sounds the depth, or the blast
of a trumpet heard from a watch-tower or minaret, have in
them something solemn and majestic.   The evening bell of a
village church, sounds cheering and hospitable to every ear,
and vividly do its strokes bring back to our recollection, with
the days of infancy, our birth-place, the place where we
learned to know our first joy, our first sorrow ; for if certain
sounds act on the nerves, those which remind us of the past,
which express a sentiment and reveal a feeling, must have
an effect of a higher kind upon the soul.   It would be difficult to mark the limit where the operation upon the senses
and that upon the soul begins or ends.   These are mysteries
which lie beyond the surface of our attainments, but of which
we have, however, many indubitable proofs.   Melodies which
we heard in our childhood, a song—the poorest as music or
poetry—if it bring to our mind recollections of earlier and
happier times, if it remind us of places and occurrences, or
more still of persons whose memory lies near to our heart,
who can doubt that its effect will be powerful, and a thousand
times more so, than a composition infinitely richer, more regular, more harmonious and scientific ?   The *Rans des Vaches*,
is originally nothing but a melody composed of the three
notes of a chord, played by the shepherd upon the horn of a
cow, and is scarcely more than a signal of the cowherd of
the Alps ; hence its name *Kuhreigen* in German ; *Rans des
Vaches* in French.   Its charms, therefore, are not in its
music, but in the recollections of home and infancy.[1]   Its
sounds, like those of *Erin-go-bragh*, or *Lochaber no more*,

were heard until the IV. cent. of our era, when Probus restored it, and
thus probably destroyed the cause of the phenomenon.—See Letronne
Sur la Statue Vocale de Memnon, Paris, 1833.   Compare Anders *Sur la
Statue de Memnon.—Gazette Musicale de Paris*, Vol. i.

[1] " On chercherait en vain dans cet air les accens énergiques, capables
de produire de si étonnans effets.   Ces effets, qui n'ont aucun lieu sur les
étrangers, ne viennent que de l'habitude, des souvenirs de mille circon-
stances qui, retracés par cet air à ceux qui l'entendent, et leur rappelant

speak more strongly to the memory and the heart than to the ear. At these accents, as by enchantment, past years, with all their joy and sorrow, rise as from the tomb, and surround like phantoms the imagination of the exile. National airs are, in this respect, most deeply affecting, and volumes upon volumes might be filled with facts gathered in the Irish and Scotch regiments, in the American and Peninsular wars, in India and elsewhere, of their wonderful effect when heard in a foreign land. Soldiers and settlers feel, according to the character of the melody, raised to the utmost excitement, or moved to the deepest dejection. " We were at a ball," wrote a few days ago a young Scotchman, from one of the islands in the Pacific Ocean ; " we danced and were happy : when all at once, to please me, a Scotch tune was struck up. It seized me with such power, that I was quite overcome : I could stand it no longer, and was obliged to leave the company, in order to hide my tears and my emotion." How deeply a simple tune, heard in our youth, can strike into the recollection of the past days of our existence, is illustrated in a remarkable instance which happened in the Glasgow Lunatic Asylum, and which was told to the author by the very persons concerned in it. Some patients in the ladies' ward met in the evening in the room of the matron. They took tea, sang, and were cheerful. A Scotch song, however, disturbed the harmony of the party : it caused such violent emotion in one of the patients, that they were obliged to remove her from the company. The following day she came to see the matron, and said, " Do you know why I wept so much yesterday in hearing that song ? It reminded me of some circumstances of which I had long since lost all recollection." Gradually, in retracing step by step, occurrences and events of long-forgotten years, she came to a clear understanding and sound appreciation of

leur pays, leurs anciens plaisirs, leur jeunesse, et leur façon de vivre, excitent en eux une douleur amère d'avoir perdu tout cela. La musique alors n'agit pas precisément comme musique, mais comme signe commemoratif."—J. J. Rousseau, *Dictionaire de Musique*, art. *Musique*.

her own situation ; and not many weeks passed before she was restored to health and to her family.

All these effects scarcely belong as yet to music in its highest acceptation. As an art, it moves in a loftier sphere ; and owes, on the one side, nothing to the nerves, and on the other, nothing to remembrance. When out of the depth of imagination, and supported by the resources of science, a lofty idea appears, clothed in beautiful and analogous forms, perceptible to one of our senses,—then we have before us a work of art ; not *mechanical* art, which tends to satisfy some material exigencies, or serves some practical purpose, but which, as a free creation, is sufficient for and in itself, which in its individual completeness reveals to us a lofty thought, or awakens and satisfies some intellectual interest. Art is the earthly symbol of the creative power—the divinity in man : its object is, the perfectibility of mankind—the embellishing, ennobling of human existence. Man is endowed with a triple nature ; he can therefore not derive a true, a permanent enjoyment, from productions purely material ; his moral and intellectual powers must equally be occupied, find nourishment and satisfaction.

In the range of fine arts, those which penetrate the deepest with the least material element, must stand the highest. Music and poetry, therefore, occupy the first place : the latter is the communicating medium of the mind ; the former, of the soul. All other arts, painting, sculpture, architecture, are composed of grosser materials ; of tangible, visible elements ; of wood and of stone, of marble and of colour. They imitate living nature, but in them is no movement, no life, no action ; all is at rest, all is quiet, all is death. In music and poetry there is actual life ; there are accents of joy ; there are sighs and tears ; there is an ocean, with its calms and its passions, its restlessly going and coming tide : and all this action, all this life, is manifested in no representation of any outward object : they wield their power in untangible sounds, unembodied in any outward form, imperceptible to every eye. These two arts are born as twins ; their etherial origin stamps them as inseparable ; and in this double nature they are the most popular of all arts, and as old as man. It is this indefiniteness, this aerial nature of music, which makes an analysis of it so difficult, and which is the reason that mediocrity can risk a public exhibition in this, with much less danger of detection, than it can in any other of the arts. From the same cause, a good work will more easily escape attention, and will not always at first have that rank assigned to it which it deserves. The disadvantage is greater still when compositions purely instrumental are concerned, in which no assistance from the language of poetry comes to aid the language of sound.

The more the cultivation of the mind approaches perfection, the more complete will be the development of the musical taste; and we recede in the same proportion from the dry combinations of harmony, which are not animated by any genius, as from the empty sounds of a melody, which passes meaningless away. We will want compositions, in which melody, harmony, and rhythm combine in beauty and truth, and in which mind and understanding, imagination and feeling, at the same time attract and satisfy.

We learn from the great masters, that the manly and energetic character, the power and originality of the man of genius, do not manifest themselves in the employment of a great material mass, any more than by the greatest number of strokes on instruments of the greatest volume. We know works in which all arms and windpipes are set in motion, the trombones and drums thunder like artillery upon the deafened and defenceless ear, yet, with all this, we find therein no music : how different from the gigantic power developed by a Palestrina, an Orlando Lasso, a Marcello, a Clari, in *four*, in *three*, in *two* simple voices ! The great, the majestic, the imposing in art, are recognizable more in the design than in the colouring, more in the conception, the disposition and symmetry of the whole, than in the disproportionate details. " Let us all learn from Händel," says Beethoven, " to produce so great effects with so few means." The degree of sensibility, of elevation of soul, and a creative power, is, as it were, the distinctive mark of the artist,

which is stamped upon his work, and which raises it so high
above ordinary ones.   Men of taste will therefore seek the
influence and power of music, in another region than that
in which the greatest perfection in mechanical effects is alone
admired.   Composers or players who so excel, are not always, in our opinion, the greatest artists, nor the most deserving of the name.   We require something more than
dexterity, than skilful execution.   Many artists have attained this sort of excellence, whom we find but little calculated to inspire us with the taste and the love of the beautiful.   See the numerous musical prodigies that land from all
parts, and multiply like ants.   These applauded musical
stars are a part of what might be expected from the favour
with which mere mechanical effects are received.   It is a
mischief that has made great inroads in the domain of art:
it moves on with a speaking trumpet, calling all to come
around and admire it.   We are tired indeed of that unmeaning noise which says nothing to the soul, of the difficulties
surmounted by mere dexterity, and at expense of thought;
of the artifices without number, which do nothing to initiate
us in the true beauties of the most powerful of all arts.   We
know not what one day will become of music, if people allow themselves to be caught in those skilful snares by which
mountebanks pass for musicians, and a masterpiece of skill
and patience for a masterpiece of art.   No better warning
can be held out to the stream of corruption in which the
real art of music seems to combat for breath and life, than
in the simple, but energetic sentence pronounced by Roch-
litz, one of its truest admirers and greatest judges :—" Down
with musical composition that expresses nothing.   If music
is the language of our sentiments, that which expresses no
sentiment cannot be music."

Without doubt it is capable of being embellished, by yield-
ing at times to a more passionate development, and more
scientific combinations ; only we must not confound the
principle of the art with the means of enhancing its value.
" Music," says Thibaut, " will not appear to us of divine origin, unless the sensations which it procures for us transport

us into the ideal world; the composer who cannot attain
this, is nothing but a mechanician or a journeyman."[1]   In all
the other arts, the work of the artist finds more easily its own
place: its distinctive character is more easily recognized, its
symbols are more visible in every aspect.   Music, too fugitive,
resembles a vision: it evaporates at the same moment that
it appears; you only hear, as it were, the light rustling of its
garment, the vibration of its wings, its accent of joy and grief,
and you feel just as you do at the instant you awake from
a dream; your heart palpitates, and you repeat, like an echo
in the distance, the same sounds, the same accents.   Here
we may say what elsewhere has been applied to poetry:
Music, " in its purest effect, is a wonder; and the belief in it
a wondrous belief;"[2] or exclaim with Cicero, (*Rem videam,
causam nescio,*) " The effect I see, the cause I cannot penetrate."

Our studies, our enquiries and researches concerning the
science, the history, the philosophy of music, may, on account
of its supernatural power, its universality, be summed up in
the words of Bettina,[3] " I would fain know what music is;
I seek it as a man would seek eternal wisdom."

O music! thou art the evening twilight of this world; thou
risest high above our griefs and tears, until thy rays melt in
the morning dawn of the eternal!

---

[1] *Ueber Reinheit der Tonkunst.*

[2] Die Poesie in ihrer reinsten Wirkung ist ein Wunder, und der
Glaube an dieselbe ein Wunderglaube.—*W. Müller.*

[3] Göthe, *Briefwechsel mit einem Kinde.*

III.

HAVING observed the various effects of music upon our sensations, we might at once approach the question of its power, influence, and importance upon the education of youth; but we must for a moment look around us, and see if there are not physiological and psychological reasons in its favour. In examining our musical organs—the voice that produces sound and the ear that receives it—we are struck with amazement at the wonders of their construction. The cause of the beauty and charm of the human voice, its flexibility and character, differing in age, sex, and individual, as much as the faces of men from each other, and the ear, mysterious channel, through which sound penetrates and strikes with power and certainty the inward man, remain, as yet, undefinable enigmas which have escaped every analysis, and will perhaps continue to baffle human science and enquiry; yet, both are an inheritance of nature, a common gift which, with more or less delicacy, belongs to all mankind. This is an important fact which should not escape the friend of education; for, if education has any object in view, it must be to develope our natural dispositions and faculties, and bring them to bear upon our future mental and moral advancement. But the marvellous construction of the ear, and the equally marvellous effect of the voice, are not the only points to which we would wish to direct attention; there is in the nature of our senses, in the diversity of their action, another powerful argument in favour of the cultivation of music.

Taste, smell, and feeling, are inferior senses, the lowest in the scale, and scarcely ever capable of reaching beyond the mere animal nature. The highest refinement of these consists in a keener relish for some things, and dislike to others. Hearing and seeing—the ear and eye—although they act equally as physical organs, are, nevertheless, susceptible of a higher cultivation, and can be elevated and ennobled. They reveal themselves in awakening deeper sensations, and pass beyond the mere external man. These senses ennobled, are offended at whatever is low, trivial, and inharmonious, and only find enjoyment in dignity, beauty, and grace ; they are the link between the outward and the inward world of man. Through their medium, tastes and distastes will be keener in all that relates to order and harmony. At first they bear only upon objects of the physical world, yet soon they will penetrate into a more spiritual sphere, and seek what is morally excellent and beautiful. It is in this moral power of the eye and ear, that the necessity and importance of their cultivation must be sought. Nothing in education can be substituted for the refinement and taste conveyed to man through the fine arts. Science developes and enlarges certain mental faculties, seeks physical results from physical causes, builds upon matter and fact; in the one the anatomical knife, in the other the chemical apparatus, in a third the arithmetical figure, are the starting points ; armed with these weapons, men of science form their theories, their systems and hypotheses, and reach, one after another, in the world of intellect, to great results and great discoveries. How often has this been attained at the expense of all other faculties! giants in intellect and reasoning, in analysing, dissecting, and compounding, but with no heart, no humanity, nothing which reveals the nobler attributes, the higher destiny of man. Instruction of the mind has been erroneously taken for training and education. The mind, therefore, has been enlarged, but the man has been left in his infancy. To such there is but one temple, that of reality. That which cannot be measured with the compass, which cannot be proved by figures, does not exist. For him there is no power but steam, no ties which link man to man, but railroads. But too often he neither believes in virtue nor justice; history and philosophy, in short, the most vital, the most affecting questions of the thinking man, are to him objects of derision and ridicule. Art and literature have no greater enemies than such half-instructed,

half-educated men, commonly called men of science. It is
they who, after the performance of a work of a Händel or a
Beethoven, the reading of a Milton or a Shakespeare, would
ask, with the mathematician, after he had listened to the
reading of a Homer, what does this prove ? [1]   What is poetry, what is art in general, to so cold and coarse a nature,—a
calculating machine, a living engine ?   Stop the wheel of
the machine, let out the steam of the engine, and both will
resemble a bagpipe with a hole in its bellows.

The object of the fine arts, of poetry and music especially,
is man, man in his moral being, in his deepest and loftiest
thoughts and aspirations.   They reach and penetrate, in
a manner peculiar and admirable, into the hidden recesses
of that being, and, by their influence and sympathy, warm
and stimulate it with a purifying flame, shield it from con-
tamination, and shed a lustre and beauty over the duties it
is called upon to perform.   We may learn from without, from
general instruction to do what is right and just, because it
is a duty or a law, which under certain penalties we may not
transgress ; but he who is really accomplished, does what is
good and just, not only because it is a duty, but because it is
an imperative necessity of his more refined nature.   In doing
otherwise, he would violate that nature, destroy that grace
and harmony with which his soul is filled, and place himself
in opposition with his more generous, his nobler self.

It remains now to be seen whether it is the eye or the ear
which operates most powerfully upon man, and which of
them leaves the deepest impressions.   The mere sight of suffering can make the chords of our pity and compassion vibrate
powerfully ; but the broken sounds which acute pain, or
poignant grief, wring from the breast of the unfortunate,
touch us more deeply.   Sounds have a hidden force, and

---

[1] Well may be applied to music and all other arts, what Rousseau so
well says in regard to Homer : " Les autres poètes écrivoient, dit-il, Ho-
mère seul avoit chanté ; et ces chants divins n'ont cessé d'être écoutés
avec ravissement, que quand l'Europe s'est couverte de barbares qui se
sont melés de juger ce qu'ils ne pouvoient sentir."—*Essai sur l'Origine
des Langues*, chap. VI.

the impressions which are made through the sense of hearing, are more lively and thrilling than those which only
affect the organ of sight. Leibnitz says (*Picturæ explica-
tiores, soni fortiores*) :—" Painting explains better, but sounds
have more power." It is only the outside, the surface of
things, which is accessible to the eye. " The ear," says
Herder, " penetrates the deepest, and affects more powerfully
than any sense, the whole nervous system." In the description of exterior nature, of all that is measurable and limited
by space, music is totally powerless, and yields the supremacy
to painting and the plastic arts;[1] but where the interior life,
the sensations of man, are to be moved, music stands the
first; its effects are the most striking, the most immediate.
A mixture of colours, without harmonious arrangement, may
offend the sight; but discordant, powerful, and unexpected
sounds, can so affect the ear, that every nerve suffers, and is
deeply shaken. Painting can touch, can charm, can elevate,
but music makes the heart thrill with delight, and fills the
soul with rapture. There exists a most intimate and a most
mysterious connection between the vibrations of the air and
those of the heart; every external sound finds there an echo;
every appeal a reply; mirth and sadness, pity, hope and remembrance, affection in all its phases of joy and grief, find a vi-
brating string in that harp of divine workmanship—the human
soul. In this secret relation between sense and feeling, the

---

[1] A *school* has lately risen in France, in which imitation of external
nature, description of events and accidental occurrences, are represented
in music. Not only audible, but visible nature, *high* and *low*, *white* and
black, clouds, rivers, mountains, and precipices, are painted by musical sound. At the first glance it must appear evident how little connection musical description or painting can have with real art. In the midst
of the many enthusiastic admirers of the so called *fantastic* school, it has
found the appreciation it deserves among men of more refined taste. A
French writer says on the performance of the *Shakespeare symphonie* of
Romeo et Juliette:—" In the midst of a tumult of horns and double
basses, I wanted to know the signification of it : I looked into the descriptive programme, and found the words, ' The gardens of Capulet, SILENT
and DESERTED.' I read there too, he continues, ' *Romeo sentait les premi-
ères atteintes du poison.*' Les violons ont fait entendre un bruit strident ;
un admirateur enthousiaste s'est écrié : *comme c'est bien cela la colique !* ' "

nerves and their corresponding sensations, lies the mystery and the power of music. By adapting the melodious inflections of the voice, their character, tone, and colour, to the sentiment which we intend to express, we govern, with an almost supernatural force, the human breast, and produce in thousands, at the same moment, the emotions which we individually felt, or wished to call forth. No art can wield with such admirable suppleness the most delicate movements of the soul, or be made to pourtray so vividly the most indefinable and mysterious sensations. No; no art has ever exercised over the human breast so decided an empire.

Thus we see that the cultivation and refinement of our senses is not so trifling an object in education as it might appear, and that the outward and the inward man, whose messengers they are, are intimately linked together, give and receive impressions; that neither without the other can rise or fall; that when the one ascends the scale of perfectibility, the other cannot remain in constant infancy.

He who is inaccessible to music, is defective in the harmony of his senses, is deprived of the nobler faculties which elevate man above the brute. Let him then boast of his unmusical nature, his unpoetical ear, his dislike or indifference to any of the fine arts; he has characterized himself; he has pronounced his own sentence. Shakespeare has left a monumental epigram to him who has "no music in his soul:" he may try in vain to efface it, it will stand and be true to the end of time.[1] Of what lofty, what exalted enjoyments he is deprived, those only know who have drank from the celestial fountain hours of happiness and rapture. In the enjoyment of works which, in thought and form, are congenial to us, we rise beyond this world, place an im-

---

[1] "We can only sing songs," says Luther, "with a pious, good, and cheerful heart; it is impossible to sing, at least any thing good, in the presence of a dull or bad man." A Roman cardinal expresses Luther's and Shakespeare's thoughts with a little more dogmatical emphasis, and abandons such men, without ceremony, to the devil, because he and his like hate all harmony. "Qui musicam non callet, seu nullo oblectamento animi illam audit, ex diabolo est, nam solus ille omnem harmoniam respuit."

mensity of space between the physical and spiritual part of ourselves; we are transported, as Schiller says, " to the spheres of the gods." We live a soul-existence, in unattainable exclusiveness from all that is earthly. This immersion into the ocean of thought and feeling, is the noble privilege of man; it is the seal of his higher destiny, and can, therefore, not be traceless in its passage. Called to ourselves from the inward to the outward world, reminded of our cares and our wants, has no impression followed us thither? Have we left the ideal world in which we lived, no matter how long, how short a time, at the threshold of this? Impressions of so sublime a kind are not so easily effaced. Their traces will still be found in the daily transactions of life. Where there is light, there is shadow; man stands between both; the shadow he casts upon the sand, is a representation of himself—the object lighted from above. A man, susceptible of lofty thoughts, deep, pure feelings, holy raptures, with a soul open to truth in music, to beauty in poetry, will, in daily life, not be forsaken by his better self.

When we, therefore, look upon the mysterious origin of music, the unaccountable effects of the voice, and the sensitiveness of the ear, its wonderful operation between the external nature and the internal man, between our senses and our soul, the universality of its language, its application to all ages, all nations, and all climes, to every individual in all stages of civilization and society, then we must exclaim, that there is a deep sense, a deep philosophy in music; that it might be a powerful auxiliary in directing the destiny of the human family. This should be done in schools, where the boy prepares and arms himself for the school of life and endurance; where, between mirth and play, he advances unconsciously towards the days of combat and adversity. Arm him, then, with all that is great, true, and beautiful. Teach him to think and to feel. Arm him with knowledge, with science! above all, arm him with art! and what is art, but the unchangeably, the eternally beautiful! It stands a faithful friend by our side in active life, and whispers warning to our soul in silent solitude.

IV.

Effect of Simple and Complicated Music—Is Modern Music inferior in its
Effects to that of the Ancients ?

HAS music really degenerated ? has it lost the magic power it
once possessed ? Where are then the miracles equal to those
with which ancient history is so filled ? And, is music worth
acquiring, if it has fallen from its former throne, and if, in
the course of ages, it has lost its charm, its power aud grandeur ? These are the usual remarks, to which every one
gives his own conclusions, more or less based upon sound
judgment and attentive observation. Music, in its effects, is
the same now as it was, and will be so to the end of time.
If we examine all those melodies which have produced extraordinary effects upon individuals, upon multitudes or nations, and thus have acquired historical importance, we shall
find that their power is not derived from science or artistical
combination, but is founded in truth, nature, and simplicity.
These are the great engines of influence in musical composition and performance. It is a power more frequently found
in melodies of popular and instinctive origin, than in works
of art ; or, if met with in the latter, it is because those same
qualities are predominant. In the scientific and difficult, the
musician, the composer, as well as the performer, will be
admired ; but it is by his simplest strains that he will captivate and subdue his hearer, that he will reach his deeper
affections. Whenever we find a melody in the mouth of a
whole nation, whenever an air is heard that produces strong
feelings of excitement or despondency, we may be certain
that it stands away from the refinements of art, and is powerful in its effects in proportion to its simplicity. To this
must be added the constant association of the two sister arts,

poetry and music. What in the language of music is too
vague, too indefinite, acquires, through poetry, its real character, form, and colour. All poets of antiquity were musicians. Music without poetry, poetry without music, were
things unknown. If ancient music had any advantage over
ours, it was owing to the intimate union of both. The poet-
musician was of a higher cast: what music wanted in thought,
it received from the poet: what to poetry was unattainable
in feeling, charm, and transport, the musician supplied in
his turn. Music is more poetical than poetry itself: where
words are inadequate to an overwhelmed bosom, be it in joy
or grief, where poetry stands at its extreme limits, where
excessive feeling strikes the stammering tongue with helpless-
ness, there music begins to rise, and opens, with unequalled,
with magic power, the gates of the wonderful, the celestial,
and the infinite. In the superiority of the Grecian poets
consisted, and therein only, the superiority of the Grecian
music. Homer, and all the early bards of Greece, were not
only poets, but musicians and singers. Such was Hesiod; such
also were Sappho and Alcæus, the two children of Lesbos.
How beautifully significant is Horace's ode on the effect of
the singing of Sappho and Alcæus in the Orcus, when he
says: " they were worthy of the sacred silence that surrounded them ; the multitude, filled with admiration, approached
nearer and nearer, until shoulder pressed on shoulder."[1] At
the side of Sappho, in the poetical world, the most splendid
star of antiquity, Pindar, was a musician, and the son of a
musician of Thebes. Æschylus, Sophocles, Euripides, the glorious triumvirate of ancient tragedy, were not only the poets,
the musical composers and choreographers, (χοροῦ διδάσκαλοι)
but even the musical performers of their dramas. Who then
can understand the ancient Grecian poets, deprived of half
their attributes? Although the melodies have been lost to
us, yet there is an ideal music in them, without which no
scholar will pretend to understand their full poetical worth,
far less their metrical and rhythmical cadence and melo-

---

[1] " Densum humeris bibit aure vulgus."—*Od.*, Lib. xi. 13.

dy. The chorus is the mother of the Grecian tragedy, and
the ideal of the Grecian popular and national songs. But
who can approach them without music ? or can, perhaps, a
translation, the most successful translation of a Voss, a
Müller, a Tieck, or a Schlegel, of a Shakespeare or a Pope,
give us a distant idea of that musical charm, that poetical
perfume which intoxicates us in ancient poetry ? Approach it
in its native garb, in its Greek idiom and Greek costume, or
it closes, like the sensitive flower, its bosom and its charms.
It is the Greek language, the melody of its lines, which gives
you a distant foreboding of its music. Music and poetry are
here like the two birds which have but one life ; separate
what has been born inseparable, and both will die.[1]

Without entering thus into the spirit of classical art and
literature, without nourishing our soul with the beautiful of
which they are so replete, and of which they are such perfect and inimitable models, classical studies are nothing
worth. What avails it to know the Latin and Greek alphabet, grammar, and syntax, and to have approached, as a
stammering schoolboy, some of the easy classics of either nation ? If this is what you call classical education, you are
right to say that you do not see (and who would say the contrary ?) what connection music has with Greek. When
schools and universities do not reach beyond the grammati-

---

[1] Herder says about the music in Pindar's Odes : " We stand like in
the stream of Tantalus ; and as the musical stream flows hence, we seek
in vain to grasp the golden fruit."—*Stimmen der Völker in Liedern.*
vol. vii.

In speaking of *popular songs, ancient ballads*, and especially that of
Shakespeare's *Twelfth Night*—

Come away, come away death,

he says, as beautifully as truly : " Let such lines be translated, how different will they appear, even in regard to their sentiment, when you
take away all its external attributes or form in tone and melody, all
that mysterious and indescribable something, which, with music, stream-
like fills our soul ! (*was uns mit dem Gesange stromweise in die Seele fliszt.*)
Open the relics of ancient poetry, translate any thing you like, and as
beautifully as you may, but without the musical accent, the melody,—
and see then what remains."—*Ibid.*

cal analysis of Greek poetry, then poetry itself is, and must remain, an unknown land; far more so still, the indispensible sister attribute, the music of their poetry. You flatter yourself and your schools by calling them classical; but the classical consists not in the grammar, it consists in literature and art. Instead of giving to your students (to use the bombastical style of some church writer,) a *glance at the temple,* instead of making them Peripatetics in its portico, and allowing them to look through the key-hole, throw the gates open, and lead them into the sanctuary, that there they may drink at its source the knowledge of classical art, which, like a sacred fire, will purify their thoughts, elevate their taste, refine their manners, embellish their life, imbue them with the laws of order and harmony, and render them better and wiser in life and action. " Grecian art is a school of mental refinement, (*Humanität*); a poor man is he who does not regard it as such."[1]

Was Grecian music more powerful, because we read that rocks and forests followed the singer, that walls, temples, and cities rose at the sound of his voice and lyre? Icelandic chronicles tell us the same of Scandinavian mythology almost in the same words: " Odin excelled all men in the art of poetry, eloquence, and music, and could sing airs so tender and melodious, that even rocks would expand with delight, while the spirits of the infernal regions stood motionless

---

[1] " Die Griegische Kunst ist eine Schule der Humanität ; unglücklich ist wer sie anders betrachted."—Herder, *Die Humanität der Griechen,* vol. xv.

Through the influence of classical literature upon refined education, the languages—Greek as well as Latin, and all other studies which lead to it—were called *studia humaniora,* or *humanitatis,* and, lastly, *humanity,* which expression is in England erroneously given to Latin alone. If, for their polishing and refining influence sake, the classical studies are not called humanity, we do not understand its meaning. There is certainly very little humanity in *us, a, um,* and quite as little in τύπτω, τύπτεις ; and it is without doubt, that humanity is to be roused in the education of boys, whom even Plato called the most unmanageable of all animals, ὁ παῖς πάντων θηρίων ἐστὶ δυσμεταχειρισ-τότατον ; which Ficinus elegantly translates with—*Puer omni bestia intractabilior.*

around him."[1]   When Orpheus sang, the oak had an ear,
Ixion's wheel stood still, and the Danaides forgot their endless toil.   This all tells of the wonderful effects produced by
music, and the works that were achieved through its aid.
Take away the allegoric garb, and you will find that the poet-
musician was no less than the instructor and benefactor, the
legislator of cities and provinces.   Through the charm of
poetry and music, he acquired among savage tribes an attentive ear, sang of great men and great deeds, inspired them
with a love for the good and the just, for virtue and order.
Through his power of eloquence and fascinating musical nar-
ration, they erected walls, cities, and temples, submitted themselves to the laws they had listened to, and had learned to
love and to sing.[2]   Similar effects were produced with similar
elements among nations of other climes.   "Who is not acquainted with the miracles of the bards and the scalds ? with
the marvellous effects produced by the troubadours and minstrels ?   how the eager people gathered around them, and
what a new world was opened to their sight ?   How sacred
were those songs in which the people learnt the history, the
traditions, and with them, the language and manners of their
nation !   They were simple but powerful, full of energy and
action: they were an appeal to the heart, and by the severity
of their accents, became a piercing dart to the soul open to
truth."[3]

We have a faint echo of the songs of ancient Israel and
ancient Greece, in those which the Christian Church borrowed

---

[1] Snorris *Heimskringla*, and Mallet's *Northern Antiquities*.

[2] The laws of Greece, as well as those of all ancient nations, were sung.
Aristotle says : " Why have we in Greece no other word for *law* than
$νόμος$? (song.)   Was it because, when writing was as yet unknown,
they sang the laws, that they might not be forgotten, as it is still the
custom among the Agathursi ?"

Διὰ τί νόμοι καλοῦνται οὓς ᾄδουσιν ; ἢ ὅτι πρὶν ἐπίστασθαι γράμ-
ματα ᾖδον τοὺς νόμους, ὅπως μὴ ἐπιλάθωνται· ὥσπερ ἐν 'Αγαθύρσοις
ἔτι εἰώθασι ;—Arist. *Probl.* xix. 28.

[3] Herder's *Lieder der alten Voelker*, vol. vii.

from both, and transmitted to us in the Greek and Roman Churches, by written and oral tradition. The Antiphones, hymns and psalms, are remains of Grecian and Hebraic music. Both lived for nearly two thousand years in the mouth of the eastern and occidental nations, and still they stand before us living monuments of piety and enthusiasm, models of simplicity, truth, and grandeur. These sacred hymns and psalms were for ages popular melodies of all Christian nations : they resounded in dungeons and catacombs, and accompanied man from the cradle to his grave. Their simplicity is such, that often they have no more notes than syllables, and with all this, who can hear without emotion, the " *Te Deum Laudamus*" of Ambrose, or the funeral song, " *Jam moesta quiesce querela*" of Prudentius, both productions of the fourth century ? The *Pange Lingua*, the *Veni Redemptor gentium*, the *Veni Creator*, were for centuries the war songs of the French armies.[1] After Charlemagne, it was the song of Roland (Cantilena Rolandi) that inflamed them with enthusiasm. Among the Slavish nations it was St. Adelbert's Hymn, the *Boga Rodziça*, which resounded in every church and upon every field of battle.

Music at all times has seen its miracles : A song—the poorest as music or poetry—if it bring back recollections of earlier or happier times, if it remind us of places and occurrences, or of persons whose memory lies near to our heart, who can doubt that its effect will be powerful, and a thousand times more so than a composition infinitely richer, more regular, more harmonious, and more scientific would be ! The singing of the Jewish captives may have been little more than the rhythmical and melodious recitation of a psalm, yet the Babylonian soldiers liked to listen to those songs of Zion, which overwhelmed with grief and tears the exiled children of Israel. The choruses in the Grecian tragedies, which consisted in a monosyllabic recitation, a melodious and rhythmical declamation, rising and falling, growing and diminishing in power and expression, simple, but true in thought

---

[1] *Chapelle-Musique des Rois de France*, par Castile-Blaze, p. 32.

and form ; yet what terror did they not produce in the
Eumenides of Æschylus, and what tears in that touching
farewell scene of Euripides Alcestis ! After the taking of
Athens by Lysander, one of the Thebans proposed, that
Athens should be destroyed, and all the citizens deprived of
their liberty. While the leaders of the enemy's army were
celebrating their victory in the banquet hall, one of the guests
sang the melody of the chorus of Euripides, " *O daughter of
Agamemnon, Electra, I come to thy humble dwelling.*" So
great was the emotion, the feeling of compassion which it
excited among the listeners, that it saved Athens from destruction, and the citizens from servitude.[1]

The wonders which the ancients attributed to music, although related by the greatest historians and philosophers,
we are much inclined to take for fables, for " Tales of a
Thousand and One Nights." But do not our own days tell
us of similar wonders achieved by this art ? If ancient history relates that Timotheus could, according to the choice of
his melody, excite or calm Alexander's soul; that Tirtæus
was able to inflame for death or victory the Spartan army;
have we not instances near our own times of similar effects ?
effects, indeed, which stand in nothing behind the reputed fables of antiquity. In the fifteenth century, in Granada, did
not the whole mass of the people shed tears when they heard
the ballad of the Moors, on the taking of Alhama ? did not
the simple and pathetic song of Schah-Culi, at the siege of
Bagdad, save the life of 30,000 inhabitants ?[2] Was not, a
century ago, the *Rans des Vaches* forbidden, under pain of

---

[1] Plutarch's *Life of Lysander.*

[2] When Amurat IV. conquered Bagdad in 1638, he gave orders to
massacre before his eyes, 30,000 inhabitants. Schah-Culi found means to
be brought before the irritated Sultan, and in singing to the harp the la-
ment of the suffering Bagdadians, Amurat was moved to tears ; the massacre, already commenced, was countermanded. In softening this blood-
thirsty tiger with his strains, still sung among the Turks and Persians,
and known under the name of *Muselie* or *Percerfi Bagdati Fetichi,* (the
taking of Bagdad,) he is deservedly called the Persian Orpheus.—See To-
derini on the *Literature of the Turks,* and *Encyclopädie der Musikali-
schen Wissenschaften,* Vol. vi., p. 160.

death, because, to the memory of the sons of Switzerland, serving far away from their country, it recalled their native hills so powerfully, as to make them desert their ranks, or die of grief? Have we not witnessed the *Marseillaise Hymn*, wherever it was heard, exciting indescribable enthusiasm: the workmen quitting their shops, abandoning wife and children, and running in their shirt-sleeves to swell the ranks of the republican army? Deeds, which seemed beyond human power, were accomplished whenever the Marseillaise was struck up:[1] and even at this moment its power is electric upon the French; its intonation still strikes with awe and terror the most valiant armies of royalty. It is, therefore, kept in constant thraldom; always feared, always watched like a lion ready to break forth from its den, and spread, a second time, desolation and carnage over half the nations of Europe. Similar effects were produced by the *Polonaise of Kosciuszko* and the *Third May* in the combat of Poland for independence; similar enthusiasm excited among the Neo-Hellenists the Δεύτε παῖδες τῶν ʽΕλλήνων; similar excitement produces daily still the *Gamel Norge* among the Norwegians. For the same reason, the nursery song has often a power over our feelings, that no work of musical genius could attain. J. J. Rousseau, when speaking of his aunt Suzon, when a child, says:—" Would one believe, that an old dotard, like myself, worn out with cares and troubles, should find myself weeping like an infant, while I murmur, with a broken and trembling voice, the songs of my childhood." [2]

It is known that the aria, *Ombra adorata aspetta* of Zingarelli's *Romeo e Giulietta*, so remarkable for its simplicity, caused an unheard-of emotion: as in the Eumenides of Æschylus, many people fainted, and women were carried away. Carpani relates,[3] that when Bertoni's opera, *Arta-*

---

[1] The words of the Republican General are known, who asked for a " supply of 1000 men, or a new edition of the Marseillaise;" or another, who reported: " J'ai gagné la bataille; La Marseillaise commandait avec moi."

[2] *Confessions de J. J. Rousseau.*

[3] Carpani's *Biography of Haydn.*

xerxes, was being performed in Rome, the character of Arbace was represented by a celebrated singer.   At the famous judgment scene, the maestro had introduced some pauses to the instrumental accompaniment, after the words, *E appur sono innocente!*   The action, the music, the art, and expression of the singer, had transported the whole audience. After these touching words, Arbace, perceiving the continued silence of the orchestra, turned round to the conductor, with somewhat of temper, and said: well, what are you all about ? who, recalled to himself, replied : we weep.   In truth, audience and orchestra, carried away by the power of his expression, remained mute and motionless, listened and wept.

In many instances, when misfortune has struck too deeply into the heart, and ravaged, with little mercy, its dearest affections, when all the energies have been paralyzed, and tears, that great source of comfort, dried up, music has often come in unexpected, simple, touching strains, and presented a balm which medical science sought for in vain, a balm which, with its invisible source, appeared to be administered by an angel of comfort, a messenger from higher spheres.[1]

Thus we see that simple compositions have at all times operated more powerfully upon individuals and people than complicated scientific compositions ; and, therefore, it can be nothing but idle speculation to pretend that, in modern times,

[1] In the year 1778, the celebrated singer, Raff, came to Naples, where resided, at that time, the Princess Belmonte Pignatelli, who, brooding over her grief at the loss of her husband, had fallen into a state of total insensibility and stupefaction, and was fast approaching the grave.   No tear brought relief to the breaking heart; medical skill had been tried in vain.   In this extremity of desolation, her waiting woman, as a last resource, arranged that, while seated one evening in one of her summer houses, Raff should sing, as by chance, from a distance.   He, with an unpretending voice, sung that simple melody of Rolli, *Solitario bosco ombroso.*   The Princess seemed at first insensible, but soon the head rose ; she opened the half-closed eyes, gazed as if awaking from a dream, and scarcely had Raff finished the first verse, when, fully conscious, she burst into a flood of tears, which continued for several days uninterruptedly. Thus her life was saved, and her spirits, by degrees, recalled to their former energy.—See Schilling's *Encyclopædie der Tonkunst*, art. *Raff.*

music has either no longer that wonderful power which it had among the ancients, or that their music was then in its infancy, compared with the more harmonious and the more scientific development of ours. The power of music is still undiminished; its application to youth, and to the people, has only to be learnt.

As simple music, then, produces the greatest effect, why should not every one find an opportunity to learn it?— In order to make the instruction in this art a really moral instruction, a powerful agent in the advancement and progress of individuals and nations, let us associate the simplest music with the best and noblest lines of poetical composition. Let us, with songs and poetry, with lessons of lofty thought and practical truth, store the memory of the young. What we are taught to sing, we never forget. The songs which we learnt in our youth, are the sweetest and most lasting recollections of man.

V.

Music among the Ancients, an essential part of Education.—Estimation in which Music was held by the Egyptians and Hebrews, by the Sages, Legislators, and the Founders of the different Schools of Philosophy in Greece.

THE music of the ancients, their technical acquirements, their scientific principles of this art, are to us a great mystery. Hundreds of years have passed since the last strains of their music were heard. In vain we listen to their songs of praise or of triumph, of hope or of contrition ; in vain we seek for them among their ruins, their temples, and their monuments ; these sounds are hushed ; they are gone to the grave with those who sought in them delight and comfort. The most minute and the most learned treatises have been written on the subject, but they leave us in the dark as we were before. No description, no explanation can help us. Sounds, sounds we want, living sounds carried upon the breath of man, or a notation of which we possess the key ; a writing in accordance with our measure, our musical compass, to be our guide through the infinity of auditive space. One canto of a Rhapsodist, one stanza of the Paeans, one scolion, one ode of Sappho or of Pindar, in its musical accents, would reveal to us the nature of the Grecian music. The only

Φράζου λάβε, λάβε, λάβε,

the terrible cry of the awakening furies in Æschylus' Eumenides ;[1] one strophe of their invocation *to the Night*,

Μᾶτερ ἅ μ᾿ ἔτιχτες, ὦ μᾶτερ
Νύξ,[2]

would give us more insight into the music of the Grecian tragedies, than the investigations of many centuries have been able

[1] V. 125.   [2] *Eumenides,* v. 312.

to accomplish. But with the nations, to a great extent, disappeared their monuments of history, their monuments of art; some temples only, some statues, escaped the general destruction, and a limited portion is left to us of Greek and Roman literature. Of the Phœnicians, no direct tradition has survived the storm of time. Of the Egyptians, nothing but their obelisks, pyramids, and a few hieroglyphics. Of that people, called the holy people, the people of God, a nation of priests, of their history, their poetry, their music, we know only what can be gathered from those fragments contained in the holy scriptures, and in the writings of the Talmudists.

What, then, is it that remains for us to tell about the music of the nations of antiquity? of their music as science, its technical principles and development? Almost nothing. The only point of which we can speak with certainty, in which we stand upon firm ground and have nothing to fear from future theories, is, that the ancients had a music, a music full of effect and power; that it was associated with every festivity of public and private life, with the laws and the religion of their country; that it was studied, honoured, recommended by their legislators, by the wisest men of all nations; and that it formed a part of moral cultivation, a branch of the education of youth. Egypt has been the cradle of the arts and sciences. The Greeks and Hebrews were only its disciples. It must certainly be a most interesting question, how music was appreciated by a people so renowned for their wisdom as the Egyptians. To their schools came the learned, the philosophers, the lawgivers of all nations. In them Moses was educated;[1] there studied Solon[2] and Pythagoras there learned philosophy, the political and sacred sciences. Plato passed there thirteen years of his life. In regard to the Egyptians, therefore, we may say with Cicero: "Audiamus enim Platonem quasi Deum Philosophorum."[3] Plato makes frequent usage of their principles of government, and

---

[1] Strabo, lib. xvi. Philo, *De Vita Mosis*, lib. i.

[2] Plato, *Symposium*. Plutarchus, Συμποσιακῶν, p. 153.

[3] Cicero, *De Natura Deorum*, lib. ii.

presents them often as a model to Greece, namely, in regard
to music.   In their general outlines, they might be still a
model to us; and if ever again music is to be earnestly, carefully and successfully applied to education, then what the
Egyptians did in the education of the young, what Plato ad-
vises the statesmen of Greece to imitate, must again become
a reality to us.   Though we may have little to learn from the
ancients in the mechanical art, yet in practical wisdom, in
the philosophy of life, they might be still our masters.   They
have been so in our religion, and until this hour the disciples
and priests of Memphis[1] are our masters, our high priests,
our prophets; and their doctrines are our doctrines, their
laws our laws.   The fine arts were cultivated in Egypt, and
applied to the education and the refinement of the people.
Greece followed its example, improved them, and carried to
its last limits their perfection.   If we acknowledge the works
of the Greeks as the highest models of art, why not learn
from them the application of art for the furtherance of the
welfare, the mental and moral culture, the happiness of men
and of nations ?   In reading Plato's *Laws* and *Republic*, we
find that it was the opinion of the first legislators of Egypt,
that to render man happy in society, his sentiments of pleasure and pain must be regulated, that his feelings and expressions of joy and sorrow must be subjected to moderation.
Convinced also that the feeling of delight experienced by
music and rhythm, was as a divine blessing given to man, as
a means to cure or to prevent passions or vice, the source of
all evil, so destructive to individual or social harmony, they
sought for songs and dances, in which the noblest expressions
of the voice were united with the most dignified, the most
graceful movements of the body.   The songs and dances were
intended to express the mental state of the wise, the virtuous,
the temperate; and by means of poetry, melody, and rhythm,
they sought to inspire the young with the love of courage
and moderation.[2]

[1] Strabo calls Moses a priest of Egypt : Μώσης γάρ τις τῶν Αἰγυπ-
τίων ἱερέων.—STRABO, lib. XVI. p. 760.

[2] That ὄρχησις, as a branch of education, or as a part of Grecian tra-

Music was regarded as subordinate to poetry, and the poet-musician was subject to a great penalty, if his writings had any other tendency, than to excite an admiration of what was good and virtuous. Education with them consisted in the art of guiding the young towards what the law, in conformity with reason, had recognized as good, and what had been acknowledged as such by the oldest and the wisest of the nation. To be ignorant of music and dancing, signified with them to be ignorant how to moderate and to regulate words and actions: they united the good with the useful; dancing and grace were inseparable; and a man was only then considered accomplished, when he was in full possession of these united qualifications.

Moses, educated as a child of Pharaoh, learned from the Egyptians, according to Philo and Clemens of Alexandria, arithmetic, geometry, and *all the branches of music*, viz. rhythm, metre, harmony, its theory, and its practical application to the voice and to instruments.[1] Throughout the whole of the Scriptures, we find that music was an inseparable companion of the Israelites, in joy and grief, in private and public festivities: in sacred rites, priests, prophets, and kings sang and played on instruments, with the

gedy, cannot mean jumping or leaping like fawns, monkies, and satyrs, or like the drunken worshippers of Dionysos, as Mr G. H. Lewis, (see *Classical Museum*, vol. II. p. 344,) or Bishop Blomfield, (*Museum Criticum*, vol. II.) would make us believe, is evident from every line in which it is mentioned as such. If the tragic dance was something else than lofty movement, majestic carriage, and graceful step, regulated by musical rhythm, how is to be explained the dancing in the religious festivities mentioned in the biblical writings? The movements of the "*old men figuring up and down the stage*," as his Lordship elegantly expresses himself, may not have been so entirely deprived of tragic pathos, as to offend the taste of the Athenians, whose monuments of art sufficiently shew us, how well they knew the difference between the beautiful and the ridiculous, and how little they need our indulgence in their appreciation of the dignified and graceful.

[1] " Itaque numeros, geometriam, universamque Musicam, rhythmicam harmonicam, metricam, sive contemplativam, sive per instrumenta vocesque promentem se modis variis, accepit ab Ægyptiis doctoribus."—PHILO, *De Vita Mosis*, lib. I.

multitude of the people.   The love for music among the
Hebrews was the stronger, as it was sanctioned and commanded by their legislator, and as it became in days of triumph, of exile and captivity, the sole interpreter of the emotions and sentiments of this, at all times, enthusiastic people.

In Greece, music was one of the elements of the education
of the young ; but their music appeared in the wider acceptation of the word, as mental cultivation through poetry and
music.   When speaking of applying music to education, we
mean nothing else.   Poetry is indispensable to vocal music ;
and it is vocal music only we think indispensable in education.   Lycurgus, following the example of Minos, king of
Crete, inspired the Spartans through music to heroism, and
taught them to sing, and thus to cherish the laws of the state.
" It is certain that the close union of music with the culture of
respect for the laws, contributed a great deal to raise music
to that high rank which it afterwards occupied in education."[1]

Music and poetry seemed a trifling art at first to Solon,
an object of play and amusement only ; but he learned from
the Egyptians, that upon the golden wings of these sister
arts, every great thought, every philosophical sentence,[2] can
be carried into the heart and memory of the singer, and all
those who stand listening about him.   From that time until
his death, the great lawgiver of Athens devoted himself to

[1] Wachsmuth's *Hellenische Alterthumskunde*, i. p. 450, and ii. p. 374.
Lycurgus, when he came to Crete, engaged Thales to put the laws he
destined to Sparta into verse, and to compose the music.   Strabo, lib.
x.   Comp. Plutarch, *Life of Lycurgus*.

Τοὺς Λακεδαιμονίων νόμους ἐμελοποίησε Τέρπανδρος.   Clemens
Alex. *Strom.* i. 308.

" D'après tous les témoignages (des anciens) on peut donc assurer,
que les Lacédémoniens durent presque toutes leurs vertus civiles et
militaires aux effets de ce goût pour la musique dont Lycurgue leur
avait fait un besoin."—Villoteau, *De l'Analogie de la Musique avec le
Language*, vol. ii. p. 263.

[2] Τῇ δὲ ποιήσει κατ' ἀρχὰς μὲν εἰς οὐδὲν ἄξιον σπουδῆς, ἀλλὰ παί-
ζων, ὡς ἔοικε, προσχρήσασθαι καὶ περίαγων ἑαυτὸν ἐν τῷ σχολάζειν·
ὕστερον δὲ καὶ γνώμας ἐνέτεινε φιλοσόφους, &c.   Plutarchus, *Life
of Solon*, 3., p. 80.

poetry ; composed in verse the *different ages of man*,[1] *his laws, his philosophical works*, the history of the Atlantides, and a great number of elegies.[2]

Music, in its wider acceptation, contained the lessons of obedience to the state and its laws ; it inflamed to heroism ; it taught order, (εὐκοσμία,) in manners, in walk and appearance, moderation, temperance, and veneration of old age, religion ; and in general, (the ἀρετή,) every virtue of a good citizen.[3]

Out of the poetical genius of the Greek nation, arose the genius of their philosophy. At first, it was not separated from poetry, but we soon see the development of ideas regarding the theogony and cosmogony, the origin and the final destiny of man, give rise to different schools, which, each following its own way, ended, one after another, in the Ionic, the Pythagorean, the Eleatic, the Atomistic and Socratic, the Stoic and Epicurean Schools.

Most of these have treated of music extensively, and given it a place in the education of youth. Their principles in this respect are far from being superannuated, and deserve once more to become an object of serious thought. Before truth and wisdom, before the spiritually beautiful, of which art is the earthly representative, Pythagoras, Socrates, Plato, and Aristotle, equally bowed their head, in thought, reverence, and humility ; for, in the beautiful is truth, and the really

---

[1] Clemens of Alexandria has preserved this little work to us in book vi. *Strom.* Compare Philo the Jew on the *Creation of the World.*

[2] Plutarch, *Life of Solon*, p. 106 ; and Diogen. Laert. *De Vitis Philosophorum*, lib. i.

Luther followed the footsteps of Solon : he not only translated the ancient Latin hymns, but wrote his Catechism and the Confession of Augsburg into verse, in order to have them sung by the people. Henry of Göttingen set even the former into four parts.

[3] Wachsmuth, ib. vol. ii. p. 375.

Beautifully has this been expressed by Barthelémy, *On the Music of Ancient Greece :* " Au lieu de s'amuser à rémuer nos petites passions, elle (la Musique Grecque) va réveiller jusqu'au fond de nos coeurs les sentiments les plus honorables à l'homme, les plus utiles à la Société, le courage, la reconnaissance, le devouement à la patrie ; c'est que de son heureux assortiment avec la poésie, elle reçoit un caractère imposant de grandeur et de noblesse."—*Voyage du jeune Anacharsis en Grèce.*

true and really beautiful is virtue.[1]   Out of the darkness of
human inquiries after knowledge and wisdom, they sought
the inspirations and sublime pleasures which music and poetry
offered them.   They themselves were either poets or musicians, or listened with delight to the poetical and musical
effusions of others.   Their appreciation and their cultivation
of music has a higher signification to us, as the great object
of their inquiries was man, his natural propensities, his
mental and moral faculties, his will, and his final destiny.
Through them music received its philosophic stamp, its dignity, as a means of contributing to thought and strife, to life
and futurity.

Pythagoras's whole system of education and philosophy was
intimately interwoven with music.[2]   Nobility of sentiment
and religious feelings should flow harmoniously, through musical and poetical inspirations, into the soul, and stimulate to
noble actions and pursuits.   He knew the power of music in
all its branches, studied its natural laws, and practised it,
with wonderful effect, as art, now to stimulate, and then to
calm the spirits, and thus to harmonize all the human faculties, and to subordinate to the better will every passionate
excitement.[3]   His deeper knowledge and more profound acquirements in the art and science of music, command the

[1] So much, among the Greeks, was the idea of beauty blended with
moral excellence, that they scarcely separated the one from the other:
καλός, therefore, signifies the physically as well as morally beautiful;
and καλός ἀνήρ, we would, in the most cases, be obliged to translate,
with a noble, a virtuous, or an excellent man.   It is quite in the Grecian
spirit that the German speaks: " Von einer schönen Handlung, einer
schönen Seele."

[2] Ἡγούμενος πρώτην εἶναι τοῖς ἀνθρώποις τὴν δι' αἰσθήσεως προ-
φερομένην ἐπιμέλειαν, εἴ τις καλὰ μὲν ὁρώη καὶ σχήματα καὶ εἴδη,
καλῶν δὲ ἀκούοι ῥυθμῶν καὶ μελῶν, τὴν διὰ μουσικῆς παίδευσιν
πρώτην κατεστήσατο, διά τε μελῶν τινῶν καὶ ῥυθμῶν, &c.—Iambl.
V. P. i. c. 15.

[3] Pythagoreis moris fuit, et cum evigilassent, animos ad lyram exci-
tare, quo essent ad agendum erectiores; et quum somnum peterent, ad
eandem prius lenire mentes, ut si quid fuisset turbidiorum cogitationum,
componerent.—Quintil. Institut. ix. c. 4.
Pythagorici, cum diurnas in somno resolverent curas, quibusdam

more respect, as he placed music in education in the first rank, and subordinated to it even what they called γραμματική. Thus music was an essential part of study to the Pythagoreans. Our soul, according to them, consisted of harmony, and from what could affect the senses, they hoped to renew the intellectual and primitive harmony of the faculties, which men had lost.[1]

Socrates lamented all his life that he had neglected music in his youth; he applied himself to it in his old age, and replied to the inquiries of the curious with Solon's words: "It is better to learn such an art in old age than never."[2]

The day before his death, an Athenian musician sung to him a poem of Stesichorus, accompanied by the lyre: Socrates was so charmed, that he prayed the singer to repeat it until he had learned it. The young man, surprised, asked of what use it would be to him, as he had to die so soon: the sublime answer of Socrates was, "That I may leave this life richer in knowledge."[3] Here we find one of the greatest sages of antiquity, in the face of death, filled with the highest thoughts on the immortality of the soul, taking music for the solace of his last earthly hours, and making of it his companion to the gates of eternity.[4]

To Plato, music was a sacred art; she was the link which tied man, in his earthly exile, to his primitive celestial home, and as a pure companion of virtue, should captivate our heart for all that is good and beautiful. The moral education,

cantilenis utebantur, ut eis lenis et quietus sopor obreperet.—Boethius, *De Musica*, i. c. 1.

[1] Schiller expresses the same idea beautifully thus: "Man has lost his dignity, but art has saved it: truth still lives in fiction, and from the copy the original will be restored."

[2] Κρεῖττον ὀψιμαθῆ ἢ ἀμαθῆ.—Ammian. *Marcell.* 28, 4.

[3] Ut aliquid sciens amplius e vita discedam.—Ibid.

The same Ammianus tells us a similar fact of Solon, who, as a very old man, wanted to learn an ode of Sappho. He replied to the inquiring musician with almost the same words: ἵνα μαθὼν αὐτὸ ἀποθανῶ: *that I may know it before I die.*

[4] See Beger's *Die Würde der Musik im Griechischen Alterthume*, p. 56. Dresden.

therefore, should begin with music.[1] To nourish the soul
with music was of the highest moment; for she penetrates
into it, and captivates it with irresistible power. The sense
of the beautiful and the good is strengthened, and the dislike
of what is common or bad will be deeply rooted, even in that
age when reason does not yet teach us to like the one, or to
fly the other.[2]

With the principles of Socrates, he united a predilection
for the laws and institutions of Egypt, and thought that,
music being so powerful an agent on the mind, all songs for
youth and the people at large, should be examined and approved by law, and that, if music were left to its fate, effeminating songs, and songs destructive to the morals, might become general, and by enervating the noble faculties of man,
endanger the state:[3] for, want of order and want of taste in
music, is the sister of bad thought, bad language, and habits;[4] and, on the contrary, earnestness and dignity in music, are nearly allied with noble sentiments.[5] In his *Prota-
goras*, where he speaks of education, he says: " That boys
should learn the songs of the best poets, that their souls
might become familiar with rhythm and harmony, in order
that they themselves might become milder, their mode of life
better regulated, so that, both in word and deed, they should
acquire earnestness, energy, and consistency; for the whole
life of man requires order and harmony."[6] He strove un-
ceasingly to combat the opinion of those who would see

---

[1] Παιδείαν εἶναι πρώτην διὰ Μουσῶν τε καὶ ᾿Απόλλωνος.—*De
Legg.* ii. 2.

[2] Ib. ii. 1.

[3] Οὐδαμοῦ γὰρ κινοῦνται μουσικῆς τρόποι ἄνευ πολιτικῶν νόμων
τῶν μεγίστων.—*De Rep.* iv. 424. c.

[4] ᾿Αῤῥυθμία καὶ ἀναρμοστία κακολογίας καὶ κακοηθείας ἀδελφά.—
Ibid. iii. 401. a.

[5] Σώφρονός τε καὶ ἀγαθοῦ ἤθους ἀδελφά τε καὶ μιμήματα.—*Ibid.*

[6] Πᾶς γὰρ ὁ βίος τοῦ ἀνθρώπου εὐρυθμίας τε καὶ εὐαρμοστίας
δεῖται.—*Protagor.* 326, 8. Comp. Πᾶσα ἡλικία καὶ σύμπας βίος ἅπασα
δὲ πρᾶξις μουσικῇ μόνῃ τελέως ἂν κατακοσμηθείη.—Arist. Quintil. *De
Musica*, i. p. 2.

nothing in music but a means of recreation and pleasure. In the second book of his laws, he says: " Most persons say, that the only purpose of music is to give pleasure, but this is a profane, an unholy language : To look on music as a mere amusement, cannot be justified. Music which has no other aim, must neither be considered of value, nor worthy of reverence." Plato's views of art and music have been generally accepted by all superior intellects, although many sages and writers of antiquity have reduced to a greater reality the ideal of the Platonic opinions.

Such also was Aristotle. He who, in all things, especially in political principles, opposed Plato, agreed with him entirely in regard to music. According to him, music should not only be studied for the sake of its power on the morals and manners of a people, but even for the sake of its cheering and recreative influences.[1] It should be considered a part of the education of youth, because it accomplishes two objects—the attainment of the end for which we live, and the recreation on the road to this end. He went farther still, and said, that it was not enough to listen to music only to feel all its advantages, but that it was necessary to practise it. Real enjoyment supposed true understanding, which could only be obtained by practical study.[2]

With the decay of the liberty of Greece, habits and manners degenerated, and with them the fine arts. In the chains of the conqueror, in the servitude of foreign princes, the noble Greek fell into the servitude of the senses. He who, in the days of the glory of his country, had thought, and had combated, sought now nothing more than pleasure and debauchery. Music then became, what it is often now, the companion of revelry. Hence the dislike or the disappreciation of some of the philosophers, who, in their stern virtue, combated against the stream of passion and corruption; hence their condemnation even of music. The cynics, the sceptics, and stoics, were so rough, so exclusive and intolerant in their principles, that, in their eyes, nothing had worth, neither the beautiful in nature nor the beautiful in

[1] See 3d and 4th chap. of *Arist. Pol.*   [2] See Appendix I.

art, but virtue alone. Pure joy, according to former philosophers, a child of heaven, was, under Diogenes and Antis-
thenes, banished as effeminating. Effeminating, especially,
was that enjoyment which is the effect of art. Every tender
and delicate feeling for humanity, every consideration of
mental or bodily suffering, was, to them, effeminacy and
weakness. Zeno, harsh, cold, and rough in life as in principles, did, however, not disdain, like many modern puritans,
to abandon himself to amusements of a grosser kind, and
drank more wine than his morals allowed him to take.[1]   In
such moments, when his eye was sparkling, and his whole
face beaming with delight, the uncouth and rougher nature
of the bear would soften, and become even sweet and amia-
ble (ἡδὺς ἐγίνετο καὶ μείλιχος.) [2]   They understood the coarser,
but not the more delicate part of the nature of man. Nature
was their highest principle. Life, thought, and action, should
be according to nature, πάντα κατὰ φύσιν; but they understood
it in the sense of *naturalia non sunt turpia*, and not in that
more noble acceptation of Juvenal, *non aliud natura, aliud
sapientia dicit.* Such principles must have made their school,
the dirty school, and their persons, outcasts of society, and a
real fright to all the five senses.

The opinion of the Epicureans, who made music only sub-

[1] There is a striking resemblance between the school of Zeno and some
more modern stoics. Pure pleasures, enjoyments, such as fine arts, such
as music give, are to be avoided as effeminating, or as seducing snares of
Satan. Man should always be grave, always nearer to a tear than to
a smile. During the day, even in business, their soul is keeping sabbath ; they are in speech, and in appearance, saints and sages ; but in the
evening they give to their wife and children the melancholy sight of a
slave in delirium ; they sing like a cow, and walk like a giddy chicken.
They are, with all this, of higher and sounder principles ; their morals
are not as easily alarmed as those of a Grecian cynic. Their philosophy can bear a drowning once a day, and intoxication shows both the
dignity of a man, and to what *quantum* he can carry the noble privilege
of his species.

That such grosser natures must be enemies of refined arts, speaks, O
Music ! thy highest praise !

[2] *Athen. and Diogenes Laert.*, vii., 26.

servient to pleasure, deserves no further attention. The principles of Epicurus, who, upon his Elysian gardens, placed the inscription, that pleasure was the highest good,[1] have been well judged, even by Plutarch, who places at the side of Epicurus, the king, Ateas of Scythia, who swore that he preferred rather to hear his horse neigh, than the music of the celebrated Ismenias.[2]

Sextus Empiricus, at last, goes so far as to wage war against music;[3] and it suffices to prove the depth of his philosophical principles, that he says, Epicurus was to him as high an authority as Plato.

Polybius differently appreciated the moral influence of this art. He says, that music was necessary to soften the character of the Arcadians, who lived in a cold, dull country; and that the inhabitants of Cenethæ, who neglected music altogether, surpassed all other Greeks in cruelty, and in the number of crimes that were there committed.[4] However strange this may sound to our ears, the words of Polybius carry with them great weight. He was himself an Arcadian; his talent, judgment, and virtue, were equally admired; he was not less a great practical statesman than an historian; and for his generosity, disinterestedness, and true patriotism, might well be called one of the last of the Greeks.

The learned Plutarch, who might be considered as a link between the ancient and the new era, who, although he lived in the second century after Christ, belonged, as priest of Apollo, to ancient Greece, has transmitted to posterity many treasures of the history and philosophy of antiquity. Among others, he has left us a Dissertation *on Music*, in which the history and the laws of this art, its beauty, importance, and sublimity, its former grandeur and subsequent decay, form the principal object. In speaking of the power and the importance of music, he begins with the remarkable words : " The

---

[1] Hospes ! hic bene manebis, hic summum bonum voluptas est.

[2] Ὤμοσεν ἥδιον ἀκούειν τοῦ ἵππου χρεμετίζοντος.

[3] Sext. Emp., *Adversus Musicos.*

[4] Polybius' *Hist.*—We give the whole quotation of this remarkable passage in Appendix II.

greatest deeds of eminent generals contributed only to save some warriors, a town, or a nation, from danger; but they made those warriors, those citizens, and inhabitants of a country, neither better nor nobler : arts and sciences alone are fundamental conditions of a truly happy life, of which not only a family, a state, or a people, but all humanity, feel the influence ; they deserve, therefore, a truly warm and earnest acknowledgment before all heroic deeds in war."

After having examined all the different opinions of the Greek philosophers on this art, he says :—" The Greeks did, not without reason, feel the utmost desire to instruct the young in music, to form, by its means, their mind and moral feelings; for music lent assistance to every serious action, and stood at the side of man even in the dangers of war."[1]   The ancient simple music is, as an invention of the gods,[2] to be kept in holy reverence.   " Music is something so superior, so divine, so great—something so beautiful and so sublime, that our forefathers were right in keeping it in high estimation in education."[3]   The ancient Greeks had only music for worship and for education.

Amongst the Romans, Cicero and Quintilianus agree that music is one of the most powerful agents in ennobling mankind.   " I agree with Plato," says Cicero, " that nothing has so much effect on tender minds as music."[4]   One can hardly say how far its power extends, for the indolent can be stimulated, the excited can be quieted.   " *Namque et incitat languentes et languefacit excitatos, et tum remittit animos, tum contrahit.*[5]

---

[1] Τῶν γὰρ νέων τὰς ψυχὰς ᾤοντο δεῖν διὰ μουσικῆς πλάττειν τε καὶ ῥυθμίζειν ἐπὶ τὸ εὔσχημον ·   χρησίμης δηλονότι τῆς μουσικῆς ὑπαρχούσης πρὸς πάντα καὶ πᾶσαν ἐσπουδασμένην πρᾶξιν, προηγουμένως δὲ πρὸς τοὺς πολεμικοὺς κινδύνους.

[2] Σεμνὴ κατὰ πάντα ἡ μουσικὴ θεῶν εὕρημα οὖσα.

[3] Σεμνὴ ἡ ἁρμονία, καὶ θεῖον τι καὶ μέγα.—ἡ ἁρμονία ἐστὶν οὐρανία, τὴν φύσιν ἔχουσα θείαν, καὶ καλὴν καὶ δαιμονίαν.

[4] *De Leg.* ii., 15.

[5] Cicero has elsewhere expressed a similar thought in these words:— " Nihil est tam cognatum mentibus nostris, quam numeri et voces, quibus

We may, therefore, draw towards the conclusion, and say, that as far as our knowledge of the nations of antiquity extends, according to their own records, we find music held in high estimation, honoured and cultivated by the wisest, the greatest, and the best of men, be they called legislators, sages, or prophets. All nations have considered it a divine gift, sublime in the temple, and cheering at the family hearth; of national festivities the brightest ornament, and in solitude the inseparable companion, the faithful friend of man. As its origin was, by all nations, looked upon as divine, so its true abode was with the gods; and when man, passing through the gate of death, had to leave behind him all earthly possessions, music alone followed him into the mansions of the blest, into eternity; its charms were sought in the Elysium and the Walhalla, as well in Odin's Hall as in Mahomet's Paradise. In the creeds of all nations music has been *eternalized*, by the rougher Scandinavian as well as the more refined Greek; and, according to the Christian doctrines, music will be everlasting:—" There shall be heard a great voice of a multitude, as the voice of many waters, as the voice of mighty thunderings, singing, Hallelujah, glory, honour, and power unto the Lord."

et excitamur et lenimur, et languescimus, et ad hilaritatem et ad tristitiam deducimur."—Cic. *Orat.*, iii. 51.

VI.

Art among the Romans.—Music in the Christian Era, especially in the British Islands.

THE British nation has frequently been compared to the Romans, and the British empire to that of the Roman Cæsars. The comparison may hold good in many points, but, fortunately for Great Britain, not in all. For, if from Athens we turn our eye to Rome, Rome even in its brightest days, we find ourselves, in regard to those manifestations which denote the mental and moral superiority of men and nations, as in a desert. Roman philosophy, Roman art, and Roman literature, stand to that of the Greeks, as the statue of the Gladiator, or the Farnese Bull, to those sublime groups of a Laocoon, or a Niobe. "Poetry had no native growth in Rome," says Schlegel; this might be said of every art where a deeper feeling, a loftier imagination, a more refined taste, more genius, more humanity, were required. "The Greeks were a nation of artists, and the Romans a practical people." [1] This may appear to many a title of their pre-eminence, and prove the truth of the comparison of the British and Roman nations. But beware of the consequence. There is something terrible in a nation of utilitarians. Where every mind is engrossed with material interests—where every action, every acquisition of knowledge, is calculated by its future produce—where high and low, those who possess much, and those who possess nothing, strive with all their energies, and strain every nerve from the first to the last day of the year, and from the first to the last of their life, to ac-

---

[1] Schlegel, *Dramatic Art and Literature;* See *Roman Theatre.*

quire more and more wealth and power, to displace the one, to outstrip the other—where nothing has value but what can be exchanged for coin, a society in which material interest is the centre of gravity; in that society there is a deeply-rooted cancer at the source of health and life, which, soon or late, will pay the penalty of the violation of the laws of nature, and the total neglect of the nobler faculties of man.[1]

Compare, then, the practical Romans, with the more ideal Greeks; with them, who made a deeper study of man, his good and evil propensities, his higher destiny, the feelings were not altogether disregarded in education. Heart and mind should harmoniously strive towards the same end of perfection. Compare them, and you will find that the Romans, far from excelling in the fine arts, left their cultivation to the Greeks and Etruscans residing at Rome.[2] The arts were to them articles of luxury, introduced as a corrupting element, both betokening and advancing degeneracy. " In the triumphal processions, the fights of the gladiators and of wild beasts, all the magnificence of the world, all the wonders of every clime, were brought before the eye of the spectator, who was glutted with the most violent scenes of blood. On nerves so steeled, what effect could the more refined gradations of tragic pathos produce ? rope-dancers and white elephants were preferred to every kind of art. Desirous as were the Romans to become thorough Hellenists, they wanted for it that milder humanity, which is so distinctly traceable in Greek history, poetry, and art, even in the time of Homer. From the most austere virtue, which buried every personal inclination, as Curtius did his life, in the bosom of fatherland, they passed with fearful rapidity to a state of corruption, by avarice and luxury, equally without example. Never in their character did they belie the legend, that their first founder was suckled, not at the breast of a woman, but of a ravenous

[1] Powerfully is this subject treated in the celebrated work of Regier *Des Classes dangereuses de la Société.*—See Appendix.

[2] " Artists were not held in high estimation, and the arts never flourish where they are not honoured."—Dr Schmitz's *History of Rome*, p. 256.

she-wolf. They were the tragedians of the world's history, who exhibit many a deep tragedy of kings led in chains, and pining in dungeons; they were the iron necessity of all other nations; universal destroyers, for the sake of raising at last, out of the ruins, the mausoleum of their own dignity and freedom, in the midst of the monotonous solitude of an obsequious world. To them it was not given to excite emotion by the tempered accents of mental suffering, and to touch with a light and delicate hand every note of the scale of feeling. Of all their ancient greatness, nothing remained to them but the contempt of pain and death, whenever an extravagant enjoyment of life must finally be exchanged for them."[1]

These are the words of the man, whose acquaintance with ancient and modern art and literature has scarcely been equalled. They express the sentence of posterity upon one of the greatest nations that ever lived, a practical nation, but a cruel, a hard, a corrupted one—a scourge to mankind, a curse to humanity; and at whose tomb we have neither tears nor sympathy. From them we would have little to learn in art, if a few master spirits, and above all, Horace, as a splendid star, worthy of Greece, Horace, the Roman Alcæus, had not enlivened the darkness of the Roman night. And, with all his splendour, he is but a child of Greece; his genius had been nourished with the genius of Greece,[2] as Pindar's with that of Corinna.

If we turn from this great Roman cemetery—upon which a few noble monuments of art, an Ovid, a Virgil, and a Lucullus, stand at the side of Horace—to the British islands, another spectacle of a surprising nature will present itself.

We hear it daily repeated, that Great Britain has neither taste nor leisure for music, and that its cultivation must be sought with those who are less occupied, and have nothing better to do. In a time when almost all Europe is cultivating this art, and begins to associate it with life, when all continental states extend its influence, and give it an impor-

[1] Schlegel, ibid., p. 209.
[2] Princeps Æolium carmen in Italos,
    Deduxisse modos.—*Hor. Od.* iii. 30.

tant share in the education of the young, we find it in the British islands, but mainly in the north of Great Britain, utterly neglected in school and church and families, burdened, persecuted with national prejudices, and in a state of infancy, with regard to its theory and practice, its history and philosophy, unequalled by any other nation. In those times, on the contrary, when all the Occident was still a land unknown to civilization, when wars, and unceasing migrations of northern and Asiatic tribes, kept all Europe in total barbarism, we find music cultivated to such a degree in these isolated islands, that we can say with certainty, that it was never any where more popular, more generally cultivated, or in closer connection with the whole public and private life of a people. The generality of its practice, as our skeleton of facts will shew, seems indeed fabulous, and appears to us, considering its present standing and insignificance, almost like a dream of fairy-land.

Historians have preserved facts concerning the harp of the Celts, which reaches almost to the commencement of the Christian era. Diodorus of Sicily, who wrote in the first half century, says, that the bards sang their poems to instruments like lyres, (ταῖς λύραις ὁμοίων.)[1] The bards stept between the hostile armies with their swords drawn, and their spears extended, and by their eloquence, or by irresistible enchantment, often prevented the effusion of blood. Ammianus Marcellinus (390 of our era) says, that the bards celebrated actions of illustrious men in heroic poems, which they sang to the sweet sound of the lyre.[2]

Skill on this instrument constituted a part of the usual acquirements of the educated class among the Celts as well as the Danes and Anglo-Saxons: in the sixth century, one-third of the male population of Ireland were harpers.[3]

At the convivial repasts of the Anglo-Saxons, the harp passed from hand to hand through all the company. The Saxon poet, Cædmon, in the 7th century, not being able to

---

[1] Lib. v., c. 31, p. 314. Edit. Bipont.   [2] Lib. xv., c. 9, p. 89.
[3] Walker's *Irish Bards*, p. 53.

play on such occasions, used to retreat, in order to conceal his ignorance of an art so generally practised among his countrymen.[1]

Bards were considered sacred in their person and property, and their houses were sanctuaries; a harp was considered an indispensable possession, of which a family, in legal pursuits, could not be deprived.[2] The veneration which surrounded the bard, and all that belonged to him, gave him the privilege to pass and repass, in safety, between hostile armies. Thus king Alfred sang (878,) as harper in the Danish camp; and sixty years later, Anlaf, the Danish king, in that of Athelslane.[3]

Adamnan, the Abbot of Iona (700,) says, that singing with accompaniment had been the custom in Ireland among the profane poets or bards, from *remote* and *unknown* time.[4]

In the life of Dunstan, the biographer, a contemporary of the saint (X. Cent.,) says, that the holy man took with him, on his journeys, according to custom, the cythara, called harp in the mother tongue.[5]

The Christian church of the Culdees, of which Bangor in Wales, Banchor in Ireland, and Iona in the Western Islands, were the principal establishments, in many points at variance with Rome, had its own ritual, liturgy, and chant. About that early period (IV. Cent.,) when St. Ambrose endowed the occidental church with his tunes of sublime inspiration, the Culdees had their own tunes; and, according to the specimens preserved to us, not less sublime, and in no degree

[1] Beda, *Historia Ecclesiastica*, lib. iv., c. 24.

[2] " The ancient Britons lived and breathed in poetry ; in their political maxims, preserved to our times, they place the poet-musician beside the agriculturist and the artist, as one of the three pillars of social existence." —Thierry's *History of the Norman Conquest*, l. i., p. 53.

See *Trioedd.* beirdd ynys Prydyn, sec. xxi., No. 1. Archaiology of Wales, iii., 283.

[3] See Yugulphus and William of Malmesbury.

[4] Cantum cum modulatione in usum fuisse inter poetas profanos seu Bardos, idque *more antiquo, ab immemorabili.*—Adamnam.

[5] Sumpsit secum Cytharam, quam, paterna lingua, harpam vocamus.

inferior to those of Rome.[1] We learn from Venerable
Bede[2] and Bishop Stillingfleet,[3] that the contest between
the Roman and British churches commenced with their respective chants.   The singers were sent from Rome, monks
well skilled in the art: they eventually gained the hearts of
those who listened to them ; and thus the Roman chant prepared the way for Roman worship and Roman power.[4]

Throughout the middle ages the harp continued to be popular in Ireland.   Irish harpers and Irish harps were titles
of excellence over all Europe.   When Gruffudd ab Cynan,
(circa 1100,) a Welsh prince, produced a new code of musical
regulations for his Cambrian subjects, a number of Irish bards
were invited to Wales, to give their assistance, which was acknowledged with obligation on the part of Caradoc, the historian.[5]   In the works of that patriotic and learned Bishop
of St David's, Gerald, the Cambrian, who, during his opposition to Henry II., had travelled in Ireland, France, and Italy,
we read that Ireland stood, in regard to skill on musical instruments, without comparison, first among the nations he
had seen.[6]

Galileo, the father of the astronomer, who devoted almost

[1] See Muratori's *Anecdota,* de Antiphonario vetustissimo Monasterii
Benchorensis in Hibernia, tom. iv., 121.

In antiquissimo antiphonario *Benchorensi* habes hymnum quando com-
municarent Sacerdotes : *Sancti venite, Christi corpus sumite.*—Abbas Ger-
bertus *De Cantu et Musica Sacra,* tom. i. p. 459.

[2] *Historia Ecclesiastica,* lib. iv. c. 18 ; and Vita Abbat. Weremoth.

[3] *Origines Britannicae.*

[4] B. Biscop Psallendi ordinem *juxta Romanum* introduisse in patri-
am suam Nordanhymbriam.—Beda, *Hist. Abbat. Weremoth,* p. 195., anno 678 ; and *Eccles. Hist.,* iv., 18.

De omnibus ejusdem provinciæ monasteriis ad eundem (archicantorem
Johannem,) qui cantandi periti erant, confluebant.—*Ibid.*

We know from Æddius, that he was the first, after the Culdees had
been driven away (Scottis ejectis), who instituted the Ecclesiastical Roman Chant (qui cantus ecclesiasticos antiphonatim instituerit) in the
monasteries of Northumberland.—Mabillon. *Annal.,* t. i., p. 414 and 494.

[5] Powell's *History of Wales,* pp. 115, 191.

[6] In musicis instrumentis, prae omni natione quam vidimus, incom-
parabiliter est instructa (gens Hibernia).—*Topog. Hib.,* c. ii., p. 739.

a whole life to the study and inquiry of ancient music, says, in speaking of the harp in Italy: "This very ancient instrument was brought to us from Ireland, as Dante has recorded, where they are excellently made, and in great numbers, and the inhabitants of which island have practised on it for very many centuries."[1]

The harp was such a constant companion of persons of rank, that no one was allowed to be ignorant of it; and no bishop, no abbot, no priest, travelled without the harp; "for in playing on it, they found, in their piety, great delight."[2]

Also, in Wales, harps were to be found in every family; and the same writer, in describing the primitive manners of the Welsh, and their hospitality to strangers, says, that, "Those who arrive at an early hour are entertained with the conversation of young women, and the music of the harp, till evening; for here every family has its harps provided for this very purpose. Every family, too, is here well skilled in the knowledge of that instrument."[3]

Remarkable is his passage on the music of Scotland. Those who only know Scotland of the nineteenth century, would not believe in that almost fabulous cultivation of music, 700 years ago, had we not before us historical documents of such weight and importance. High as he places Ireland, "Scotland has not only equalled but far excelled it; so much so, that Scotland is now regarded as the fountain of the art."[4]

The Caledonian bards were in existence so late as the eighteenth century; their last representatives were Rode-

[1] *Dialogues on Ancient and Modern Music.* By Galileo. P. 143. Printed in 1582. Also, in Lord Bacon's *Sylva Sylvarum,* a high compliment is paid to the Irish harps.

[2] Episcopi et abates et sancti in Hibernia viri Citharas circumferre, et in eis modulando pie delectari consueverant.—*Geraldus Cambrensis,* l. c.

[3] Geraldus' *Cambr. Cambriae Descriptio,* c. ix.

[4] (Scotia) non tantum *aequiparavit* Hiberniam, verum etiam in musica peritia *longe prævalet et præcellit ;* unde et ibi quasi *fontem artis requirunt. Topographia Hiberniae,* Distinctio III., c. xi., apud Camdeni Anglic. Francofurti, 1602.

rick Morison[1] and Murdoch Macdonald, the former at Dun-vegan Castle, the latter in that of Maclean of Coll. The bagpipes have usurped the place of the harp; a poor substi-tute for the nobler instrument and the nobler race of poet musicians.

The harpers were of the household of kings and princes.[2] They slept in the bed-chamber of the kings,[3] and ate out of their plates, and drank out of their cups,[4] and were at all times admitted into the king's presence.[5] So high was the estimation in which they were held, so superior their skill,[6] so many their privileges, so great the honours bestowed on them, that, on the one hand, they grew arrogant, exacting, and overbearing; and, on the other, vagabonds, idlers, and rogues, assumed their dress and appearance, in order to en-joy their privileges and distinctions. Laws, therefore, were found necessary to repress the arrogance of the harpers, and also to protect their dignity and respectability from encroach-ments of idle adventurers. Acts were passed to prevent their asking for the king's buckle which fastened his cloak,[7] or for

[1] *Essay on the Highland Music,* by Macdonald, p. 11.

[2] In Domesday Book, the king's minstrel had lands assigned to him as stated officer. See also, Dr. Percy, v. 1., Introd. p. 64.

[3] Buchanan's *History of Scotland.* See Ethodius 25th, and Fethalna-chus 38th, king of Scotland.

[4] Froissart tells this of the four Irish kings, who had submitted to Richard II. at the end of the fourteenth century, and were put under the care of Henry Castide, to be taught English manners. They refused to submit to them, and *would not be deprived of their good old customs.*

[5] See interesting anecdote in Walsingham's *History of England.*

[6] Those who are inclined to depreciate, in consequence of the popu-larity of the harp, the skill required for playing it, have perhaps never seen or heard the performance of a good Welsh harper. There are still some rare blind harpers to be heard, who are able, to the amazement of every musician, to handle the triple-stringed harp (three rows of strings) in diatonic and chromatic compositions, with a talent, and in a style, with which modern harpists, with all the improvements in pedals, can only with difficulty compete. The power of performance, together with the counterpointed style, in which some Welsh harpers excel, have given us, of harp and harp-music, and of the bards, in Wales at least, a higher idea than any we could have formed before.

[7] See Walker's *Irish Bards,* p. 53.

the prince's horse, hawk, or greyhound.[1]   That the dignity
of the harper must have been very enviable, as it was capable of satisfying the most exorbitant ambition, has been
proved in many instances.   John of Salisbury treats the great
people of his time as following Nero in their extravagances
in behalf of the gold and silver dresses, and embroidered
garments of the minstrels.[2]

The number of those who wished to pass for harpers and
minstrels grew, by degrees, to an enormous amount.   Every
mountebank, every tale-teller, every beggar, those who danced,
or played tricks of buffoonery and legerdemain, wore the
cap and cloak of the minstrel, and as such lived upon public
hospitality.   That privileged race, therefore, so well received
in every feudal castle, and fondly beloved by the mass of the
people, revered during the barbarous ages and the time of
chivalry, became, by degrees, the terror and plague of the
country.   Laws of great severity were passed against " minstrels," " songsters," and " tale-tellers ;" but it would be an
act of injustice to throw the blame upon, and to pronounce
judgment against, the true harpers and minstrels.   If we examine the texts of those legal acts with minuteness, we shall
find that they were as much a protection of real minstrelsy
as of the country.   That of Edward I. (1315), begins thus :—
" Forasmuch as many idle persons, *under colour of minstrelsy*
. . . . have ben, and yet be, receaved to meate and
drynke, and be not therewith contented yf they be not largely
considered with gyftes," &c.   The law, therefore, restrains
the number of minstrels to be admitted in the houses of pre-
lates, earls, and barons, to three or four a day, and that none
come to " meaner men," unless desired.   Edward IV. (1489),
complains, in a letter, that a number of persons falsely assume the privileges of minstrels.[3]   The increased severity
of the law seemed to increase the number of such vagabonds.
In vain should the *ear be cut*, or *burned with a hot iron for a*

---

[1] See Jones' *Welsh Bards*, p. 28.

[2] John of Salisbury, in his *Rigordus*, 1185.

[3] *Percy's Relics.*   Introduct., pp. 69, 70.

first offence, and the man be *hanged for a second;* acts followed acts, the one more bloody than the other, yet they were still repeated under James VI. (1579, c. 75),[1] and even more than a century later, this kind of vagabondage existed to a most alarming extent. Fletcher of Saltoun computes, in 1698, the number of such characters who, as a real plague, wandered through the counties of Scotland alone, to more than a hundred thousand.[2]

With the introduction and spread of Christianity, there arose a new instrument of music, the organ, producing indescribable effects; and, remarkable as it may appear, it seems that the organ was in general use in North and South Britain and Ireland, many years before it found a place in the churches of France and Italy.[3] During the thirteenth century, when Italy was recognized as the most eminent school for the practice of that most sublime of all instruments, Florence was visited by organists from all parts of Europe, to hear and see the famous blind performer, called, in consequence, *Francesco Cièco,* and the equally celebrated *Antonio,* surnamed *Dagl' Organi.* Many English and Scottish monks were among those who went to learn and study, and who brought back, over the sea, the knowledge which they had acquired.[4]

In the reign of Queen Elizabeth, whose time produced a Shakespeare, a Bacon, and a Milton, gave also birth to Tallis, Bird, Bull, and many other composers, whose works are still

---

[1] " All minstrels, not avowed in special service by some of the Lords of Parliament, or great Barons," &c.

[2] Second *Discourse on the Affairs of Scotland,* p. 145.

[3] Vide Busby's *History of Music,* Vol. i., p. 264; and O'Connor, *Rerum Hibernicarum Scriptores Veteres,* Vol. iv. *De Organorum et Psalmodiæ usu in vetustis Hibernorum Ecclesiis.*

[4] We have seen and heard, in our own times, the famous Antonio, of whom it might be observed, that as many persons went from Cadiz, the remotest part of Spain, to Rome, in order to see the historian Livy; so, many most excellent musicians have come from England, *and the most distant regions of the north,* crossing the sea, Alps, and Appennines, in order to hear the performances of Antonio.—*Christophero Landino, Comment. on Dante.*

sung and admired.   England then possessed a school of its
own, a school which could compete with the most renowned
of Europe.   Music was then generally understood, and knowledge of this art considered a necessary adjunct of a liberal education.   Part singing, especially, was then, as the multitude of
compositions of madrigals and canons shew, daily practised
in families, and as under the Anglo-Saxons, the harp, so singing in parts, was in general use after repasts and banquets.
A curious and remarkable instance of the knowledge of music in those times, has been preserved to us in the following
lines :   " Supper being ended, and music-books, *according to
the custom*, being brought to the table, the mistress of the
house presented me with a part, earnestly requesting me to
sing.   But when, after many excuses, I protested unfeignedly
that I could not, *every one began to wonder*, yea, *some whis-
pered to others, demanding how I was brought up*." [1]

What was the position of music in Scotland at that time,
we may learn from many historical facts, which, as clearly
as Morley's Dialogue, explain and characterize the whole
period.   The extent to which the inhabitants of Edinburgh
practised singing and instrumental music, is to be found in a
most curious and interesting incident which occurred on the
arrival of Queen Mary from France, when many of the inhabitants, to the number of *five* or *six hundred*, attended during
several nights, under the windows of the Abbaye of Isle-
bourgh,[2] (Holyrood,) where the Queen was then staying,
and played on the violins or *rebecs*, and sang psalm tunes.[3]
Whatever may have been the character of the performances,
the above fact fully shews, that Edinburgh had then as many
violins and violinists as perhaps now all Scotland.   Music

[1] Morley's *Treatise on Practical Musick.*

Thomas Morley, Gentleman of Queen Elizabeth's Chapel, one of the
most celebrated masters in composition,—died 1604.

[2] Edinburgh was frequently so named by French writers of that period.

[3] Brantôme, who accompanied the Queen, says in the *Dames Illustres :*
" Ils lui donnèrent une aubade de méchants violons, et de petits rebecs,,dont
il n'y en a pas faute dans ce pays là."   John Knox, however, is more
favourable in his account of the performance : he remarks in speaking of

schools existed almost in every town;[1] and remarkable is
the statute of King James VI., (issued in the year 1579,)
who, as a last and vain effort, tried to save them from utter
decay.

When we now speak of the organization of music schools,
or of music to be added to the daily branches of instruction,
we appear to Scotchmen[2] as if we were speaking in a dream.
In times so utterly industrial, it passes the limits of the understanding, when there is question of the cultivation and
diffusion of an art. However, it is a comfort to say, that it
was not always so, as King James's statute most evidently
shows: "For the instruction of the youth in the art of music and
singing, quhilk is almaist decayit, and sall shortly decay, without tymous remeid be providit, our sovereign lord, &c. . . .
requestis the Provest &c. . . . to erect and sett up ane sang
scuill, with ane maister sufficient and able for instruction of
the youth in the said science of music, as they will answer to
his hienes upoun the parrell of their fundationis."

That at that time still considerable skill in music and part
singing existed, show us, as well the collections of psalms
which were then published in Scotland,[3] as those occasional
appearances of the people, who in the streets sang, *two thousand persons in number*, psalms in four parts, at the sound of

the Queen : " The melodie lyked hir weill, and she willed the same to
be continued sum nychts after with grit diligence."

[1] There were music schools in Ayr, Irvine, Paisley, Glasgow, Cupar,
Dunbar, Lanark, Aberdeen, Dundee, Elgin, and St Andrews.—Vide in
James Melville's *Autobiography*, concerning his musical studies at St An-
drews.

[2] Especially to the Town-Council of Edinburgh.

[3] The psalm tunes published shortly after the Reformation, are in four
and five parts, and in *seven* different cliffs, five of which would be now unintelligible hieroglyphics to the greater number of the amateurs and musicians of Scotland. The parts are besides printed, two on one page, and
two, but inverted, on the other. This manner of printing is an evident
testimony that reading in parts was a common practice in families and
churches, where two and two were sitting opposite each other on a table
or in a pew, and read from the same book. Compare " *the Psalmes of
David in Prose and Meeter, with their whole tunes in foure and more parts,
with same Psalmes in Reports.* Printed at Edinburgh by the heires of
Andrew Hart, *Anno Dom.* 1635."

which, as the historian says, *heaven and earth resoundit, and singer and listener were moved to tears.*[1]

We close here the series of documents concerning the high cultivation of music in the British Islands. We have met with incontestable facts, proving that music has as favourable a soil in Great Britain and Ireland, as elsewhere. Without the annals of past centuries, however, such an assertion would find an unbelieving ear. The present state of this neglected art (in Scotland at least,) is so destitute, that without the faith in the universality of music, and without a glance into the history of past ages, it would be too great a stretch of imagination, to believe that music ever was a popular art, far less to such a fabulous extent; for out of hearing of the concert-rooms and theatres, we stand, in regard to music, in a land of exile; we tread the ground of a cemetery. We ask in vain for the schools, the choirs, the works and masters of former days. A misunderstood piety has carried them to the grave. A gift that providence found worthy of giving to man, should have been found worthy of preserving: but it is not so. Silence surrounds us on every side; the children are silent in the schools; silent is the united multitude in churches, or if they raise their voices and mean to sing, it is in a style, compared with which the singing of a Moravian congregation of the Hottentots would appear as a choir of angels. The teacher of the people in the church, and the teacher of the people in the school, have not felt the absence of this heavenly art of sound within their walls. Instead of seeking it above their horizon, as a sublime power to open the heart and the understanding, they seek it in the lower regions, and look down upon it, from their imaginary throne of superiority, as upon a lovely woman, both the mother and the victim of debauchery and seduction.

Yes, it is far in space and time, from the shriek of the engine-whistle to the simple and sublime chants, the sacred

---

[1] Calderwood the historian has furnished us with the most minute description of this incident, which happened at the return of Durie, one of the town ministers, from exile.—See also the *Letters and Journals of Robert Bailie*, edited by David Laing, vol. III.

musical inspirations of the fathers of the church ; it is far
away from the Forth and the Tweed to that dwelling in
Wittenberg, where a Mathesius, a Melancthon, and a Luther
passed half nights in singing mottets, and the *dulces exuviae,*
the last words of Virgil's *Dido*.[1] It is a long time from our
days to those of Zuinglius, who could sing and play,[2] and
nevertheless, could speak as a Demosthenes, and die upon
the field of battle.

If history tells us that music may be a luxuriant plant of
the British soil, these men teach us that music is also a religious art; that it is a sacred legacy of the fathers and founders
of Christianity, and of the founders and martyrs of the Reformation ; a legacy, which in the hands of those who should be
its guardian priests, instead of being watched and guided, cultivated with zeal, with care and jealousy, has been allowed to
sink deeper and deeper, more and more neglected in church
and school, and more and more deprived of all its sacred attributes.   How well would the words of Zuinglius be applied
to his misled, his degenerated followers !   " If thou knewest
what music is, the evil spirit of ambition, power, and controversy, the demon of riches, luxury, and avarice, would instantly be driven out of thee."

What a terrible sentence must, to their ear, appear the
words of the energetic and learned author of the Reformation,
when he says : " I do not think that through the scriptures
all fine arts should be condemned, as many would-be theolo-
gians do : I want to see the arts, especially that of music, in

---

[1] Mathesius, (*Historien von Luthers Leben*, Bl. 155,) who was frequently a guest on these occasions, says, " We often sang the last words
of Virgil's *Dido*.   Master Philippus (Melancthon) also sang with us."

[2] Vide Bullinger.   In the MS. preserved at Zurich, this writer says of
Zuinglius, " That although his adversaries called him the Evangelical
Piper, he continued to cultivate music with great modestie ;" and when
Faber (afterwards Bishop of Vienne) reproached him for his cultivation
of music, he said, in his noble simplicity : " Tu ne sais pas, mon cher
Faber, ce que c'est que la musique : J'ai, il est vrai, appris à jouer du
luth, du violin, et d'autres instruments : Ah, si tu connoissais le son du
luth celeste, l'esprit malin de l'ambition et de l'amour des richesses qui te
possèdent sortiraient ainsi de toi."

the service of him who has given and created it."[1]   Therefore he mentions: " Children must learn to sing, and teachers
must be able to teach it.   Music stands nearest to divinity !
. . . I would not give the little I know, for all the treasures
of the world ! She is my shield in combat and adversity, my
friend and companion in moments of joy, my comforter and
refuge in those of despondency and solitude."

[1] Preface to his *Geistlichen Liedern*.   Wittenberg, 1544.

VII.

Music then, as we have shown, stands in connection with education, with classical and popular education ; and the objection that its cultivation has no native soil in the British Islands, is proved to be unfounded. That it is also a part of religious training, has in a few words sufficiently been expressed. But all obstacles, all prejudices, are not therefore removed, and at every step new ones arise and obstruct our path. We hear many teachers and directors of educational institutions say, that already a great deal of time and attention on their part, and too great a share indeed on the part of the parents, was already given to music, and that the time its study requires, was altogether out of proportion with other branches of instruction ; and that, after all, they could not see in what consisted the superiority of those who had acquired superiority in music ; and that even many musicians were far from being an ornament to society, and luminaries in the moral world ; that, on the contrary, they seemed even to have been more prodigally provided with human weakness than the rest of mankind, and that their thirst for knowledge and wisdom, revealed itself only in their unquenchable thirst for all good things of this earth.—These objections are serious ; they place music before a high tribunal. Here it stands before the bar of an implacable judge—experience—before whose terrible sentence even the authority of a Plato and a Luther must remain mute and of no avail. This is a language which is not uncommon, and which, applied to a considerable portion of the craft, is unfortunately too true. As

a great share of the still existing fears for a musical education, especially for young men, is attributed, and rightly so,
to the social meetings to which music might lead, and to that
dense atmosphere in which a number of musicians are known
to live and exhibit their skill and talent, it is necessary, before speaking of general musical education, to say a few
words on the education of those whose principal and exclusive study and profession it is.

The abuse which professional men make of the art, has
its source in a too superficial, too partial, too one-sided development of their faculties. The mind and the heart, as
said before, should be developed simultaneously, and receive
nourishment from the cultivation of the understanding and
of the sentiments. Nothing is so baneful in its consequences
as the unfolding of one faculty to the prejudice of the others;
the connection between the different branches of human
learning is too intimate, too delicate, to admit of the attention being devoted exclusively to one alone. The ignorance
of musicians has been often remarked. J. J. Rousseau said
a great deal in these few words : " *les musiciens lisent peu ;*"
their inebriety also is proverbial, and has acquired for them
a lamentable celebrity. These facts bear a date of long
standing, for, besides the very ancient proverb of the church,
cantores amant humores, translated in French by *Ivrogne
comme un musicien*, Titus Livius tells us, that when the
censors forbade the flautists to eat and drink in the temples, they quitted the city of Rome, and went to dwell at
Tibur. There being then no musicians for the religious
service, the senators were much embarrassed. But the Ti-
burians came to their aid. The decided passion of the Tibi-
cinists for drink was known : their hosts invited them to a
great feast. Their throats, dried up by the flute, were frequently moistened by wine, until at last, by dint of continued
libations, every one of them, without exception, fell dead
drunk ; in this state they were transported back to Rome,
and were not a little surprised when they awoke on the
forum, under the shouts of the populace. The Senate then
laid hands on them, but, instead of punishment, they were

henceforth allowed to continue eating and drinking, for it seems that nothing short of this could set the flutes again agoing. This miserable failing, so derogatory to the noble profession of musician, and which probably has produced the Latin diction, *musice vivere, musice œtatem agere*, for a life of debauchery, is perpetuated in many of its followers; for we learn that under Louis XIV. the principal band of musicians received on the fête days of St Louis and St Martin, bread and wine to their hearts' content. The minstrels used to partake of the latter to such excess, that they almost always appeared before the king with their eyes starting from their sockets, no longer in condition to play in time; and notwithstanding the conductor's staff, *gavots, minuets,* all would go pell-mell, to the utter despair of the royal auricles. Even the king of the minstrels, in spite of the high dignity with which he was invested, saw neither notes nor musicians, and could distinguish no sharp from a flat. J. J. Rousseau relates of his professor of music, M. Lemaître, what might be still said of many others: " He was as good a drinker as he was a musician; his inspiration augmented in proportion as the liquid in his bottle diminished; and if he were captivated by the charms of composition, he was no less so by those of wine." [1] On proceeding with this original sin of musicians, we may sometimes find it among eminent composers; among those who, while moving in the regions of high tragic poetry, are, in reality, walking, like Robert Macaire, upon the upper leather of their boots. These are not proofs of a high vocation, although they may be found even in men of genius; but they are, to a certainty, proofs of a deficiency of general education, or of the cultivation of one faculty at the expense of all others. A man may be a star in his profession, and there possess great eminence, and yet be, in every other sphere, in infantine ignorance. A great mathematician, a superior chemist, an excellent lawyer or physician, may be a very uneducated man. Education extends over the moral and intellectual faculties, harmonizes all the various

---

[1] *Confessions de J. J. Rousseau.*

branches of knowledge; and, in this union, it manifests itself not only in thought and action, but even in language, in manners, and external bearing. If, therefore, we find among a certain lower order of musicians, those propensities which have caused them so sad a celebrity, and created against music such apprehensions, it is evident that their art stands beyond the reproaches which their intellectual inferiority, their deficiency of general education, alone deserves. Every thing holy may be abused, religion as well as art ; yet they remain unchanged, though often administered by unworthy hands.

But even this abuse of music, why make it a subject of reproach to music itself, or to musicians, when, on the contrary, musicians should ask you to account for it ? Does not Plato, for twenty-two centuries, warn the legislators of the abuse of music, and recommend to their care its purity ? Has he not foretold, that unless its sacred character, its power and importance, were jealously preserved to the youth, to the nation, to the state, it might be turned, in corrupted hands, against the youth, against the nation, and against the state ? Whence does music receive its greatest injury, its deepest wounds ? From those who should be its natural guardians, the most jealous defenders of its beauty and purity—the parents of children, and the managers of schools, especially schools for female education. To study music is, to them, nothing but to learn to *play the piano*. You may have talent, or you may have none, you must learn it under penalty of being taxed with having received but an indifferent education. In what, then, consists this study of the piano ? In sitting so many hours *daily* before the instrument, having the fingers curved, and stretched, and trained ; and after having thus passed, in the most tedious and thoughtless of all studies, the most precious and invaluable hours of life, what knowledge has been acquired ? Have they become musicians for their pains ? Has the science of music been revealed to them ? Have they learned to understand, to judge, to analyze a musical composition in its technical construction and poetical essence ? Or, have they learned to produce, after their own impulse, a musical thought, to develope it, and, in a momentaneous inspiration, to make the heart speak in joyful or plaintive strains, according to their mood of mind? Nothing of the kind. A few have learned to play a *sonata*, perhaps a *concerto*; a greater number have reached variations, but by far the greatest majority only quadrilles! This playing of quadrilles, this training of the fingers, mothers complacently call *accomplishment*, a *refined education;* and musicians who look with contempt upon musical study and musical works of this description, can they be surprised when the art to which they have devoted themselves, is not appreciated, not understood? What can we expect, when its whole destiny is left in the hands of matrons of boarding-schools, who, generally, are clear-sighted enough to make it an important *item* of their business, withdraw the lion's part from what is due to the teacher, but are ignorant of its very alphabet.[1]

If, in musical education, great errors are committed by teachers, the greatest of all arises from their submitting to the tyranny of these matrons, and their complacency in satisfying the wishes and the vanities of the parents. Unacquainted with music, its loftier purposes, and even with its mechanical department, the latter are over-anxious, in their paternal solicitude, to hear their offspring play or sing great pieces. The day is fixed beforehand, when, at a certain party, the young prodigy should take the whole company by surprise. The teacher, or governess, are alone initiated into the secret; and

[1] Every cow in Switzerland knows the bells of her own herd, and distinguishes the air (Rans des vaches) of her herdsman from that of any other; but we know managers of boarding-schools, where the pianoforte tinkling is going on from morning to night, to the great delight of the quarter bills, who flatter themselves that they cannot distinguish Rule Britannia from God Save the Queen. Their musical knowledge seems to extend as far only as that of Dr Johnson, who could distinguish a drum from a trumpet, and a bagpipe from a guitar. Boswell, his biographer, says, that he was very fond of the bagpipe, but instead of admiring it, as other people do, at a certain distance, he put his ear close to the great drone, which was certainly a little beyond what the nerves of an ass might be able to stand, and which would be enough to drive to insanity the most unmusical of all brutes.

these poor martyrs of ignorance try every means to show the
star in all its magnitude. The day, the great day, arrives;
the company begin to gather; the grandpapa has taken his
arm-chair, and now, O misery! begins the musical entertainment.   Papa feels quite uneasy; mamma is in a fever; and
the juvenile Corinna is all but fainting.   However, the glorious moment has come when the sun is to rise and dazzle
every eye. We all have heard such prodigious performances.
One bar after the other makes slowly its appearance, and is,
as it were, forced out; when she sings, it is in stammering
notes that she produces the eloquent *A te o cara*, or, *Una
furtiva lagrima*.   Often overcome with fear and emotion,
not of the music, but of the heads and candles around her,
she stops short, goes on again, but, alas! the black and white
keys begin to melt into each other, and to interchange
colours, until—all is darkness and confusion.   So ends the
first musical entertainment, and so begins the musical career
of young persons in general : each party-day is a new disap-
pointment for the family and visitors, and a day of deep distress for the poor victim of such vanities and follies.

It is very certain that music, so acquired, must become
irksome and tedious, that it can offer no enjoyment for the
moment, no nourishment for the mind, and throughout a
whole lifetime, no compensation for the time, the money,
and the tears it has cost.   In going directly against the purpose, it would be unreasonable to expect to attain it.   We
would wish to learn and love music; but you teach us to
dread and to hate it :—a system which resembles that of the
night police, who carry lanterns, that the thieves may see
them from a distance.   Well may we say to those parents,
and boarding-school Minervas, that music is a dangerous art,
if thus it becomes, in their unholy hands, an instrument of
torment to the young, or if it has to pass as a blighting
blast over the happy days of youth, and is, thanks to them,
a handmaid of vanity, an empty, idle, stupid show, on the
one side, and a greedy, cunning speculation, a vile, contemptible trade on the other.   Well may we say to the musician,
who thus sacrifices his dignity, betrays the art, and, as a sor-

did usurer, sells it to the highest bidder, what Schiller said
to the literary tradesman: " Unhappy mortal! who, with
science and art, the noblest of all instruments, effectest and
attemptest nothing more than the day-drudge with the
meanest; who, in the domain of perfect freedom, bearest
about thee the spirit of a slave."

" But," continues he, " how is the artist to guard himself
from the corruption of his time ? By despising its decisions.
Let him look upwards to his dignity and his mission, not
downwards to his comforts and his wants."

As we do not expect to change this degrading system
of musical education, unless the parents show a better understanding and a higher appreciation of the art, it is to
them we expose the necessity of a total reform in musical
tuition, and say, either release the child entirely from this
odious, mechanical, and stupifying study, good only for
nourishing ostentation and self-conceit, or make it a rational,
intellectual, and noble agent of moral education and mental
refinement. The more solid, the more elementary the beginning, the sooner the end is attained. All those who learn
music with the view to shine, will never learn it to satisfy
the better judge. They will find the general road too long,
and, unlike common mortals, begin where others finish ; fly
without wings. They learn, by heart, like a bird, a *Cavatina* and a great *Aria*, and display their science in drawing-
rooms, turning henceforth—a living hurdy-gurdy—in endless rotation, from the Cavatina to the Aria, and from the
Aria to the Cavatina. How different those who have learned
thoroughly the principles of music ! they sing every choral
or solo composition, though never seen before.

As soon as we approach music with more earnestness and
intelligence, as soon as we ask for its deeper sense, its worth,
we find that neither a common mechanical study, nor a common acquaintance with some of the inferior musical productions, can suffice. Music has its different spheres in which
it moves, different according to its character and its tendency. In its lowest, it has no other aim than to reach the
ear, to please, to charm it, to amuse for a moment, and

then to pass hence with the same breath of air which brought it. To this sphere belong the greater part of those musical compositions which have as yet reached the generality of amateurs. The endless variations, those numerous songs, duets, and trios, in which a foreign language and exotic melodious form have the great share of attraction, belong to this class. Many songs, glees, and other vocal compositions in the native language, are not, in their poetical and musical thought and form, much more deserving of attention. Hours of study spent on such, often worse than senseless combinations of words and sounds, are hours lost in life.

Music has its low and lofty branches; like architecture, it has its gradations, its huts, its palaces, and cathedrals. The greater part of the playing and singing multitude, have not yet extended their acquaintance beyond the hut and cottage region of the art. Or, if we take painting as our measure of comparison—arias, duets, and trios, vocal or instrumental, however beautiful, belong only to that rank of musical composition, in which stands a *portrait* or *genre* painting, scenes of common life, like Adrian van Ostade's village fairs, groups of dancers, drinkers or fiddlers; or like Morillo's Savoyards, monks, and beggars. Quartettes, overtures, symphonies, though the latter have, by the genius of Mozart and Beethoven, been placed upon the broadest, the grandest basis, and have risen to an almost unproportioned height, will never reach beyond the standard of the landscape. They stand at the side of those vivid and elegant scenes of a Canaletto, and now speak the touching pastoral language of a Poussin in his Arcadia, or disclose nature, like a Salvator Rosa, in all her grandest, wildest, most terrific moods. Choral and orchestral compositions, in which music and poetry go hand and hand in the development of a lofty, a moral, or sacred idea, rank with historical works in painting, with temples and cathedrals in architecture, in glorious supremacy over the humbler divisions of the art. In this region we meet those great spirits who, with their works, have both enlightened and astonished the world; an Animuccia and a Perugino, a Palestrina, at the side of a Michael

Angelo, an Orlando Lasso, a Philippus de Monte, a Siciliani, a Morales, a Vittoria, vying with a Titian, a Tintoretto, a Correggio. Here we meet those glorious names of an Allegri, a Durante, Lotti, Caldara, the Scarlattis, and Bachs, and Hasse, and Handel, grouped together like the Pleiades of the musical constellation. Compare with such names and works, those which we find in the musical library of our amateurs. You will see the sphere in which they move: then you will often peruse a number of large volumes, without finding one single composition which would captivate the interest of a real musician; not one which he would think good enough to be put into the hands of his pupils or children. What sacrifices, what hours, what precious years, are wasted in the acquisition and practice of a kind of composition, which, in reality, belong only to, what we might call, the musical infirmities and excrescences! Such compositions are the productions of musical merchants, written for the market, and calculated upon the ignorance of the customers. The distance of such a musician to a Palestrina, a Handel, a Mozart, can only be measured by that from an *ignis fatuus* to one of the luminaries of the ether above us. The same space lies between works of their creation; the one is like an earthen pot fit for common purposes; the other, the lofty effusion of a lofty mind, sprung from the immeasurable depths of the feelings and emotions of a noble heart, aiming at the beautiful, the great, and the infinite. In them all is spirit, enthusiasm, and poetry. Whoever approaches the sphere in which they breathe, feels himself elevated, and upon the wings of genius, carried away into other zones, other climes, more congenial with the spiritual, the immortal man. There he lives with a Raphael, a Schiller, a Mozart, in the regions of the ideal, and tastes, in those moments of light and purity, joys which the world can neither grant nor take away, which no recollection can either darken or efface. Their works are not temporary in their effect; they leave traces wherever they pass, indelible remembrances. " *They cease,*" says Zelter, " *but they are not done; in them there is no end.*"

Should such works of genius exist in vain? Should they remain a dead letter to the most of us? Should a ballad, a glee, a madrigal, close our musical horizon? Is there nothing more beyond this narrow space of atmosphere, in which we turn and return like a water-wheel, without moving one step in advance? Can we remain in this musical infancy? Have we not to rise out of this circle of musical trivialities, and, through a closer acquaintance with its technical and scientific principles, try to approach nearer to the sanctuary of the temple of art, and to be initiated in its loftier inspirations? There are elements enough about us, to raise music from its lowest to its highest station; and soon we might be able to say, in every school, in every institution, with Zelter: "Our chorus is now nothing less than a vast organ, which I can set a-playing or stop with one movement of my hand, and can make it, like a telegraph, denote and express great thoughts;—an organ, every pipe of which is a rational, voluntary agent, and which may realize our highest conception. Our choir is a school, whose end is wisdom, whose means, poetry, harmony, and song."[1]

[1] Zelter's *Briefwechsel mit Göthe.*

VIII.

Vocal Music: its influence upon the Health of Children, and upon the Development of the Physical Organs.

WE have spoken, in the former part of this work, of the nature of the various senses; we have deduced the necessity of the cultivation of the ear from its power, its direct and immediate influence upon the moral faculties, and the intimate connection existing between both; and have now reached the moment when we must shew, in all their special bearing, the influence which the cultivation of vocal music exercises upon the development of our external organs, and indicate the ways by which it unfolds by degrees the internal nature, the moral part of man.[1]

The various parts of the human body, in order that they may be kept in a healthy and active condition, require to be exercised according to the different functions assigned to them by nature. We are provided with a voice having the two-fold power of articulating words, and of uttering musical sounds. We may thence conclude, that both singing and

[1] For more particulars, we must refer the reader to the Introductory remarks contained in our Elementary Manuel, *Singing for the Million,* where the subject is treated under the following heads:—

1. *Influence of Singing on Physical Education in general, and on the health of children in particular.*

2. *Influence of Singing upon Moral Education.*

3. *The most suitable Age for Instruction in Singing.*

4. *Singing Exercises and Songs for Children.*

5. *Simultaneous Instruction in Elementary Schools.*

6. *Musical Education in Germany.*

From p. i. to p. **xxiii.**

speaking contribute to maintain, and even to improve, the healthy state of the various muscles and other organs, called into action when these physical faculties are exercised.

One of the first benefits arising from vocal instruction, is improvement in speaking. It has been justly asserted, that singing is the most effective means of improving the organs, if naturally good, and of correcting them if defective. In the manner of speaking, as well as of singing, as in the voice itself, there is a marked difference in different persons. This difference consists in more or less facility of utterance, more or less agreeableness of pronunciation, and in the peculiar tone with which nature has provided each individual. However various the shades of voice and tone, the practice of singing will be for all, we are sure, a never-failing means of improvement.

Instruction in singing serves to develope and cultivate not less the sense of hearing, the organs of which, like those of the voice, are not equally perfect in every individual. A great error will therefore be committed, in depriving those children of singing lessons who do not, in the first instance, evince a decidedly musical disposition, or what is popularly termed a musical ear. That quality is developed much more slowly in some persons than in others; there are some, indeed, in whom it seems totally deficient; but its absence often proceeds from their seldom or never having heard singing, and from their consequently not having had the opportunity of imitating the tones of others. By listening to singing, we learn to distinguish the relative position of the notes uttered by the voice; our ear thus becomes practised, and able to convey the nicest distinction of tone to the seat of perception. Thus, by endeavouring gradually to imitate others, we succeed in rendering the organs of voice capable of reproducing the sounds which the ear has received.

We come now to consider the influence of singing on the health of children. One of the prejudices most obstinately maintained against teaching children to sing, arises from an opinion frequently broached, that singing, if practised at a tender age, may have a baneful influence on the health, and

occasion pulmonary affections. It is not long since this idea
prevailed in Germany also ; but the most minute investigations, made by governments as well as parents, have proved
it to be quite erroneous. From the many thousand instances
of contrary results, the German people have at last learnt the
utter fallacy of this notion, and have not only ceased to dread
singing as being injurious to health, but go so far as to consider it one of the most efficacious means, not only for refining the ear, for developing the voice, but also for giving
strength and vigour to all the physical organs it calls into action. Nothing is better calculated than the practice of singing, to produce the power of free and lengthened respiration.
In proportion as matter is soft and plastic, it receives impressions the more readily and indelibly. The human body
is necessarily subject to this physical law ; and its mysterious
union with the living principle, and with spirit, must contribute to increase rather than diminish the effect of that law.
Childhood is the fittest period to receive to its fullest extent
all the advantages resulting from this branch of instruction.
All the organs of the voice are then soft and flexible, and
susceptible of the slightest impression. The lungs expand
with unobstructed ease ; the muscles and nerves connected
with the throat and chest, yield readily to the action of respiration ; the ear receives and conveys sound with facility,
and ideas communicated at that early epoch of life are not
easily effaced.

On the whole, then, we are convinced that singing, or, as
it may be termed, the art of extending and managing breath,
is one of the best preventives of, and surest remedies for general weakness of the chest ; and that its use, provided always
it be proportioned to the other physical powers of the singer,
is calculated to exert a most favourable influence on delicate
constitutions, to impart vigour to the organs connected with
the lungs, and thus to conduce to a healthy state of those
important functions of the body.

Those who assert, that children who learned to sing early
have lost their voices, do not take into account the thousand
accidents and changes to which their constitution, by our

effeminate training, may be subjected ; disease of any kind, violent colds, and whatever else may have weakened the chest, and destroyed the former better quality of the voice. At that period of life when the voice undergoes a change, boys lose theirs altogether ; the notes of a higher pitch disappear one after another, till, by degrees, a new one presents itself upon a lower octave of the scale, in the form of a Tenor or a Bass. Often an excellent Treble is, in the space of a few months or a few weeks, replaced by a Bass of the roughest kind. Although the Female voice does not undergo such a remarkable transformation, it nevertheless changes its whole character : a low voice often becomes a high one, and a high one descends and becomes a Contralto ; a good voice changes into an indifferent one, and *vice versa*. This depends entirely upon the development of the bodily frame and the state of health, so that no one can say, with certainty, what the voice of a child will be at a more mature age. The loss of voice is therefore unjustly attributed to *early singing*, unless injudiciously chosen exercises, or too high notes, have occasioned efforts beyond the power of the voice and chest. Besides, every one knows that children, playing in the open air, often exercise their vocal powers more in *one* hour, by violent exclamations, than a judicious teacher would ask them to do in a year.

The earliest age, that of six or seven years, is the most appropriate for learning to sing ; voice and ear, so obedient to external impressions, are rapidly developed and improved, defects corrected, and musical capabilities awakened. Experience of many years, and observation of every day's occurrence, have taught us, that a considerable proportion of the numerous children with whom we have met, could *at first* neither sound a single note, nor distinguish one from another ; ALL, without exception, have acquired ear and voice, and some of them have even become superior in both to their apparently more gifted companions ; in others, the very weak or indifferent voices have in a short time become pleasing, strong, clear, and extended.

Children, from five to six years of age, some of them unacquainted with the letters of the alphabet, have learnt to read music, to a considerable extent, in unison and parts, and to sing, with astonishing precision, imitations and fugues of Hiller, Rink, Fuchs, Teleman, and other great masters. So thoroughly acquainted have they become with the pitch of sound, that, without the least hesitation, they name the notes of which melodious phrases are composed, as soon as sung or played ; and it is remarkable, that in this exercise the youngest, and those who had at first to contend with the greatest difficulties, appeared the most acute and ready.

This improvement is more or less rapid. Some children having no ear at first, became awakened to the distinction of sound in a few days, some in a few weeks, and others after months only.

After having seen in a thousand instances, what interest, what intense pleasure children, we might say infants, take in their little singing lessons, after we have seen the astonishing progress they make, we are convinced that, through the medium of such early instruction, musical dispositions may be awakened in a surprising degree. Thus a taste, a true appreciation of this beautiful, innocent, and delightful art, may be created at a very early period, and its charming effects extended over a whole existence.

We have seen children whom their parents believed to be totally devoid of any taste or faculty for music, attend singing classes with the most unexpected success. Their interest in music grew, and with it their knowledge and their voice. With several children, a few weeks practice sufficed to change the entire character of their voices, which, though at first weak and indifferent, and of almost no extent, became strong, extended, clear, and, in some cases, of even a fine quality. Such instances are best calculated to dispel the prejudices existing against musical instruction at an early age.

It would be useless, however, to expect such results from individual tuition. We know by experience, that when children are brought together, they imperceptibly impart cheerfulness, and stimulate each other to exertion and activity ; thus, the influence of singing upon the ear and voice, and in the health and morals of the pupils, will be increased tenfold, when aided by the participation of numbers in this pleasurable exercise; the delicate and nervous child will gain strength and confidence, and the slow and indolent be roused. Imitation, that powerful spring of human action—the example of their little companions, their progress, and even their mistakes—furnish the teacher with the means of making his lessons more interesting and successful, than he could ever render them by individual tuition, however great his zeal or talent. And so we find, that the children take that intense interest in their lessons which, at their age, is in general only bestowed on play; at home, the influence of singing extends itself to their habits and dispositions, and consequently to their moral character.

In short, such facts certainly speak in favour of the musical nature of the youth of Great Britain, and we wonder if we shall again have to listen to the old-fashioned prejudice, 'that Music can only grow on German or Italian ground, and that England is not a musical country.' But cannot the senses, which are common to us all, be in England, as well as in Germany, cultivated, refined, and *educated?* for it is education that developes the dormant faculties of nature, awakens the latent spark of genius, and unfolds, in wondrous ways, the secret powers of heart and intellect.

With regard to young persons, comparatively less advantages are to be expected than from children. The nerves and muscles to be exercised in singing have no longer the same elasticity; the voice and ear are less flexible; and the teacher has lost that creative power, which he possessed in so high a degree during the period of infancy. Then he could awaken musical faculties, form an ear, call forth a voice, inspire a love for music, and break through every obstacle. If we consider, besides this, that young persons are overwhelmed with varied studies, and cannot have their thoughts so concentrated upon this branch of instruction, we may say, with certainty, that those who have not learned the elements of vocal music before their 10th or 12th year, have lost the most favourable period of their life—a loss which nothing but zeal and perseverance, and particular musical talent, can redeem. Throughout life, the difference between a musician from infancy, and one from more mature age, will be visible at a glance. The latter may possess musical knowledge and taste ; the former will possess both, with deeper musical feeling, more power, and greater certainty of judgment. In the one, music will be an acquirement; in the other, a feeling, a new sense interwoven with the constitution, a second nature. With children, the teacher has a power of creation ; with adults, he is dependent on circumstances ; he educates in the one case, in the other he has to amend the defects of education. The errors and prejudices in regard to vocal instruction are so great, that in general it is begun only when it should cease, and when the greatest care of the teacher alone can avert fatal consequences. It must, however, be evident to every intelligent mother, that when the voice changes its scale and character, and assumes another for life, it is no time to begin to sing ; on the contrary, this is the time not to sing, or to do it with great care, avoiding every violent exertion ; then a voice may be destroyed, not in infancy, when every trial is gain, every exercise is strength.

Besides the physical difficulties, another, not less prejudicial, presents itself ; and this is, the defective musical education which young ladies have previously received in the tedious and mechanical study of the piano. Instead of learning the poetical part of music and its higher bearings, the pupils in general pass year after year in the drudgery of seeking mechanical perfection, hardly even acquiring the exterior form, and never looking below the surface for a thought or the connexion of ideas. If, in learning music, it is not the object to learn its meaning, to understand and enjoy the deeper sense hidden under the beauty of the form, it is scarcely worth the trouble, and certainly deserves not, as a mere fashion, the sacrifice of so much labour, and so many of the most interesting moments and best years of life.

Singing is the foundation of all musical education, and ought to precede the study of any instrument. In singing classes, children learn to read at sight, and are made acquainted with the general elements of the art, before their attention is called to the mechanical part of it. Thus prepared, they appreciate and enjoy the study of an instrument, instead of finding it, as is usually the case, tedious and interminable. Years of pianoforte instruction may be spared in following this more rational plan, universally recognized and adopted in Germany, with such practical advantage.

In order to remedy, as far as possible, this kind of musical education, adults will have to begin from the commencement, and pass, though more rapidly than children, over the elementary parts. Notwithstanding the obstacles which scarcity of time for practice, and more hardened natural organs, oppose, they may still attain a considerable facility in reading in parts; the voice may be cultivated, rendered more flexible, and above all, more expressive. The principal object of the teacher must be to draw the attention to the more poetical part of music; to explain the variety of form, the difference of character and style, and the consequent expression in the performance of solo compositions. Thus he may still succeed in imparting, as far as practicable, a thorough knowledge of its theory and practice; and, at the same time, cultivate the taste and judgment that are so indispensable for understanding and enjoying works of art. A deeper feeling of the beauties of music, and a more intellectual penetration of its value, will result from the study of the works of great masters; more serious compositions will thus gain an attraction and a charm, which they did not before possess. Thus we place an elevating element of thought in the room of a trivial and unmeaning amusement, with which so many hitherto have alone been acquainted, and to which they have almost exclusively devoted their time and attention. But whatever be the result at that age, it is unquestionable that all these purposes will be better and more effectually attained by those who have been brought up from their infancy with music, who have known it as the companion of their youth, and to whom it has necessarily become a study, full of interest and attraction, as delightful and consoling as it will be inexhaustible.

Before we approach the examination of the moral influence of music, we conclude by recapitulating the principal heads in the preceding remarks :—

1*st*, The earliest period of life is the best for the cultivation of the musical faculties. The musical organs are then easily developed, and defects corrected.

2*d*, Instead of being prejudicial to health, singing has been found a powerful means of strengthening the lungs, throat, and chest.

3*d*, Singing is the foundation of all musical education ; it ought to precede the learning of any instrument.

IX.

Moral Influence of Music.—Songs for Children, their Poetical and Moral Character.

THAT music has a great power over man, and is capable of producing deep emotions, we all know, and we all have, once in our life at least, experienced: how sublime are the effects of a simple tune played on an instrument, or the solemn peal of the organ! and can it be believed that the human voice, the most impressive of all musical sounds, when joined to words, which speak at once to our feelings and our reason, does not, when thus adorned and rendered more significant, exert a greater and more beneficial influence upon our whole being than any other excitement? and must not this influence be materially increased, if we are ourselves the performers?

It is useless, however, to adduce further proofs, when thousands are ready to bear testimony to the vivid, the sublime, the powerful sentiments which song has often awakened within them, and to the beneficial and enduring impressions it has left behind. If such effects are felt by persons unprepared, perhaps, to receive high impressions, or in whom the gentler sensibilities have been blunted by the common drudgeries and troubles of life, how powerfully must the practice of singing, carefully adapted to this end, act upon the hearts and minds of children, whom the ills of existence have never reached, and whose soul is so innocently and defencelessly open and sensitive to impressions imparted from without. It must, therefore, be of great importance to every friend of youth, and every promoter of the interests of society, to know exactly the poetical and moral character of the compositions in which the youth of a country, the future nation, is to be instructed, and in whose hearts the impressions received, at such a tender age, will undoubtedly never be effaced. In this point consists the touch-stone of this question; here lie its public usefulness and its importance.

Juvenile poetry is in form and thought, we mean in the choice of the subject, as well as in that of the words employed to express it, of a peculiar kind. As soon as words are to be introduced into the exercises, too great care cannot be bestowed on their selection. Songs intended for children, should, in every respect, be adapted to the narrow limits of their understanding. They should present nothing abstract or inanimate, but should be full of life and action. The words of children's songs should treat of such innocent subjects as are suited to their years and feelings, if we desire that their effect upon them should be permanent and salutary. From songs of this character alone, the individual may derive benefit during his whole life, and may find in them aids to his moral and religious advancement. The child should receive from them such lessons as will add to the worthiness of the adult—lessons on all the duties he will have to perform, whether as a man, as a citizen, or as a link of that mighty chain called society.

The world appears to a child in a light totally different from that in which a grown-up person beholds it; his vivid imagination invests every object with life: in the buildings which his little hands raise out of sand, his creative fancy discovers cities, villages, and flowery fields; cards are converted into a palace; a fragment of glass furnishes a sun; a soap bubble is to him a world. The man of riper years, on the contrary, sees all his illusions vanish one by one; and as his feelings become hardened in the school of suffering and adversity, he gradually retires from the sphere of active existence, into a more abstract world of thought and recollection. He lives in the past, whilst the child—a butterfly, courting every flower, sucks its honied juice, and inhales its perfumes—knows and enjoys the present alone. In the rules, by which our choice of songs destined for children should be made, we should be guided by the nature of the infant mind itself, and should remember that the science of the child extends not further than its hand, and that the horizon of its mind closes with that of its eye.

Though there is a general dearth of songs for children, the materials for such songs are by no means so limited as may be supposed.   All nature, as it lives around us, and spreads its charms and wonders out before our eyes—nature, with its hills and dales, its brooks, trees, birds, butterflies, and flowers, affords a varied choice of subjects, fitted to attract and interest the young mind.

In thus calling the attention of the young to nature in all its marvellous manifestations, we cannot fail to impress them with due respect for every object of the animate as well as inanimate creation.   This has been overlooked in schools.   Much is done for the intellect, but little for the heart, the main-spring of human actions in the social intercourse of life.   How often are we forced to witness, in grief and indignation, the cruel pleasure that children (often intelligent and clever children in all that concerns the usual branches of instruction,) take in persecuting, and uselessly tormenting, animals, even those upon whose daily labours their own master's and tormentor's livelihood depends! General school instruction, as it is, is inadequate to develope the higher, better feelings, in children ; and in trying to make them more learned, has utterly failed to make them more humane.   Societies have been formed in all parts of Great Britain for the protection of animals.   Prizes have been awarded, punishments inflicted.   If, on one side, this proves that something is wanted in the education of the people, on the other, we can see at a glance the insufficiency of such societies.   Unless man has learnt to respect the inferior beings in the scale of creation, and is moved by higher considerations than those of reward or punishment, such societies are of no avail, and, however well intended, do not attain the object of their foundation.

The children of our schools will never forget the lessons they received in songs which charmed their years of infancy ;

they ever will remember the songs on *The Lark, The Bird's Nest, The Butterfly*, &c., &c. In shewing to them, in a few touching lines, the wondrous instinct of the *Sparrow*, the *Ant*, the *Bee*, &c., we cultivate in them that feeling of re-spect for all nature's children, which will follow them through life, and which will be their guide of conduct in all circum-stances, when seen or when in solitude. Or can a song which delighted us in our infancy, pass without leaving a trace be-hind ? Children, after having learnt by heart, and sung and enjoyed the sweet little strains on the *Fly*, would they ever forget the lessons they contain ?

> My merry little fly play here,
> And let me look at you ;
> I will not touch you, tho' you're near,
> As naughty children do.
>
> I'll near you stand to see you play,
> But do not be afraid ;
> I would not lift my little hand
> To hurt the thing He made.

The same thought, only more sententiously expressed, per-vades the little tune on *The Worm*. We quote it entire, be-cause it illustrates distinctly our views and principles :—

> Turn, turn thy hasty foot aside,
> Nor crush this helpless worm ;
> The frame thy thoughtless looks deride,
> Required a God to form.
>
> Let it enjoy its little day,
> Its little bliss receive ;
> Oh ! do not lightly take away
> The life thou canst not give.

Besides songs of this description, of whose importance in schools no one can doubt, there are also songs, intended to promote social and domestic virtues,—*order, cleanliness, obedi-ence, unity, humanity, temperance*, &c. ; thus impressing, not the letter of the laws of charity on immature minds, but the spirit of them in the memory, and so identifying them with the very fibres of the heart.

In all this we do not prescribe only vague theories, the execution of which exists but in the brain of an enthusiast, or belongs to future ages, we have seen them practically applied to the fullest extent. Juvenile compositions of that poetical and moral character which we recommend, already live in the mouths of thousands of children, and are heard in many a school and many a humble dwelling.

We should never cease, were we to tell of all the effects which, to our knowledge, the songs of children produced : they act upon the little singers, and re-act upon their parents. We know many families in which the children unite in the evening and sing their little duets, and through them charm and captivate those who hitherto sought recreation elsewhere than at their own hearth, in the society of their wives and children.

Music gives, as may easily be seen from this, to the home of the poorer classes, an additional attraction, and is a powerful, and at the same time elevating and noble substitute for those grosser pleasures which lead so many families into ruin and destitution ; and, if what has been stated before Parliament be true, that the dissipated habits of the humbler classes have, for the most part, their source in the utter want of any rational enjoyment, and especially in the total intellectual destitution of the female part of the population, it must become a matter of considerable importance to see an innocent and elevating recreation like vocal music, associated with sacred and moral poetry, become a part of the education of the people. We pity those who know music only as a luxury, and who look with a jealous eye upon this art when taught to children, who are not born in and for the drawing-room, and who, therefore, have no right to claim their share of drawing-room education. Music is no luxury, but something far higher : we do not recognize it as such even among the wealthiest.

The education of the people has become the motto of all parties : if not from sympathy, humanity, and justice, its necessity is felt as the only means of self-defence against the daily growing stream of intemperance, poverty, depravity, and crime.[1]   At the moment when popular education begins to be the all-engrossing subject of the Legislature, the warning lest mere intellectual education should exclusively occupy public attention, will neither be out of place nor out of season. Through its influence upon the youth of all classes, music must again become a serious object to serious minds, to the educationalist and the promoter of the moral advancement of the people.   Herder says: ' To fill the whole soul of a child, to impart to him songs which will leave an impression, salutary and eternal ; thus to urge him on to great actions, to glory ; to implant in his heart the love of virtue, and to afford him consolation in that adversity which it may be his lot to encounter,—how noble an endeavour, how great a work !'

These few words of a profound thinker, a pious, noble, and classical mind, shew the great importance of this question ; and we may conclude by saying, that music must again become an agent in the moral training of the people.   Associated with poetry, simple and true, as a source from which heart and memory will, throughout life, draw lessons of virtue and morality, it will again be called the friend of humanity, the sister of wisdom.

[1] We refer the reader, for further particulars on this important subject, to Appendix No. II.

X.

Music in Infant Schools, in Schools for Children, Young Ladies, and Classical Students.—Family Music.—Methods, Systems.—The Board of Education.

FROM the preceding, it can be easily seen what musical instruction is, and how its influence might be applied with advantage to the education of youth. The errors committed in female schools can, therefore, not be raised as accusations against this art. " If you pray, or if you sing," says St Paul, " pray and sing with spirit and understanding." There is neither in the contemptible finger-stretching education, in the generality of educational institutions of that kind. That those who have thus learned music, or have thus seen it taught, are no friends to it, is not surprising ; we would a thousand times prefer to see our children totally ignorant of the art, than that they should know it in its degradation.

The natural question now will be, Where should singing be taught, and how can it be acquired, according to which system, that it may become the key to all musical knowledge ; and, above all, that the moral advantages, so much spoken of in the former part of this work, may be attained ? Where shall we seek for our model ? Where are the schools in which music has been so carefully associated with real training and real education ? In Britain, France, or Germany ? or in other continental states ? Britain's period of musical supremacy has gone by ; and after having once been a country which might, in point of composition, have vied with any of the continental nations, it is now satisfied with re-echoing the productions of German and Italian masters. In schools generally, as a branch of elementary instruction, it is but in germ ; and only a few years are past since the proposition of its admission into schools, was received, by the whole House of the British Parliament, with a shout of laughter. France has, during the last thirty years, acknowledged its necessity, adopted it, by principle; but it has, in fact, scarcely ever reached the suburbs of its great capital.

In Germany vocal music is everywhere adopted; but nowhere has it received more careful attention, in the education of the people, than in Prussia. It seems, therefore, quite natural that in Germany, in Prussia particularly, we should seek the model for our musical constitution. And yet it is not so. Knowledge is acquired there, but not rightly applied; it receives no right direction, and therefore misses or destroys the very purpose for which it is intended. The theatre has too much influence; the opera too large a share in the music of all classes of society, even in schools; it is cultivated, promoted by all possible means; but that which gives to music its true importance, its power and influence, poetry, the indispensable partner, another self of this beautiful art, is not watched, not carefully enough selected, and zealously sounded in its moral bearing.

We follow, therefore, the footsteps of the ancients, and say that our music must be simple and characteristic; that the poetry must be the best, and the purest in principle, adapted in tone and form to the various ages to which we address ourselves; all that is great and good, cheering and elevating, must there find its musical and poetical accents.

In *Infant-schools*, children should learn little melodies, in poetry and music, according to the compass of their infantine intelligence and voice. They should sing *by heart* only; nothing prepares better, and developes more effectually, than such early training, the musical faculties, the ear and voice, the feeling of time and rhythm.

In schools of children, (from 7 to 12 years of age,) singing at sight must become as general as the reading of the mother-tongue. This is the true age for musical instruction; and schools of this kind are the true sphere in which it should breathe, grow, and be cultivated with care and solicitude.   Children of all grades of society, whether boys or girls, in public, private, or charity schools; in hospitals, orphan or blind asylums; all must participate in this useful and pleasurable exercise.

As we intend to give to youth, that age of song, that season of poetry, poetry and song, no child should be deprived of the simple elements which can unfold to him so many moral treasures, so many hours of happiness: what is useful to one, is useful to all; and if any instruction is to be considered universal, it is vocal music: upon its accents, moral lessons, sweet cheering lessons, are carried home, are retained in memory through life, in good and evil days.

When once acquainted with the elementary part of musical reading, and as we advance in age, a higher sphere of poetry opens itself; the style of music will grow with the child. There are numerous smaller compositions in two and three parts required, which, without being as yet of a lofty character, may be beautiful in an humble sphere.   All the finest shorter pieces of English poetry, simple in expression, noble in thought, clothed in analogous, melodious, and harmonious forms, might here find a place.   In High-schools, classical academies, and in institutions for female education, this branch of instruction will rapidly reach maturity.   The change, the animation, the cheerfulness which well-directed vocal classes will give to the inmates of houses of education, will be incalculable.   The day classes, filled up with scientific subjects, will be succeeded by those of music, in which *all* can simultaneously be occupied.   In the evening, the pupils of such institutions may again unite, and have their musical practisings.   On holidays, or evenings of rest, what can be a substitute for a little family concert, where every one can join in some appropriate composition, beautiful and elevating, in poetry and music ?   A better taste for the art will ere long manifest itself, and instrumental music may then have attractions to many who now may be justified in detesting it.   Those who begin this movement with solidity and earnestness, will not regret it; they will soon, as in

Germany, be the great models, objects of imitation to many others.[1]

Every school festivity, every examination or distribution of prizes, must be a day solemnized with music appropriate to the occasion. All the scholars must then take their part; the whole multitude of the now mute assembly of young people must become tuned and harmonized; at one given signal they must break forth in hundreds of voices, and open in solemn strains the solemnity of the day. Where is the classical scholar whose heart would not leap, in hearing hundreds of young voices strike up Fleming's simple composition of Horace's sublime *Integer vitae scelerisque purus?* who would not listen with emotion, after a silence of 1800 years, to the few specimens of ancient music: Misomedes's[2] Νέμεσι πτερόεσσα, or Pindar's Χρυσέα φόρμιγξ' Απόλλωνος? How splendidly might, after a few voices had sung the first lines, the chorus Πείθονται δ' ἀοιδοὶ σάμασιν appear, in full harmony, and sung by all the students of a High-school or a university!

If, after such modifications as time and circumstances have brought about in our day, ancient poetry and literature are still worthy of attention, those moments in which the best of the ancient poetical productions could be revived, and could again appear among us in the musical garments of which time has deprived them, would be of a high interest; they would make us more intimate with, and teach us more to enjoy, the inheritance left us by antiquity. Once more the voice of Horace and Ovid, Pindar, Alcæus, and Sappho, would be heard; and what, in the most inspired moments, their muse produced of the sublime and the beautiful, would resound again in our halls, would live on the tongue of a young

---

[1] " They began to employ vocal music as a means of education and mental refinement in the *Philanthropin* in Dessau; in the *elementary school* in Rekan, and in the *seminary* in Hanover. Encouraged by the most surprising results, one school and institution after another, imitated those models which had given the signal."—*Encyclopaedie der Tonkunst,* vol. v. article Music, p. 74.

[2] Misomedes of Crete, whom Eusebius calls in his *Chronicle,* κιθαρω-δικῶν νόμων μουσικὸς ποιητής.

generation, would again elevate, charm, and delight us. Instead of being shut up in our dusty libraries, songs will bring them nearer to our memory; the dead languages, the forgotten poets, those luminaries of the Grecian sky, will thus again rise out of their tomb: Greek will teach us music; music will teach us Greek; and the one will help us to raise the other in value and usefulness.

All these classes, at last, will reach that beautiful style, which, though scarcely known as yet, is that which gives to music its real character, its educational importance, the stamp of its lofty destiny,—*Domestic*, or *Family Music*. In a country where dramatic works have so long and so exclusively occupied the field, it is difficult to make it understood what family, what domestic music is. In the expectation that this style of composition would soon find poets and musicians, we might mention as such, the smaller pieces of Händel and Mozart, the psalms of Marcello; or, should we name the work of a more modern master, those beautiful duets of Rinck, called, in the English translation, " The Sabbath Eve!" In the character of these simple musical dialogues,[1] of which the English poet has unfortunately too much contracted the thought, is our idea of one kind of family music best personified. They have that sublime cast, that lofty tone and sentiment, which mark this kind of music as the most cheering, the most elevating. Who once has been a witness of the magic charm thrown over a family, by the true and expressive interpretation of such simple compositions; who has seen what a little paradise rises, as by enchantment, out of the few inspired strains of the poet-musician, will ever forget, what an endless ocean rolls its waves between the every-day compositions, and works, such as we understand them, and as we would fain see them domesticated under every roof, at every fireside! The music we seek to implant in the soil and in the hearts of the people, is a music, the fruits of which render us wiser, better, and happier.[2] Why

---

[1] Published by Ewer & Co., Newgate Street.

[2] Thibaut, the celebrated Professor of Law in Heidelberg, in whose house the best compositions of the 16th and 17th centuries were perform-

should not, in every family, when the day's busy stream is past, all unite harmoniously, and have one happy hour in the enjoyment of such works?

To attain all this, the means are simple: Vocal music must be acknowleged as an indispensable branch of instruction in every school. The young scholar must be made aware that he is learning something useful; as a renovating and exhilarating power, the music-lesson must be placed between those studies which require more mental abstraction. There is no hope of seeing music and poetry resume their power in education, until teachers begin to understand that an hour devoted to their acquirement, is not an hour lost, but an hour gained for school and church, for life and for society.

Another question now presents itself, that of the most suitable method of imparting to the young the necessary musical elements. Nothing is more important, and it cannot be denied, that one method is preferable to the other, as being based upon simpler principles, and more in conformity with the juvenile capacities and juvenile understanding. But should it be made obligatory on the teacher? Supposing the system he wishes to follow simple and easy, based upon the nature of the art to be learnt, and the intelligence and the nature of the child who has to acquire it, and therefore perfectly well adapted for schools,—is he to be prevented from carrying it out? Should, because one method has become the law of the land, the world of thought and of inquiry be shut up to all future improvement and progress? should all studies, all efforts, be thus declared useless and unavailable? No country has ever attempted such tyranny. Neither France nor Prussia, neither Saxony, Bavaria, nor Würtenberg, have ever dared to put such drag-shoes on human intelligence, the least of all on educational pursuits. School books are examined with care, and, above all, by men competent to judge; and when approved, they are re-

ed, relates, in his musical work, *Ueber Reinheit der Tonkunst*, of a young man, who, after hearing a composition of Lotti, was so moved, that in leaving his house, he exclaimed, " Oh ! this evening, I could do no harm to my greatest enemy."

commended, but their exclusive use is never insisted upon. Numerous methods bear, therefore, in France the words, *Approuvée et recommandée*, as motto of the minister of public instruction : so it is in Germany : hundreds of different methods are thus, at the same time, in operation : here it is the one, there the other, which produces the better result, according to circumstances or the individuality of the teacher. Make the teacher answerable for the result, but leave to him the choice of the means. He knows best how to work, in order to reach the mind of infancy. His system may not be the best, yet he will imbue it with an element without which the most perfect method remains a dead letter, a closed, an unintelligible book,—the fire of his heart, his enthusiasm.

The Board of Education in England has, during the last few years, given a half-official acknowledgment to music. It is a timid commencement of a great period in the history of music in Great Britain ; this period has, however, not begun under favourable circumstances. What is given with the one hand, is destroyed with the other. And, contradictory as it seems to the national feeling and the national habits, Great Britain is the country in which this branch of education has been made a monopoly. All other methods or systems of teaching, are under the ban of the Board of Education : far from deserving encouragement, they are treated as tares, good only to be uprooted and perish on the highway. Musical methods have breathed their last ; the philosophical stone has been discovered ! and teachers and theorists, for all time to come, may rest in peace, and stretch their limbs under the shade of this Herculean pillar of the human intellect.[1] If you really wish that music should lay hold of the

---

[1] This plan, so passionately pursued by the Secretary of the Board of Education, has found in the public press a still more violent advocate. The Athenæum, which pretends to the honour of leading the destiny of art in Great Britain, has, in its "Weekly Gossip," become the trumpeter of the new musical Joshua. Whether the musical world, especially those numerous teachers who have in this field for years exerted themselves successfully, will acknowledge such doubtful superiority, and doubtful disinterestedness, we cannot say ; we know only, that every one who has studied music seriously, must be convinced that something more

young population, and penetrate into the very heart of the
British islands, throw widely open the gates of instruction ;
surround yourself with a whole army of different teachers
and different systems ! efface the line of narrow demarcation,
and let the stream of competition carry on its waves, life and
animation, through the schools, into the people.   Give some
special encouragement to this so neglected art, and some
preference to the schoolmaster able to promote it.   Try enlarged ideas, and see whether they are not more worthy of a
great nation.   All the youth of your country will then be
instructed, never mind by what plan or system.   Let Progress be your standard, and do not force us, since we have
steamers and railroads, to travel in sedans and litters, on
horses and donkies, as our forefathers did.

In this manner you will soon see, one after another, the
schools begin the work ; the success of one will be a stimulus
to all ; and, by degrees, there will be no re-union of young
persons or young students, of children or infants, no orphans,
and no inmates of a charity school, from the Channel to the
islands of Ultima Thule, where the hundreds and the thousands will not raise their voices, and surprise and overpower
every ear and every heart.

Thus, when a competition is opened for methods and systems, as well as for poetical and musical compositions, lofty
in thought and beautiful in form, and, in every respect, fit to
take a share in the education of the people ; a new and important branch of composition will appear as by enchantment,
and extend its influence and ramifications into every school
and every family through the length and breadth of the land.
The educational and family music, scarcely known as yet
by name, will, in the midst of an ocean, in all its various changes and tempests, stand in its simplicity, purity,

is to be done for its advancement than gossiping about it ; that there is
a great distance from understanding music to talking musical trivialities ;
and that he who is guilty of the " Weekly Gossip," and therefore proves
that he stands but in the antechamber of art, should certainly not pre-
sume to judge, when so important a matter as musical education is the
subject.

and grandeur, like a rock, and bear unshaken the sway of
all the surrounding tides of style and fashion. May the
classic, romantic, and fantastic schools, combat and efface
each other ! may the lyric drama of all the continental languages intoxicate the lions of the fashionable world ! there
will be a music which appears neither upon the stage nor
the market-place, neither in concerts nor drawing-rooms, but
which modestly enlivens the school and the cottage, and
helps to instruct the people, to embellish the hour of toil and
that of rest. This style will remain uncontaminated by the
impure breath of changing fashion and passing mountebanks,
and as truly NATIONAL, form the axis, round which all others
move, appear and disappear, as figures of a *Lanterna Magica.*
In this manner you will render to the young what they have
been deprived of; you will advance the rest of Europe, and
give, even to Prussia, a glorious example of a better, a more
philosophical application of music to the education of youth.

Thus Music will again be looked at with reverence. In
churches she will fill, like a stream, the hearts of the multitude ; she will again appear as the minstrel and the harp of
old in our dwelling ; be our guardian angel, a heavenly
messenger, our teacher, friend, and comforter ; and from her
deepest dejection, from a state of servitude, corruption, and
degeneracy, rise, a new phœnix out of ashes, higher and
higher, to a glorious apotheosis.

APPENDIX I.

An opinion contrary to that of Aristotle was very often entertained in ancient and modern times. Philip of Macedon reproached his son Alexander with himself practising music, instead of being content to listen to that of others. The same opinion was expressed, in our times, by a man whose influence was considerable on the fashionable world, and whose reasonings still influence those who have been educated, or continue to educate, upon such superficial and formal principles. It was about the middle of last century that music was probably at its lowest ebb in England, and the contemptuous language used by Lord Chesterfield, in regard to its practice, may be taken as an indication of the way of thinking on that subject among the fashionable society of his day. He says, "If you love music, hear it : pay fiddlers to play to you, but never fiddle yourself. It makes a gentleman appear frivolous and contemptible ; leads him frequently into bad company, and wastes that time which otherwise might be well employed." Lord Chesterfield's condensed and sententious style, gives his precepts a false air of soundness and truth ; they have led many a weak head into the conviction, that he could not be a perfect gentleman without following the instructions, and emulating the example, of so great a master. There are thousands who mistake the outside, with all its hollowness and glitter, for the internal and essential truth, and adopt Lord Chesterfield's precepts as their manual, both in their moral and intellectual education. A mind so constituted can know little or nothing of moral and spiritual worth. Outward forms, and a little brilliant appearance in society, are the main points to which Lord Chesterfield's maxims are directed. What marvel, then, that art in general, and more particularly music, is never understood by men of this stamp, whose whole scope is not to be, but to appear perfect. His words, when more closely examined, are the expression either of consummate ignorance, or an overweening idea of what is due to dignity and decorum. That music is not for a gentleman, says as little as the known words of Charles II., that the Presbyterian religion was not a religion for a gentleman.

The opinion of Lord Chesterfield might be easily balanced with that of other men, whose names stand in history so high, that neither the frivolous nor the contemptible of his Lordship's musical anathema can reach them.

Charlemagne not only, according to Eginhard, ordered all national songs to be collected, not only instituted music schools, but sang himself with the choir in church. Almost the whole series of the Austrian emperors were practical musicians; some, even eminent composers.

Leopold I. was not only an excellent pianist, but his airs and cantatas, many of which are still extant, are proofs of his talent and skill. It is said, in the life of Leopold the Great, (published at Leipzig, 1709,) that the Emperor preferred music to every other enjoyment. In each of his four palaces, in which he used to pass alternately a certain time, there was a valuable harpsichord in his private apartment, and at this instrument he passed all his leisure hours. All the members of his chapel, musicians, leaders, and singers, were examined by himself before their reception; and it was merit only, not favour, which influenced his choice. His chapel was therefore esteemed the first in Europe. Many of the members were counts and barons, and their appointments were such as enabled them to live in a manner becoming their families. Not an opera was represented, for which the Emperor had not composed one or more airs. During the performance, he had the score constantly before him, and followed the performers with the utmost attention. When a passage made a particular impression on him, he closed his eyes, but opened them very wide when anybody in the orchestra committed a mistake; on these occasions he generally pointed out the offender.

Joseph I. inherited his predecessor's love for music. Charles VI. also held it in high estimation, promoted its culture, and was himself a performer on several instruments. During his reign, music was much cultivated by persons of the first families. His inclinations led him especially to dramatic music. The poet of his court, Metastasio, contributed not a little to this predilection. Caldara's splendid work, *Achilles*, was performed at the nuptials of Maria Therese.

Fuchs, the great composer, and author of the celebrated *Gradus ad Parnassum*, was the aulic Kapellmeister during the reign of these three emperors. In the year 1724, on the birthday of one of the Austrian archduchesses, one of Fuchs's operas was performed, which pleased the Emperor to such a degree, that he set on foot a lottery for all who performed in it, in which every one had to gain from 500 to 2000 florins.   The Emperor himself played, and conducted the performance at the harpsichord.   It was at this representation that Kapellmeister Fuchs (who stood behind the Emperor, and turned the leaves of the score,) was so much enchanted, in a passage of great difficulty, with the Emperor's skill, that he loudly exclaimed, " Bravo !" and added, " Your Majesty might be employed as a most accomplished Kapellmeister."   The Emperor turned his head, and said, " I am pretty well satisfied with my situation."

Joseph II. was also a musician, and sang very well.   The operas of Gluck, Paesiello, Cimarosa, Martini, Salieri, and Sarti, were performed at the theatre of the Court before the public in Vienna.

Frederick the Great was a passionate lover of music; and though a first-rate flute player, was not less a first-rate soldier, the terror of the Russian and Austrian armies.   After he had been rushing against the enemies' batteries, and had roared like a lion to his dispersing squadrons his favourite cry, " *Will you, then, live for ever !*" he was an hour later heard, in his tent, playing on the flute.—Alexander I., Emperor of Russia, to whom music had been, as to Frederick the Great, in the strongest terms forbidden by his father, loved and practised it all his life.—We know from what has been stated, (p. 57 and 58,) that in the most brilliant period of the English annals, the reign of Queen Elizabeth, musical skill and knowledge were so essential to persons of condition, that ignorance of the art was looked upon as a proof of low breeding, and unfitness for the intercourse of polite society.   A thousand examples of this kind might be gathered from the history of all nations. A number of the English kings were musicians : the Stuarts of Scotland were remarkably skilled in this art.   James I. was one of the first musicians of his age, and most accomplished on every instrument.

If Lord Chesterfield is an authority, Milton is another, perhaps a greater one ; and it is when speaking precisely of the education of young gentlemen, that he says, "The rest before meat may, both with profit and delight, be taken up in recreating and composing their travail'd spirits, with the solemn and divine harmonies of music *heard* or *learn'd;* either while the skilful organist plies his grave and fancied descant in lofty fugues, or the whole symphony, with artful and imaginable touches, adorn and grace the well-studied chords of some choice composer; sometimes the lute or soft organ stop waiting on elegant voices, either to religious, martial, or civil ditties, which, if wise men and prophets be not extremely out, have a great power over dispositions and manners, to smoothe and make them gentle from rustic harshness and distemper'd passions." [1]

J. J. Rousseau was not only a musical copyist, he was also a theorist and composer. His opera, *Le Divin du Village,* has seen more representations than any opera ever since performed. Upon the volume of songs composed by him, he wrote the remarkable words: "La consolation des misères de ma vie."

To conclude, we might reply to Lord Chesterfield, what Count d'Anjou answered to his cousin Louis d'Outremer, who reproached him with practising music himself, instead of doing it by deputy: "Sachez, Sire, qu'un Roi sans musique, n'est qu'un âne couronné."

[1] Milton's *Letter on Education.*

APPENDIX II.

POLYBIUS says (Hist. iv., 20): " With regard to the inhabitants of
Cynætha, whose misfortunes we have just now mentioned, it is
certain that no people ever were esteemed so justly to deserve that
cruel treatment to which they were exposed.   And since the Arcadians, in general, have been always celebrated for their virtue
throughout all Greece, and have obtained the highest fame, as well
by their humane and hospitable disposition, as from their piety
also towards the gods, and the veneration of all things sacred; it
may perhaps be useful to enquire from whence it could arise, that
the people of this single city, though confessed to be Arcadians,
should, on the contrary, be noted for the savage roughness of their
lives and manners, and distinguished by their wickedness and
cruelty above all the Greeks.   In my judgment, then, this difference has happened from no other cause than that the Cynætheans
were the first and only people among the Arcadians who threw
away that institution which their ancestors had established with
the greatest wisdom, and with a nice regard to the natural genius
and peculiar disposition of the people of the country ; I mean, the
discipline and exercise of music ; of that genuine and perfect music, which is useful indeed in every state, but absolutely necessary
to the people of Arcadia.   For we ought by no means to adopt the
sentiment that is thrown out by Ephorus in the preface to his history, and which indeed is very unworthy of that writer, ' That
music was invented to deceive and delude mankind.'   Nor can it
be supposed, that the Lacedæmonians and the ancient Cretans were
not influenced by some great reason, when, in the place of trumpets, they introduced the sound of flutes, and harmony of verse, to
animate their soldiers in the time of battle ; or that the first Arca-

dians acted without strong necessity, who, though their lives and
manners, in all other points, were rigid and austere, incorporated
this art into the very essence of their government ; and obliged not
their children only, but the young men likewise, till they had
gained the age of thirty years, to persist in the constant study and
practice of it.   For all men know that Arcadia is almost the only
country in which the children, even from their most tender age, are
taught to sing, in measure, their songs and hymns that are composed in honour of their gods and heroes : and that afterwards,
when they have learned the music of Timotheus and Philoxenus,
they assemble once in every year in the public theatres, at the
feast of Bacchus, and there dance, with emulation, to the sound of
flutes, and celebrate, according to their proper age, the children,
those that are called the puerile, and the young men, the manly
games ; and even in their private feasts and meetings, they are
never known to employ any hired bands of music for their entertainment, but each man is obliged himself to sing in turn.   For
though they may, without shame or censure, disown all knowledge
of every other science, they dare not, on the one hand, dissemble or
deny that they are skilled in music, since the laws require that
every one should be instructed in it; nor can they, on the other hand,
refuse to give some proofs of their skill when asked, because such
refusal would be esteemed dishonourable.   They are also taught to
perform, in order, all the military steps and motions to the sound of
instruments : and this is likewise practised every year in the theatres, at the public charge, and in sight of all the citizens.

   " Now, to me it is clearly evident, that the ancients by no means
introduced these customs to be the instruments of luxury and idle
pleasure ; but because they had considered with attention, both the
painful and laborious course of life to which the Arcadians were accustomed, and the natural austerity also of their manners, derived
to them from that cold and heavy air, which covered the greatest
part of all their province.   For men will be always found to be in
some degree assimilated to the climate in which they live : nor can
it be ascribed to any other cause, that in the several nations of the
world, distinct and separated from each other, we behold so wide a
difference in complexion, features, manners, and customs.   The Arcadians, therefore, in order to smoothe and soften that disposition
which was by nature so rough and stubborn, besides the customs
above described, appointed frequent festivals and sacrifices, which
both sexes were required to celebrate together ; the men with

women, and the boys with virgins; and, in general, established every institution that could serve to render their rugged minds more gentle and compliant, and tame the fierceness of their manners. But the people of Cynætha, having slighted all these arts, though both their air and situation, the most inclement and unfavourable of any in Arcadia, made some such remedy more requisite to them than to the rest, were afterwards engaged continually in intestine tumults and contentions, till they became at last so fierce and savage, that, among all the cities of Greece, there was none in which so many and so great enormities were ever known to be committed. To how deplorable a state this conduct had at last reduced them, and how much their manners were detested by the Arcadians, may be fully understood from that which happened to them, when they sent an embassy to Lacedæmon, after the time of a dreadful slaughter which had been made among them. For in every city of Arcadia through which their deputies were obliged to pass, they were commanded by the public crier instantly to be gone. The Mantineans also expressed even still more strongly their abhorrence of them; for, as soon as they were departed, they made a solemn purification of the place, and carried their victims in procession round the city, and through all their territory.

" This, then, may be sufficient to exempt the general customs of Arcadia from all censure; and, at the same time, to remind the people of that province, that music was at first established in their government, not for the sake of mere pleasure and amusement, but for such solid purposes as should engage them never to desert the practice of it. The Cynætheans also may perhaps draw some advantage from these reflections, and, if the Deity should hereafter bless them with better sentiments, may turn their minds towards such discipline, as may soften and improve their manners, and especially to music, by which means alone they can ever hope to be divested of that brutal fierceness for which they have been so long distinguished."

If Polybius were still among us, and visited our poor-houses, lunatic asylums, and prisons, he would still say, that criminals and insane are so, out of all proportion, numerous, because the first and simplest of all means of education, music, has been neglected. However ludicrous this may appear to some of our legislators and educationalists, yet nothing would be more true. If the people of Great Britain had learned music as an amusement only, they would not want to seek amusement in public houses; and there is the

source of their ruin, ruin in health and in character. The state
seems to find prisons and lunatic asylums indispensable institutions,
or it would stop the source whence the insane and criminals proceed. Shut up public houses, teach the people sober habits for
those of intemperance, and soon you will have to close the greater
number of the asylums and the jails. Would it not be better to
inspire the people with purer desires, and to provide them with
nobler amusements? Teach them in your schools those innocent
pleasures which music gives, and you will make their home more
attractive. Where is the husband debased enough, who would seek
pleasures abroad, when the mother sits by the fireside, surrounded
by her children, and sings sacred hymns or songs, appropriate in
music and poetry, to time and circumstances! Or is, then, in reality
the vice of intemperance so ineffaceable in the British Islands?
have not philanthropists gathered the most terrifying statistics of
the increase of this fearful epidemic, which undermines the physical
and moral health of families, of cities, and of the state, and augments
daily, to a degree quite alarming, the destitute and the criminal?
And are we not the authors, should they one day, in overwhelming
multitudes, range themselves in armies, and under the command of
a bold tribune, seek to revenge themselves for their depraved habits
and their crimes in which the state has nourished them, for their
bodily and mental destitution in which the state has left them, and
from which it made not even an attempt to redeem them, although
forewarned in a thousand ways?

Well may be heard here the voice of a French writer who has
studied the dangerous classes of society, and has written on them
a remarkable work. Although under different circumstances, in a
different age, his words say nothing that is not expressed in those
of Polybius; yet as they speak of the dangerous classes of that
society with which we have to come in daily contact, which live
with us in the same city, in the same street, and under the same
roof, his remarks will come closer home, and find, at least, a more
interested reception.

" The singing classes have a relation to the amusements of the
people; and for this reason it is, perhaps, that they have been
judged less favourably than those courses of instruction which had
reference to objects purely utilitarian. It has been said that they
are not in harmony with the condition of those for whom they are
designed. The objection is not a conclusive one; for the most
brilliant airs of our operas are daily hawked about our streets, and

sung in our highways. These airs, caught flying, if we may so express ourselves, by the workmen, are repeated in their shops and garrets. Why forbid them access to the punctuated music and accentuated harmonies of scientific compositions, when you cannot prevent their seizing, and rendering often with great taste, by their musical instinct alone, the airs which float through the works of our greatest masters. The municipal administration may not as yet have fully satisfied itself as to the utility of the moral and civil effects which will result from the funds granted for the establishment of these music classes; for unhappily there is, even among the enlightened, a disposition to believe that the people are not susceptible of the charm of noble or refined amusements, or of emotions which are purely intellectual. Yet it is a fact in evidence, that such amusements have an irresistible attraction for them. I am anxious to point out this error, and call attention to the facts which attest it, because it is most mischievous.

" In truth, our rulers and political economists, have reflected too little on the moral bearing of public amusements—on those especially adapted to the labouring classes. Yet amusement of some kind is a necessity of all ages and all conditions. The poorer a man is, and the more he is the slave of toil, the more needful it is that he should find diversion and refreshment of some kind for his weary spirit; and the more important that he should find it in enjoyments which are not sensual, and which, while they soothe his feelings, refine them. The human heart is naturally so unquiet, morose, and jealous a thing, so apt to make *itself* the *centre* of all its thoughts and sentiments, that the happiest man is he who can most easily find the means of escaping from his own narrow personality, to fix his attention on something which is not himself.

" Interest him in the recital of some noble action, excite him by verses or songs which give expression to lofty sentiments, or paint the beautiful features of natural scenery, and you will see him rejoice in his own emotions, mastered and melted by the omnipotence of the arts.

" Music, the most seductive and the purest of them all, is calculated, more than all, to exercise a sway over the popular heart, raising therein sensations alternately glowing and refined."[1]

In a work of the same kind—*The Claims of Labour*,—the same idea is expressed thus :—

[1] H. Regier, *Des Classes dangereuses de la Société*.

" We may remark, as bearing upon this subject, that singing lessons should be greatly encouraged in schools. There are several merits connected with this mode of instruction. It employs many together, and gives a feeling of communion ; it is not much mixed up with emulation ; the tenderest and highest sentiments may be unostentatiously impressed by its means, for you can introduce in songs such things as you could not lecture upon ; then it gives somewhat of a cultivated taste, and an additional topic of social interest, even to those who do not make much proficiency ; while to others, who have a natural ability for it, it may form an innocent and engaging pursuit throughout their lives."

The voice for an improved state of the education of the people has been raised repeatedly and eloquently by Lord Ashley, Mr Wyse, and many others. Mr Wyse, who was almost the first who brought the question of music, in its connection with a national system of education, before the British public and the British Parliament,[1] says :—Music, even the most elementary, not only does not form an essential of education in this country, but the idea of introducing it is not even dreamt of. It is urged, that it would be fruitless to attempt it, because the people are essentially anti-musical ; but may not they be anti-musical, because it has not been attempted ? The people roar and scream, because they have heard nothing but roaring and screaming—no music—from their childhood. Is harmony not to be taught ? is it not to be extended ? is not a taste to be generated, at least in the period of two generations ? Taste is the habit of good things ; " je ne suis pas la rose, mais j'ai vecu avec elle," is to be caught. But the inoculation must somewhere or other begin. It is this apathy about beginning that is censurable, not the difficulty of propagating when it has once appeared. No effort is made in any of our schools ; and then we complain that there is no music amongst scholars. It would be just as reasonable to exclude grammar, and then complain that we had no grammarians. . . . . *The elements of music should, therefore, form an integral part of all public education.* . . . . A better preservative of pure morals ; a more delightful addition to innocent amusements ; a more cheerful stimulant to all exercises, whether of labour, study, or religion, can scarcely be devised. Nor would its effects be confined to the school-room or to childhood ; it would soon penetrate the paternal dwelling ; in another generation it would be natural to the land."

[1] *Education Reform*, by T. Wyse, Esq., M.P., pp. 186 and 195.

Mr W. E. Hickson, who has done so much for education, and has devoted himself so earnestly to the promotion of music in schools, has, like a true statesman, penetrated this subject.[1] He shews how miserably deficient are our present systems of education ; how they work only upon the intellect, and upon that imperfectly, and neglect the cultivation of the heart ; how our poorer classes, especially, are taught only a few barren mechanical acquirements, such as reading, writing, and casting accounts, whilst their honest sympathies, their generous emotions, their whole moral natures, are altogether uncared for and unattended to. After urging that education should embrace a higher, nobler object than these mechanical acquirements ; that every moral engine by which the character can be influenced and improved, should be employed ; and after briefly explaining how music exerts its power, he proceeds to shew that vocal music, judiciously directed, is a most efficient means of moralization.

" Music may be regarded as having an indirect moral influence in weaning the mind from coarse and brutalizing pursuits, and from pleasures consisting in mere sensual indulgences. The reason is, that music is a means of pure and innocent enjoyment, which, in proportion as it is cultivated and directed, will approve itself to the mind, as of a higher, better, and more satisfactory character, than any of the grosser pleasures pursued by the slaves of vice.

" And here let me protest against the doctrine, that it is not part, or ought to be no part, of the business of an instructor, to teach the means of rational enjoyment to the people. That music is a means of social enjoyment, will be admitted ; and that ought to be a sufficient argument for rendering it, if possible, a means of enjoyment to the poorest of the community. After all that can be done for the amelioration of the condition of the working-classes, they will have to submit to quite enough of privation, as compared with the lot of a rich man, without withholding from them any innocent source of pleasure which we might enable them to command.

" I have no sympathy with those who think that the duty of individuals or of legislators, with regard to the masses, ends in teaching them resignation and submission, and in enabling them at best to earn their bread by the sweat of their brow ; but who

[1] A *Lecture*, by W. E. Hickson, on the introduction of VOCAL MUSIC as a branch of national education.   Taylor and Walton.

would do nothing to cheer their hearts or gladden their existence, by throwing a little sunshine into the cottage, as if nature had designed them to be merely living, moving, animated machines, existing not for themselves, but solely to furnish the means of gratification to a superior race of mortals.

" Happily, however, for the lot of the poor, nature has not left it to our own cold hearts to decide this question. Some amount of pleasurable relaxation from labour is necessary to every condition of animal existence. The slave will have it, though he work in chains for six days out of the seven, or without it he will die, and thus escape the lash of his cruel task-master. Some change of a pleasurable character, to relieve the monotony of a life of labour, is necessary for all ; but, what is most to the purpose, we can withhold it from none—we can merely choose the form it shall assume.

" This is then the real question at issue, whether we shall leave the people, while in a low moral state, to choose their own sources of gratification, (although we may know that while in that state, they will choose such as will be of a low and debasing character,) or shall we first enable them to appreciate, and then place within their reach rational and intellectual enjoyments ? In short, will you have prize-fighting, bull-baiting, gambling, Tom and Jerry amusements, a taste encouraged for witnessing executions and reading of murders ; will you have intemperance, as a means of excitement, rendered all but universal ; or will you allow an art like that of music to be cultivated in their place, and teach society to obey the laws of harmony, both in a moral and scientific sense ?"

In the same spirit are written the following eloquent lines by Dr Channing, in his *Address on Temperance* :—

" The first means which I shall suggest of placing a people beyond the temptation to intemperance, is to furnish them with the means of innocent pleasure.

" I have said, a people should be guarded against temptation to unlawful pleasures, by furnishing the means of innocent ones. By innocent pleasures, I mean such as excite moderately ; such as produce a cheerful frame of mind, not boisterous mirth ; such as refresh, instead of exhausting the system ; such as recur frequently, rather than continue long ; such as send us back to our daily duties invigorated in body and in spirit ; such as we can partake in the presence and society of respectable friends ; such as consist with, and are favourable to, a grateful piety ; such as are chastened by self-respect, and are accompanied with the consciousness that life has a higher end than to be amused. In every community there must be pleasures, relaxations, and means of agreeable excitement; and if innocent ones are not furnished, resort will be had to criminal. Man was made to enjoy, as well as to labour, and the state of society should be adapted to this principle of human nature. France, especially before the Revolution, has been represented as a singularly temperate country; a fact to be explained, at least in part, by the constitutional cheerfulness of that people, and the prevalence of simple and innocent gratifications, especially among the peasantry. Men drink to excess very often to shake off depression, or to satisfy the restless thirst for agreeable excitement, and these motives are excluded in a cheerful community. A gloomy state of society, in which there are few innocent recreations, may be expected to abound in drunkenness, if opportunities are afforded. The savage drinks to excess, because his hours of sobriety are dull and unvaried, because, in losing the consciousness of his condition and his existence, he loses little which he wishes to retain. The labouring classes are most exposed to intemperance, because they have at present few other pleasurable excitements. A man, who, after toil, has resources of blameless recreation, is less tempted than other men to seek self-oblivion. He has too many of the pleasures of a man, to take up with those of a brute. Thus. the encouragement of simple innocent enjoyments is an important means of temperance.

" These remarks shew the importance of encouraging the efforts which have commenced among us, for spreading the accomplishment of music through our whole community. It is now proposed that this shall be made a regular branch in our schools; and every friend of the people must wish success to the experiment. I am not now called to speak of all the good influences of music, particularly of the strength which it may and ought to give to the religious sentiment, and to all pure and generous emotions. Regarded merely as a refined pleasure, it has a favourable bearing on public morals. Let taste and skill in this beautiful art be spread among us, and every family will have a new resource. Home will gain a new attraction. Social intercourse will be more cheerful; and an innocent public amusement will be furnished to the community. Public amusements bringing multitudes together, to kindle with one emotion, to share the same innocent joy, have an humanizing influence; and among these bonds of society, perhaps no one produces so much unmixed good as music. What a fulness of enjoyment has our Creator placed within our reach, by surrounding us with an atmosphere which may be shaped into sweet sounds? And yet this goodness is almost lost upon us, through want of culture of the organ by which this provision is to be enjoyed."

Madame de Stael[1] says :—

" There is a whole order of sentiments, I might say, a whole order of virtues, which belong to the knowledge, or at least to the taste for music ; and it is great barbarity to deprive a numerous portion of the human race of such impressions. The ancients pretended that nations had been civilized by music, and this allegory has a deep meaning ; for we must always suppose that the bond of society was formed either by sympathy or interest, and certainly the first origin is more noble than the other."

Napoleon, the mortal enemy of Madame de Stael, had not less than herself a very peculiar predilection for music; and remarkable is his opinion on this art, expressed in these words :—" Music exercises the greatest influence upon the human passions, and acts with an uncommon power upon man. It is a duty of the legislator to encourage and to favour the study of music more than any other art. A moral composition, drawn by the hand of a master, penetrates into the deepest feelings, and operates more powerfully than any good and moral work which speaks to our reason only."

In the *Manuel de l'Instruction Primaire*, (c. vii. art. 1,) addressed to the teachers throughout France, we read, " Le chant élève l'ame et touche le cœur : il est une partie intégrante du culte, et un divertissement pour le peuple. *Il sera donc un moyen puissant d'éducation dans toutes les écoles primaires.*"

After having given more detailed regulations on the singing exercises to be applied to children, the minister of public instruction continues in the same *Manuel*, (c. vii. art. 4,) in which vocal music is considered as an essential, and not an accessory branch of popular education : "On parviendra de cette manière à faire chanter convenablement dans l'église, *à ennoblir les idées, à toucher les cœurs, à évincer les mauvaises chansons populaires, à réformer la morale publique.*"

The minister of war in France has, a short time ago, published an ordinance, in which the organization of vocal choirs is commanded in every regiment. In Germany, such bands consist often of the whole regiment. We hope to see the British army imitate such examples. Nothing is easier than to reach with whole battalions

---

[1] De Stael on *Germany*, Volume I. chap. 19th : (*On Public Institutions.*)

this result. A few of the many hours which burden the existence of the soldier, and which are so often spent in worse than idleness, might be spared during the week for musical instruction. Every regiment would soon have its vocal band, and soon we would reach those great results described by Ambert :[1]—

"La grande voix du régiment se ferait entendre ; les compagnies répondraient aux compagnies, et les bataillons marcheraient avec l'orgueil des cohortes anciennes.—Oh ! alors je n'en doute pas, les choses miraculeuses que le fanatisme faisait exécuter jadis se renouvelleraient de nos jours."

We cannot refrain from quoting, in regard to the musical instruction in regiments, the eloquent lines of Guéroult :—

"Pour donner une grande impulsion, je ne sache rien de plus efficace que l'éducation musicale de l'armée ; il faut que l'art sorte aujourd'hui de ces petits tabernacles bourgeois ; il faut qu'il descende dans le peuple, et qu'il aille chercher des recrues dans ses derniers rangs. Or, l'armée c'est le peuple assemblé, le peuple discipliné, hiérarchisé, organisé ; c'est une députation du peuple prête à recevoir le feu sacré pour le porter ensuite sur toute la surface du territoire. Le peuple est aujourd'hui la grande pépinière où les partis épuisés vont se renouveler ; rien de grand ne se fait aujourd'hui qu'en son nom, qu'au nom de ses intérêts.—Que le savoir donc soit distribué au peuple, que l'industrie s'occupe de son bien-être, il y a là pour des siècles de travaux ; mais que l'art aussi ait sa part dans les libéralités de ses puissans amis. Nous le demandons pour le peuple et pour l'art : pour le peuple, que l'art annoblira, élèvera, moralisera ; pour l'art, qui, armé de la voix puissante du peuple, pourra enfin sortir des serres-chaudes où il est cultivé, et pousser ses racines en pleine terre, en plein vent, en pleine humanité. Je le dis avec une entière conviction, le jour où l'art quittera les boudoirs pour la place publique, une révolution plus grande aura été accomplie que lorsque de l'église il est monté sur le théâtre. Oui, faisons de la démocratie en musique ; ce sera une démocratie bienfaisante, pacifique ; toute à l'avantage de tous."

[1] *Esquisses historiques des Armées Françaises,* par Joachim Ambert.

F I N I S.

PRINTED BY H. AND J. PILLANS, EDINBURGH.

April 1847.

NEW WORKS

IN

Miscellaneous and General Literature,

PUBLISHED BY

MESSRS. LONGMAN, BROWN, GREEN, AND LONGMANS,

PATERNOSTER ROW, LONDON.

CLASSIFIED INDEX.

New Works and New Editions

Messrs. Longman, Brown, Green, and Longmans,

ABERCROMBIE'S PRACTICAL GARDENER,
And Improved System of Modern Horticulture, alphabetically arranged. 4th Edition, with Introductory Treatise on Vegetable Physiology, and Plates, by W. Salisbury. 12mo. 6s. bds.

ABERCROMBIE & MAIN.—THE PRACTICAL GARDENER'S
COMPANION; or, Horticultural Calendar: to which is added, the Garden-Seed and Plant Estimate. Edited from a MS. of J. Abercrombie, by J. Main. 8th Edition. 32mo. 2s. 6d. sd.

ACTON (ELIZA.)—MODERN COOKERY,
In all its Branches, reduced to a System of Easy Practice. For the use of Private Families. In a Series of Receipts, all of which have been strictly tested, and are given with the most minute exactness. By Eliza Acton. New Edition, to which are added, Directions for Carving. Fcp. 8vo. with plates and woodcuts, 7s. 6d. cloth.

ADAIR (SIR ROBERT).—AN HISTORICAL MEMOIR OF A
MISSION to the COURT of VIENNA in 1806. By the Right Honourable Sir Robert Adair, G.C.B. With a Selection from his Despatches, published by permission of the proper Authorities. 8vo. 18s. cloth.

ADAIR (SIR ROBERT).—THE NEGOTIATIONS FOR THE
PEACE of the DARDANELLES, in 1808-9: with Dispatches and Official Documents. By the Right Honourable Sir Robert Adair, G.C.B. Being a Sequel to the Memoir of his Mission to Vienna in 1806. 2 vols. 8vo. 28s. cloth.

ADSHEAD.—PRISONS AND PRISONERS.
By Joseph Adshead. 8vo. with Illustrations, 7s. 6d. cloth.

AIKIN.—THE LIFE OF JOSEPH ADDISON.
Illustrated by many of his Letters and Private Papers never before published. By Lucy Aikin. 2 vols. post 8vo. with Portrait from Sir Godfrey Kneller's Picture, 18s. cloth.

ALLAN (J. H.)—A PICTORIAL TOUR IN THE MEDITER-
RANEAN; comprising Malta, Dalmatia, Asia Minor, Grecian Archipelago, Egypt, Nubia, Greece, Sicily, Italy, and Spain. By J. H. Allan, Member of the Athenian Archæological Society, and of the Egyptian Society of Cairo. 2d Edition. Imperial 4to. with upwards of 40 lithographed Drawings, and 70 Wood Engravings, £3. 3s. cloth.

AMY HERBERT.
By a Lady. Edited by the Rev. William Sewell, B.D. Fellow and Tutor of Exeter College, Oxford. New Edition. 2 vols. fcp. 8vo. 9s. cloth.

ARTISAN CLUB (THE)—A TREATISE ON THE STEAM
ENGINE, in its Application to Mines, Mills, Steam Navigation, and Railways. By the Artisan Club. Edited by John Bourne, C.E. 4to. with 30 Steel Plates and 349 Wood Engravings, 27s. cloth.

BAKEWELL.—AN INTRODUCTION TO GEOLOGY.
Intended to convey Practical Knowledge of the Science, and comprising the most important recent discoveries; with explanations of the facts and phenomena which serve to confirm or invalidate various Geological Theories. By Robert Bakewell. Fifth Edition, considerably enlarged. 8vo. with numerous Plates and Woodcuts, 21s. cloth.

BALMAIN.—LESSONS ON CHEMISTRY,
For the use of Pupils in Schools, Junior Students in Universities, and Readers who wish to learn the fundamental Principles and leading Facts: with Questions for Examination, Glossaries of Chemical Terms and Chemical Symbols, and an Index. By W. H. Balmain. Fcp. 8vo. with Woodcuts, 6s. cloth.

BARRETT.—A SYNOPSIS OF CRITICISMS UPON THOSE
PASSAGES of the OLD TESTAMENT in which Modern Commentators have differed from the Authorised Version: together with an Explanation of various Difficulties in the Hebrew and English Texts. By the Rev. RICHARD A. F. BARRETT, M.A. Fellow of King's College, Cambridge. Vol. I. 8vo. 28s. cloth; or, in 2 Parts, price 14s. each.

*** To be continued quarterly, in half-volumes. Vol. II. Part I. will be published on July 1st.

BAYLDON.—ART OF VALUING RENTS AND TILLAGES,
And the Tenant's Right of Entering and Quitting Farms, explained by several Specimens of Valuations; and Remarks on the Cultivation pursued on Soils in different Situations. Adapted to the Use of Landlords, Land-Agents, Appraisers, Farmers, and Tenants. By J. S. BAYLDON. 6th Edition, corrected and revised, by John Donaldson. 8vo. 10s. 6d. cloth.

BAYLIS (E.)—THE ARITHMETIC OF ANNUITIES AND
LIFE ASSURANCE; or, Compound Interest Simplified: explaining the Value of Annuities, certain or contingent, on One or Two Lives, and the Values of Assurances in Single and Annual Payments; and comprehending the Values of Leases, Pensions, Freeholds, and Reversionary Sums, in possession or expectation, immediate, deferred, or temporary. Illustrated with practical and familiar Examples. By EDWARD BAYLIS, Actuary of the Anchor Life Assurance Company. 8vo. 5s. cloth.

BEDFORD CORRESPONDENCE. — CORRESPONDENCE OF
JOHN, FOURTH DUKE OF BEDFORD, selected from the Originals at Woburn Abbey (1742 to 1770). With Introductions by Lord JOHN RUSSELL. 3 vols. 8vo. with Portrait, 48s. cloth.

*** Separately: Vol. I. (1742-1748), 18s.; Vol. II. (1749-1760), 15s.; Vol. III. (1761-1770), 15s.

BELL.—LIVES OF THE MOST EMINENT ENGLISH POETS.
By ROBERT BELL, Esq. 2 vols. fcp. 8vo. with Vignette Titles, 12s. cloth.

BELL.—THE HISTORY OF RUSSIA,
From the Earliest Period to the Treaty of Tilsit. By ROBERT BELL, Esq. 3 vols. fcp. 8vo. with Vignette Titles, 18s. cloth.

BLACK.—A PRACTICAL TREATISE ON BREWING,
Based on Chemical and Economical Principles: with Formulæ for Public Brewers, and Instructions for Private Families. By WILLIAM BLACK. Third Edition, with considerable Additions. 8vo. 10s. 6d. cloth.—Also,

REMARKS ON BAVARIAN BEER, London Porter, the Influence of Electricity on Fermentation. By WILLIAM BLACK. Being a Supplement to his "Treatise on Brewing." 8vo. 2s. 6d. sewed.

BLAINE.—AN ENCYCLOPÆDIA OF RURAL SPORTS;
Or, a complete Account, Historical, Practical, and Descriptive, of Hunting, Shooting, Fishing, Racing, and other Field Sports and Athletic Amusements of the present day. By DELABERE P. BLAINE, Esq. Author of "Canine Pathology," &c. Illustrated by nearly 600 Engravings on Wood, by R. Branston, from Drawings by Alken, T. Landseer, Dickes, &c. 8vo. £2. 10s. cloth.

BLAIR'S CHRONOLOGICAL AND HISTORICAL TABLES,
From the Creation to the present time: with Additions and Corrections from the most authentic Writers; including the Computation of St. Paul, as connecting the Period from the Exode to the Temple. Under the revision of Sir HENRY ELLIS, K.H., Principal Librarian of the British Museum. Imperial 8vo. 31s. 6d. half-bound in morocco.

BLOOMFIELD.—HISTORY OF THE PELOPONNESIAN WAR.
By THUCYDIDES. A New Recension of the Text, with a carefully amended Punctuation; and copious NOTES, Critical, Philological, and Explanatory, principally original, partly selected and arranged from the best Expositors: accompanied by full Indexes, both of Greek Words and Phrases explained, and matters discussed in the Notes Illustrated by Maps and Plans. By the Rev. S. T. BLOOMFIELD, D.D. F.S.A. 2 vols. 8vo. 38s. cloth.

BLOOMFIELD.—HISTORY OF THE PELOPONNESIAN WAR.
By THUCYDIDES. Translated into English, and accompanied by very copious Notes, Philological and Explanatory, Historical and Geographical. By the Rev. S. T. BLOOMFIELD, D.D. F.S.A. 3 vols. 8vo. with Maps and Plates, £2. 5s. boards.

BLOOMFIELD.—THE GREEK TESTAMENT:
With copious English Notes, Critical, Philological, and Explanatory. Especially formed for the use of advanced Students and Candidates for Holy Orders. By Rev. S. T. BLOOMFIELD, D.D. F.S.A. 6th Edition. 2 vols. 8vo. with a Map of Palestine, £2, cloth.

BLOOMFIELD.—A COLLEGE & SCHOOL GREEK TESTAMENT;
With shorter English Notes, Critical, Philological, and Explanatory, formed for use in Colleges and the Public Schools. By the Rev. S. T. BLOOMFIELD, D.D. F.S.A. 4th Edition, greatly enlarged and improved. Fcp. 8vo. 10s. 6d. cloth.

BLOOMFIELD.—GREEK AND ENGLISH LEXICON TO THE
NEW TESTAMENT: especially adapted to the use of Colleges, and the Higher Classes in Public Schools; but also intended as a convenient Manual for Biblical Students in general. By Dr. BLOOMFIELD. 2d Edition, enlarged and improved. Fcp. 8vo. 10s. 6d. cloth.

BOY'S OWN BOOK (THE):
A Complete Encyclopædia of all the Diversions, Athletic, Scientific, and Recreative, of Boyhood and Youth. 23d Edition. Square 12mo. with many Engravings on Wood, 6s. boards.

BRANDE.—A DICTIONARY OF SCIENCE, LITERATURE,
AND ART; comprising the History, Description, and Scientific Principles of every Branch of Human Knowledge; with the Derivation and Definition of all the Terms in General Use. Edited by W. T. BRANDE, F.R.S.L. & E.; assisted by J. CAUVIN. 8vo. with Wood Engravings, £3, cloth.

BRAY'S (MRS.) NOVELS AND ROMANCES,
Revised and corrected by Mrs. BRAY. In 10 vols. fcp. 8vo. with a Portrait, Frontispieces, and Vignettes, uniformly with "The Standard Novels," £3, cloth.—Or,

1. The White Hoods, 6s.	4. Fitz of Fitz-Ford, 6s.	8. Trials of the Heart, 6s.
2. De Foix, 6s.	5. The Talba, 6s.	9. Henry de Pomeroy, 6s.
3. The Protestant, 6s.	6. Warleigh, 6s.	10. Courtenay of Walreddon, 6s.
	7. Trelawny of Trelawne, 6s.	

BRAY.—AN ESSAY UPON THE UNION OF AGRICULTURE
WITH MANUFACTURES, AND UPON THE ORGANISATION OF INDUSTRY. By CHARLES BRAY. 12mo. 1s. sewed.

BRAY.—AN OUTLINE OF THE VARIOUS SOCIAL SYSTEMS
and COMMUNITIES which have been FOUNDED on the PRINCIPLE of CO-OPERATION. Preceded by an Essay on the Union of Agriculture with Manufacture, and on the Organisation of Industry. By CHARLES BRAY. Post 8vo. 5s. cloth.

BRAY.—THE PHILOSOPHY OF NECESSITY;
Or, the Law of Consequences as applicable to Mental, Moral, and Social Science. By CHARLES BRAY. 2 vols. 8vo. 15s. cloth.

BREWSTER.—TREATISE ON OPTICS.
By Sir DAVID BREWSTER, LL.D. F.R.S., &c. New Edition. Fcp. 8vo. with Vignette Title, and 176 Woodcuts, 6s. cloth.

BUCKLER (J. C. AND C. A.)—A HISTORY OF THE
ARCHITECTURE of the ABBEY CHURCH of ST. ALBAN, with especial reference to the Norman Structure. By J. C. and C. A. BUCKLER, Architects. 8vo. with numerous Illustrations.　　　　　　　　　　　　　　　　　　　　　　　　　　　[*Nearly ready*.

BUDGE (J.)—THE PRACTICAL MINER'S GUIDE;
Comprising a Set of Trigonometrical Tables adapted to all the purposes of Oblique or Diagonal, Vertical, Horizontal, and Traverse Dialling; with their application to the Dial, Exercise of Drifts, Lodes, Slides, Levelling, Inaccessible Distances, Heights, &c. By J. BUDGE. New Edition, considerably enlarged. 8vo. with Portrait of the Author, 12s. cloth.

BULL.—THE MATERNAL MANAGEMENT OF CHILDREN,
in HEALTH and DISEASE. By T. BULL, M.D. Member of the Royal College of Physicians, Physician-Accucheur to the Finsbury Midwifery Institution. 2d Edition. Fcp. 8vo. 7s. cloth.

BULL.—HINTS TO MOTHERS,
For the Management of Health during the Period of Pregnancy and in the Lying-in Room; with an Exposure of Popular Errors in connection with those subjects. By THOMAS BULL, M.D. &c. 5th Edition. Fcp. 8vo. 7s. cloth.

BURDER.—ORIENTAL CUSTOMS,
Applied to the Illustration of the Sacred Scriptures. By Dr. SAMUEL BURDER. 3d Edition, with Additions. Fcp. 8vo. 8s. 6d. cloth.

BÜRGER.—THE "LEONORA" OF BÜRGER.
Translated by JULIA M. CAMERON. With Six large Illustrations, drawn on Wood by D. Maclise, R.A. and engraved by John Thompson. Crown 4to. 15s. cloth.

BURNS.—THE PRINCIPLES OF CHRISTIAN PHILOSOPHY;

containing the Doctrines, Duties, Admonitions, and Consolations of the Christian Religion. By JOHN BURNS, M.D. F.R.S.   6th Edition.   Fcp. 8vo. 6s. 6d. cloth.

BURNS.—CHRISTIAN FRAGMENTS;

Or, Remarks on the Nature, Precepts, and Comforts of Religion.   By JOHN BURNS, M.D. F.R.S.   Author of "The Principles of Christian Philosophy."   Fcp. 8vo. 5s. cloth.

BUTLER.—SKETCH OF ANCIENT & MODERN GEOGRAPHY.

By SAMUEL BUTLER, D.D. late Lord Bishop of Lichfield and Coventry; and formerly Head Master of Shrewsbury School.   New Edition, revised by the Author's SON.   8vo. 9s. boards.

BUTLER.—AN ATLAS OF MODERN GEOGRAPHY.

By the late Dr. BUTLER.   Consisting of Twenty-three coloured Maps, from a New Set of Plates; with an Index of all the Names of Places, referring to the Latitudes and Longitudes. New Edition.   8vo. 12s. half-bound.

BUTLER.—AN ATLAS OF ANCIENT GEOGRAPHY.

By the late Dr. BUTLER.   Consisting of Twenty-three coloured Maps; with an Index of all the Names of Places, referring to the Latitudes and Longitudes.   New Edition, from an entirely new and corrected Set of Plates.   8vo. 12s. half-bound.

BUTLER.—A GENERAL ATLAS OF MODERN AND ANCIENT

GEOGRAPHY.   By the late Dr. S. BUTLER.   Consisting of Forty-five coloured Maps, and Indices.   New Edition, from an entirely new and corrected Set of Plates.   4to. 24s. half-bound.

CALLCOTT.—A SCRIPTURE HERBAL.

With upwards of 120 Wood Engravings.   By LADY CALLCOTT.   Square crown 8vo. 25s. cloth.

CARTOONS (THE PRIZE).—THE PRIZE CARTOONS

EXHIBITED IN WESTMINSTER HALL, A.D. 1843.   Published under the Sanction and Patronage of Her Majesty's Commissioners on the Fine Arts.

The average size of the Prize Cartoons is fifteen feet in width and ten in height.   A reduced scale of one inch and a half to the foot has been adopted; and in the process of reduction every care has been taken faithfully to preserve all the characteristic features of the originals; and the Engraving of each work has been subjected to the approval of its author.   Lithography has been chosen as the most suitable medium for producing copies of these important works.

The size of the work is large folio.   The price of the Eleven Engravings, in a neat Portfolio, £5. 5s.; Proofs before Letters, £8. 8s.

CATLOW.—POPULAR CONCHOLOGY;

Or, the Shell Cabinet arranged: being an Introduction to the Modern System of Conchology: with a sketch of the Natural History of the Animals, an account of the Formation of the Shells, and a complete Descriptive List of the Families and Genera.   By AGNES CATLOW.   Fcp. 8vo. with 312 Woodcuts, 10s. 6d. cloth.

CHALENOR.—WALTER GRAY,

A Ballad, and other Poems.   By MARY CHALENOR.   2d Edition, including the Authoress's Poetical Remains.   Fcp. 8vo. 6s. cloth.

CLAVERS.—FOREST LIFE.

By MARY CLAVERS, an Actual Settler; Author of "A New Home, Who 'll Follow?"   2 vols. fcp. 8vo. 12s. cloth.

COCKS (C.)—BORDEAUX, ITS WINES, AND THE CLARET

COUNTRY.   By C. COCKS, B.L. Professor of the Living Languages in the Royal Colleges of France; Translator of the Works of Michelet and Quinet.   Dedicated, by permission, to M. Le Comte T. Duchâtel.   Post 8vo. with View of Bordeaux, 8s. 6d. cloth.

COLLEGIAN'S GUIDE (THE);

Or, Recollections of College Days, setting forth the Advantages and Temptations of a University Education.   By **** ******, M.A. —— College, Oxford.   Post 8vo. 10s. 6d. cloth.

COLLIER (J. PAYNE.)—A BOOK OF ROXBURGHE BALLADS.

Edited by JOHN PAYNE COLLIER, Esq.   Fcp. 4to. with Woodcuts, 21s. boards; morocco, 38s. *(bound by Hayday.)*

COLTON.—LACON; OR, MANY THINGS IN FEW WORDS.

By the Rev. C. C. COLTON.   New Edition.   8vo. 12s. cloth.

COOLEY.—THE WORLD SURVEYED IN THE NINETEENTH

CENTURY; or, Recent Narratives of Scientific and Exploring Expeditions (chiefly under-taken by command of Foreign Governments). Collected, translated, and, where necessary, abridged, by W. D. Cooley, Esq. Author of the "History of Maritime and Inland Discovery" in the Cabinet Cyclopædia, &c.—The First Volume of the Series contains,

THE ASCENT of MOUNT ARARAT. By Dr. Friedrich Parrot, Professor of Natural Philosophy in the University of Dorpat, Russian Imperial Councillor of State, &c. 8vo. with a Map by Arrowsmith, and Woodcuts, 14s. cloth.

The Second Work of the Series will be

ERMAN'S TRAVELS through SIBERIA. 2 vols. 8vo. with Illustrations. [*In the press.*

COOLEY.—THE HISTORY OF MARITIME AND INLAND

DISCOVERY. By W. D. Cooley, Esq. 3 vols. fcp. 8vo. with Vignette Titles, 18s. cloth.

CONVERSATIONS ON BOTANY.

9th Edition, improved. Fcp. 8vo. 22 Plates, 7s. 6d. cloth; with the plates coloured, 12s. cloth.

CONVERSATIONS ON MINERALOGY.

With Plates, engraved by Mr. and Mrs. Lowry, from Original Drawings. 3d Edition, enlarged. 2 vols. fcp. 8vo. 14s. cloth.

COOPER (REV. E.)—SERMONS,

Chiefly designed to elucidate some of the leading Doctrines of the Gospel. To which is added, an Appendix, containing Sermons preached on several Public Occasions, and printed by desire. By the Rev. Edward Cooper. 7th Edition. 2 vols. 12mo. 10s. boards.

COOPER (REV. E.)—PRACTICAL AND FAMILIAR SERMONS,

Designed for Parochial and Domestic Instruction. By Rev. Edward Cooper. New Edition. 7 vols. 12mo. £1. 18s. boards.

₊ Vols. 1 to 4, 5s. each; Vols. 5 to 7, 6s. each.

COPLAND.—A DICTIONARY OF PRACTICAL MEDICINE;

comprising General Pathology, the Nature and Treatment of Diseases, Morbid Structures, and the Disorders especially incidental to Climates, to Sex, and to the different Epochs of Life, with numerous approved Formulæ of the Medicines recommended. By James Copland, M.D. Consulting Physician to Queen Charlotte's Lying-in Hospital, &c. &c. &c. Vols. 1 and 2, 8vo. £3, cloth; and Parts 10 and 11, 4s. 6d. each, sewed.

₊ To be completed in One more Volume.

COSTELLO (MISS.)—THE ROSE GARDEN OF PERSIA.

A Series of Translations from the Persian Poets By Miss Louisa Stuart Costello, Author of "Specimens of the Early Poetry of France," "A Summer amongst the Bocages and the Vines," &c. Long 8vo. with Illuminated Pages and Borders printed in rose-colour, 18s. boards; or 31s. 6d. bound in rose-coloured morocco *(Persian style)* by Hayday.

COSTELLO (MISS).—THE FALLS, LAKES, AND MOUNTAINS

OF NORTH WALES; being a Pictorial Tour through the most interesting parts of the Country. By Louisa Stuart Costello, Author of "The Rose Garden of Persia," "Bearn and the Pyrenees," &c. Illustrated with Views, from Original Sketches by D. H. M'Kewan, engraved on wood, and lithographed, by T. and E. Gilks. Square 8vo. with Map, 14s. cloth.

CRESY (E.)—AN ENCYCLOPÆDIA OF CIVIL ENGINEERING,

Historical, Theoretical, and Practical. By Edward Cresy, F.S.A. C.E. Illustrated by upwards of Three Thousand Engravings on Wood, explanatory of the Principles, Machinery, and Constructions which come under the Direction of the Civil Engineer. One very large Volume 8vo. £3. 13s. 6d. cloth.

CROCKER'S ELEMENTS OF LAND SURVEYING.

Fifth Edition, corrected throughout, and considerably improved and modernized, by T. G. Bunt, Land Surveyor. To which are added, TABLES OF SIX-FIGURE LOGARITHMS, &c., superintended by R. Farley, of the Nautical Almanac Establishment. Post 8vo. 12s. cloth.

CROWE.—THE HISTORY OF FRANCE,

From the Earliest Period to the Abdication of Napoleon. By E. E. Crowe, Esq. 3 vols. fcp. 8vo. with Vignette Titles, 18s. cloth.

DALE (THE REV. T.) — THE DOMESTIC LITURGY AND

FAMILY CHAPLAIN, in two Parts: the first Part being Church Services adapted for domestic use, with Prayers for every day of the week, selected exclusively from the Book of Common Prayer; Part 2 comprising an appropriate Sermon for every Sunday in the year. By the Rev. THOMAS DALE, M.A. Canon-Residentiary of St. Paul's, and Vicar of St. Pancras, London. Post 4to. handsomely printed, 21s. cloth: or, bound by Hayday, 31s. 6d. calf lettered; £2. 10s. morocco, with goffered edges.

DAVY (SIR HUMPHRY).—ELEMENTS OF AGRICULTURAL

CHEMISTRY, in a Course of Lectures. By Sir HUMHHRY DAVY. With Notes by Dr. JOHN DAVY. 6th Edition. 8vo. with 10 Plates, 15s. cloth.

DE BURTIN.—A TREATISE ON THE KNOWLEDGE NECES-

SARY to AMATEURS of PICTURES. Translated and Abridged from the French of M. FRANCIS XAVIER DE BURTIN, First Stipendiary Member of the Royal Academy of Brussels in the Class of Sciences, &c. By ROBERT WHITE, Esq. 8vo. with four Plates, 12s. cloth.

DE CUSTINE. — RUSSIA.

By the MARQUIS DE CUSTINE. Translated from the French. 2d Edition. 3 vols. post 8vo. 31s. 6d. cloth.

DE LA BECHE.—REPORT ON THE GEOLOGY OF CORN-

WALL, DEVON, and WEST SOMERSET. By HENRY T. DE LA BECHE, F.R.S. &c., Director of the Ordnance Geological Survey. Published by Order of the Lords Commissioners of H.M. Treasury. 8vo. with Maps, Woodcuts, and 12 large Pates, 14s. cloth.

DE MORGAN.—AN ESSAY ON PROBABILITIES,

And on their Application to Life Contingencies and Insurance Offices. By AUG. DE MORGAN, of Trinity College, Cambridge. Fcp. 8vo. with Vignette Title, 6s. cloth.

DE SISMONDI.—THE HISTORY OF THE ITALIAN REPUB-

LICS; or, of the Origin, Progress, and Fall of Freedom in Italy, from A.D. 476 to 1806. By J. C. L. SISMONDI. Fcp. 8vo. with Vignette Title, 6s. cloth.

DE SISMONDI. — THE HISTORY OF THE FALL OF THE

ROMAN EMPIRE. Comprising a View of the Invasion and Settlement of the Barbarians. By J. C. L. DE SISMONDI. 2 vols. fcp. 8vo. with Vignette Titles, 12s. cloth.

DE STRZELECKI (P. E.)—THE PHYSICAL DESCRIPTION

of NEW SOUTH WALES and VAN DIEMAN'S LAND; accompanied by a Geological Map Sections, and Diagrams, and Figures of the Organic Remains. By P. E. DE STRZELECKI. 8vo. with coloured Map and numerous Plates, 24s. cloth.

DIBDIN (THE REV. T. F.)—THE SUNDAY LIBRARY:

Containing nearly One Hundred Sermons, by eminent Divines. With Notes, &c. by the Rev. T. F. DIBDIN, D.D. 6 vols. fcp. 8vo. with Six Portraits, 30s. cloth; or, £2. 12s. 6d. neatly half-bound in morocco, with gilt edges.

DODDRIDGE.—THE FAMILY EXPOSITOR;

Or, a Paraphrase and Version of the New Testament: with Critical Notes, and a Practical Improvement of each Section. By P. DODDRIDGE, D.D. To which is prefixed, a Life of the Author, by A. KIPPIS, D.D. F.R.S. and S.A. New Edition, 4 vols. 8vo. £1. 16s. cloth.

DONOVAN.—A TREATISE ON CHEMISTRY.

By M. DONOVAN, M.R.I.A. Fourth Edition. Fcp. 8vo. with Vignette Title, 6s. cloth.

DONOVAN.—A TREATISE ON DOMESTIC ECONOMY.

By M. DONOVAN, Esq. M.R.I.A. Professor of Chemistry to the Company of Apothecaries in Ireland. 2 vols. fcp. 8vo. with Vignette Titles, 12s. cloth.

DOUBLEDAY AND HEWITSON'S BUTTERFLIES. — THE

GENERA of DIURNAL LEPIDOPTERA; comprising their Generic Characters—a Notice of the Habits and Transformations—and a Catalogue of the Species of each Genus. By EDWARD DOUBLEDAY, Esq. F.L.S. &c., Assistant in the Zoological Department of the British Museum. Imperial 4to. uniform with Gray and Mitchell's Ornithology; Illustrated with 75 Coloured Plates, by W. C. HEWITSON, Esq. Author of " British Oology."

₊ Publishing in Monthly Parts, 5s. each; each part consisting of 2 coloured plates, with accompanying Letter-press, giving the Generic Characters, a Short Notice of the Habits, and a Catalogue of the Species of each Genus. Part VII. will appear on the 1st of May.

DOVER.—LIFE OF FREDERICK II. KING OF PRUSSIA.

By LORD DOVER. 2d Edition. 2 vols. 8vo. with Portrait, 28s. boards.

DRESDEN GALLERY.—THE MOST CELEBRATED PICTURES
of the ROYAL GALLERY at DRESDEN, drawn on Stone, from the Originals, by Franz Hanfstaengel: with Descriptive and Biographical Notices, in French and German. Nos. I. to XLIV. imperial folio, each containing 3 Plates, with accompanying Letter-press, price 20s. to Subscribers; to Non Subscribers, 30s. Single Plates, 12s. each.

₊ To be completed in a few more numbers.

DRUMMOND (DR. J. L.)—LETTERS TO A YOUNG NATU-
RALIST, ON THE STUDY OF NATURE AND NATURAL THEOLOGY. By JAMES L. DRUMMOND, M.D. Author of "First Steps to Botany," &c. Second Edition. Post 8vo. with Wood Engravings, 7s. 6d. boards.

DRUMMOND.—FIRST STEPS TO BOTANY,
Intended as popular Illustrations of the Science, leading to its study as a branch of general education. By J. L. DRUMMOND, M.D. 4th Edit. 12mo. with numerous Woodcuts, 9s. bds.

DUNHAM.—THE HISTORY OF THE GERMANIC EMPIRE.
By Dr. DUNHAM. 3 vols. fcp. 8vo. with Vignette Titles, 18s. cloth.

THE HISTORY OF EUROPE DURING THE MIDDLE AGES. By Dr. Dunham. 4 vols. fcp. 8vo. with Vignette Titles, £1. 4s. cloth.

THE HISTORY OF SPAIN AND PORTUGAL. By Dr. Dunham. 5 vols. fcp. 8vo. with Vignette Titles, £1. 10s. cloth.

THE HISTORY OF SWEDEN, DENMARK, AND NORWAY. By Dr. Dunham. 3 vols. fcp. 8vo. with Vignette Titles, 18s. cloth.

THE HISTORY OF POLAND. By Dr. Dunham. Fcp. 8vo. with Vignette Title, 6s. cloth.

THE LIVES OF THE EARLY WRITERS OF GREAT BRITAIN. By Dr. Dunham, R. Bell, Esq. &c. Fcp. 8vo. with Vignette Title, 6s. cloth.

THE LIVES OF BRITISH DRAMATISTS. By Dr. Dunham, R. Bell, Esq. &c. 2 vols. fcp. 8vo. with Vignette Titles, 12s. cloth.

DUNLOP (JOHN).—THE HISTORY OF FICTION:
Being a Critical Account of the most celebrated Prose Works of Fiction, from the earliest Greek Romances to the Novels of the Present Age. By JOHN DUNLOP, Esq. 3d Edition, complete in One Volume. 8vo. 15s. cloth.

ECCLESTON (JAMES.)—A MANUAL OF ENGLISH ANTIQUI-
TIES. By JAMES ECCLESTON, B.A. Head Master of Sutton Coldfield Grammar School. 8vo. with numerous Illustrations on Wood. [In the press.

ELLIOTSON.—HUMAN PHYSIOLOGY:
With which is incorporated much of the elementary part of the "Institutiones Physiologicæ" of J. F. Blumenbach, Professor in the University of Göttingen. By JOHN ELLIOTSON, M.D. Cantab. F.R.S. Fifth Edition. 8vo. with numerous Woodcuts, £2. 2s. cloth.

ENGLISHMAN'S GREEK CONCORDANCE OF THE NEW
TESTAMENT: being an Attempt at a Verbal Connexion between the Greek and the English Texts; including a Concordance to the Proper Names, with Indexes, Greek-English and English-Greek. 2d Edition, with a new Index. Royal 8vo. 42s. cloth.

ENGLISHMAN'S HEBREW AND CHALDEE CONCORDANCE
of the OLD TESTAMENT; being an attempt at a Verbal Connection between the Original and the English Translations: with Indexes, a List of the Proper Names and their occurrences, &c. &c. 2 vols. royal 8vo. £3. 13s. 6d. cloth; large paper, £4. 14s. 6d.

EPHEMERA.—A HAND-BOOK OF ANGLING;
Teaching Fly-fishing, Trolling, Bottom-fishing, Salmon-fishing; the Natural History of River Fish, and the best modes of Catching them. By EPHEMERA, of Bell's Life in London. Fcp. 8vo. with Illustrations, 9s. cloth.

ESDAILE (DR. J.)—MESMERISM IN INDIA;
And its Practical Application in Surgery and Medicine. By JAMES ESDAILE, M.D. Civil Assistant-Surgeon, E.I.C.S. Bengal. Fcp. 8vo. 6s. 6d. cloth.

ETHERIDGE (J. W.)—THE SYRIAN CHURCHES:
Their Early History, Liturgies, and Literature. With a literal Translation of the Four Gospels from the Peschito, or Canon of Holy Scripture in use among the Oriental Christians from the earliest times. By J. W. ETHERIDGE, Author of "Horæ Armaicæ." 12mo. 7s. 6d. cloth.

FAREY.—A TREATISE ON THE STEAM ENGINE,
Historical, Practical, and Descriptive. By JOHN FAREY, Engineer. 4to. illustrated by numerous Woodcuts, and 25 Copper-plates, £5. 5s. boards.

FAWN (THE) OF SERTORIUS.

2 vols. post 8vo. 18s. cloth.
" As a work that contains lively and graphic pictures of life and manners in a distant age, we commend it to the perusal of our readers."—CRITIC.

FERGUS.—HISTORY OF UNITED STATES OF AMERICA,

From the Discovery of America to the Election of General Jackson to the Presidency. By the Rev. H. FERGUS. 2 vols. fcp. 8vo. with Vignette Titles, 12s. cloth.

FITZROY (LADY). — SCRIPTURAL CONVERSATIONS BE-

TWEEN CHARLES and his MOTHER. By Lady CHARLES FITZROY. Fcp. 8vo. 4s. 6d. cloth.

FLORA.—THE SPECIMEN FLORA;

Or, British Botany exemplified by Plants from a Collector's Cabinet. Arranged by the Author of "The Pictorial Flora." 8vo. 21s. in watered silk.

FORSTER.—THE STATESMEN OF THE COMMONWEALTH

OF ENGLAND. With an Introductory Treatise on the Popular Progress in English History. By JOHN FORSTER, Esq. 5 vols. fcp. 8vo. with Original Portraits of Pym, Eliot, Hampden, Cromwell, and an Historical Scene after a Picture by Cattermole, £1. 10s. cloth.

The above 5 vols. form Mr. Forster's portion of the Lives of Eminent British Statesmen, by Sir James Mackintosh, the Right Hon. T. P. Courtenay, and John Forster, Esq. 7 vols. fcp. 8vo. with Vignette Titles, £2. 2s. cloth.

FORSTER (REV. C.)—THE HISTORICAL GEOGRAPHY OF

ARABIA; or, the Patriarchal Evidences of Revealed Religion. A Memoir, with illustrative Maps and an Appendix, containing Translations, with an Alphabet and Glossary of the Hamyaritic Inscriptions recently discovered in Hadramaut. By the Rev. CHARLES FORSTER, B.D. Author of "Mahometanism Unveiled." 2 vols. 8vo. 30s. cloth.

FORSTER (REV. C.)—THE LIFE OF JOHN JEBB, D.D. F.R.S.,

late Bishop of Limerick. With a Selection from his Letters. By the Rev. CHARLES FORSTER, B.D. Rector of Stisted, and formerly Domestic Chaplain to the Bishop. Second Edition. 8vo. with Portrait, &c. 16s. cloth.

FOSBROKE.—A TREATISE ON THE ARTS, MANNERS,

MANUFACTURES, and INSTITUTIONS of the GREEKS and ROMANS. By the Rev. T. D. FOSBROKE, &c. 2 vols. fcp. 8vo. with Vignette Titles, 12s. cloth.

FROM OXFORD TO ROME;

And, How it fared with some who lately made the Journey. By a COMPANION TRAVELLER. Fcp. 8vo. with Frontispiece, 6s. cloth.

GASCOYNE.—A NEW SOLUTION, IN PART, OF THE SEALS,

TRUMPETS, and other SYMBOLS of the REVELATION of ST. JOHN : being an Attempt to prove that, as far as they are fulfilled, they denote the Rise, Increase, and Maturity of the Man of Sin, and the Coming of our Lord Jesus Christ for his Destruction. By the Rev. R. GASCOYNE, A.M. 18mo. 5s. cloth.

GERTRUDE.

A Tale. By the Author of " Amy Herbert." Edited by the Rev. WILLIAM SEWELL, B.D. of Exeter College, Oxford. New Edition. 2 vols. fcp. 8vo. 9s. cloth.

GILBART (J. W.) — THE HISTORY AND PRINCIPLES OF

BANKING. By JAMES WILLIAM GILBART, General Manager of the London and Westminster Bank. 3d Edition. 8vo. 9s. boards.

GLEIG.—LIVES OF MOST EMINENT BRITISH MILITARY

COMMANDERS. By the Rev. G. R. GLEIG. 3 vols. fcp. 8vo. with Vignette Titles, 18s. cloth.

GOLDSMITH. — THE POETICAL WOKRS OF OLIVER

GOLDSMITH. Illustrated by Wood Engravings, from the Designs of G. W. Cope, A.R.A., Thomas Creswick, A.R.A., J. C. Horsley, R. Redgrave, A.R.A., and Frederick Tayler M te- bers of the Etching Club. With a Biographical Memoir, and Notes on the Poems. Edi d by BOLTON CORNEY, Esq. Square crown 8vo. uniform with " Thomson's Seasons," 21s. cloth ; or, bound in morocco, by Hayday, £1. 16s.

₊ One Hundred Copies, £2. 2s. each, printed on prepared paper of great beauty.

GOOD.—THE BOOK OF NATURE.

A Popular Illustration of the General Laws and Phenomena of Creation. By JOHN MASON GOOD, M.D. F.R.S., &c. Third Edition, corrected. 3 vols. fcp. 8vo. 24s. cloth.

GOWER.—THE SCIENTIFIC PHÆNOMENA OF DOMESTIC

LIFE, familiarly explained. By CHARLES FOOTE GOWER. New Edition. Fcp. 8vo. with Wood Engravings, 5s. cloth.

GRAHAM.—ENGLISH ; OR, THE ART OF COMPOSITION :

explained in a Series of Instructions and Examples. By G. F. GRAHAM. New Edition, revised and improved. Fcp. 8vo. 7s. cloth.

GRANT (MRS.)—LETTERS FROM THE MOUNTAINS.

Being the Correspondence with her Friends, between the years 1773 and 1803. By Mrs GRANT, of Laggan. Sixth Edition. Edited, with Notes and Additions, by her son, J. P. GRANT, Esq. 2 vols. post 8vo. 21s. cloth.

GRANT (MRS.) — MEMOIR AND CORRESPONDENCE OF

the late Mrs. Grant, of Laggan, Author of " Letters from the Mountains," " Memoirs of an American Lady," &c. &c. Edited by her Son, J. P. GRANT, Esq. 2d Edition. 3 vols. post 8vo. with Portrait, 31s. 6d. cloth.

GRATTAN.—THE HISTORY OF THE NETHERLANDS,

From the Invasion by the Romans to the Belgian Revolution in 1830. By T. C. GRATTAN, Esq. Fcp. 8vo. with Vignette Title, 6s. cloth.

GRAY (THOMAS).—GRAY'S ELEGY,

Written in a Country Churchyard. Illuminated in the Missal style. By OWEN JONES, Architect. Imp. 8vo. 31s. 6d. elegantly bound in patent relievo leather.

GRAY.—FIGURES OF MOLLUSCOUS ANIMALS,

Selected from various Authors. Etched for the Use of Students. By MARIA EMMA GRAY. Vol. I. 8vo. with 78 plates of Figures, 12s. cloth.

GRAY AND MITCHELL'S ORNITHOLOGY.—THE GENERA

Of BIRDS ; comprising their Generic Characters, a Notice of the Habits of each Genus, and an extensive List of Species, referred to their several Genera. By GEORGE ROBERT GRAY, Acad. Imp. Georg. Florent. Soc. Corresp. Senior Assistant of the Zoological Department, British Museum ; and Author of the " List of the Genera of Birds," &c. &c. Illustrated with Three Hundred and Fifty imperial quarto Plates, by DAVID WILLIAM MITCHELL.

In course of publication, in Monthly Parts, 10s. 6d. each ; each Part consisting generally of Four imperial quarto coloured Plates and Three plain, and accompanying Letterpress ; giving the Generic Characters, short Remarks on the Habits, and a List of Species of each Genus as complete as possible. The uncoloured Plates contain the Characters of all the Genera of the various Sub-families, consisting of numerous details of Heads, Wings, and Feet, as the case may require, for pointing out their distinguishing Characters.

*** The work will not exceed Fifty Monthly Parts, of which Thirty-Six have appeared.

ORDER I.—Accipitres, has been completed, and may be had separately. Imperial 8vo. with 15 coloured and 12 plain Plates, £2. 8s. boards.

GREENER.—THE GUN ;

Or, a Treatise on the various Descriptions of Small Fire-Arms. By W. GREENER, Inventor of an improved method of Firing Cannon by Percussion, &c. 8vo. with Illustrations, 15s. boards.

GRIMBLOT (P.)—LETTERS OF WILLIAM III. AND LOUIS

XIV. and of their Ministers. Illustrating the Domestic and Foreign Policy of England during the period which followed the Revolution of 1688. Extracted from the Archives of France and England, and from Family papers. Edited by P. GRIMBLOT. 2 vols. 8vo. [In the press.

GUEST.—THE MABINOGION,

From the Llyfr Coch o Hergest, or Red Book of Hergest, and other ancient Welsh MSS.: with an English Translation and Notes. By Lady CHARLOTTE GUEST. Parts 1 to 6. Royal 8vo. 8s. each, sewed.

GUICCIARDINI (F.)—THE MAXIMS OF FRANCIS GUIC-

CIARDINI. Translated by EMMA MARTIN. With Notes, and Parallel Passages from the works of Machiavelli, Lord Bacon, Pascal, Rochefoucault, Montesquieu, Burke, Talleyrand, M. Guizot, &c.; and a Sketch of the Life of Guicciardini. Square fcp. 8vo. with Portrait, 7s. boards; or bound in morocco by Hayday, 14s.

GUTCH.—A LYTELL GESTE OF ROBIN HODE :

With other Antient and Modern Ballads and Songs relative to this celebrated Yeoman. To which is prefixed, his History and Character, grounded upon other Documents than those made use of by his former Biographer, " Mister Ritson." Edited by J. M. GUTCH, F.A.S. and adorned with Cuts by F. W. FAIRHOLT, F.A.S. 2 vols. 8vo. with numerous Wood Engravings, 30s. cloth.

GWILT.—AN ENCYCLOPÆDIA OF ARCHITECTURE;
Historical, Theoretical, and Practical. By JOSEPH GWILT, Esq. F.S.A. Illustrated with upwards of 1000 Engravings on Wood, from Designs by J. S. GWILT. 8vo. 52s. 6d. cloth.

HALL.—NEW GENERAL LARGE LIBRARY ATLAS OF
FIFTY-THREE MAPS, on Colombier Paper; with the Divisions and Boundaries carefully coloured. Constructed entirely from New Drawings, and engraved by SIDNEY HALL. New Edition, thoroughly revised and corrected; including all the Alterations rendered necessary by the recent Official Surveys, the New Roads on the Continent, and a careful Comparison with the authenticated Discoveries published in the latest Voyages and Travels. Folded in half, Nine Guineas, half-bound in russia; full size of the Maps, Ten Pounds, half-bd. russia.

HALSTED.—LIFE AND TIMES OF RICHARD THE THIRD,
as Duke of Gloucester and King of England: in which all the Charges against him are carefully investigated and compared with the Statements of the Cotemporary Authorities. By CAROLINE A. HALSTED, Author of "The Life of Margaret Beaufort." 2 vols. 8vo. with an Original Portrait and other Illustrations, £1. 10s. cloth.

HAND-BOOK OF TASTE (THE);
Or, How to Observe Works of Art, especially Cartoons, Pictures, and Statues. By FABIUS PICTOR. New Edition. Fcp. 8vo. 3s. boards.

HANSARD.—TROUT AND SALMON FISHING IN WALES.
By G. A. HANSARD. 12mo. 6s. 6d. cloth.

HARRIS.—THE HIGHLANDS OF ÆHIOPIA;
Being the Accout of Eighteen Months' Residence of a British Embassy to the Christian Court of Shoa. By Major Sir W. C. HARRIS, Author of "Wild Sports in Southern Africa," &c. 2d Edition. 3 vols. 8vo. with Map and Illustrations, £2. 2s. cloth.

HAWES.—TALES OF THE NORTH AMERICAN INDIANS,
And Adventures of the Early Settlers in America; from the landing of the Pilgrim Fathers, in 1620, to the Time of the Declaration of Independence. By BARBARA HAWES. Fcp. 8vo. with Frontispiece, 6s. cloth.

HAWKER.—INSTRUCTIONS TO YOUNG SPORTSMEN
In all that relates to Guns and Shooting. By Lieut.-Col. P. HAWKER. 9th Edit. corrected, enlarged, and improved, with Eighty-five Plates and Woodcuts by Adlard and Branston, from Drawings by C. Varley, Dickes, &c. 8vo. £1. 1s. cloth.

HAYDON.—LECTURES ON PAINTING AND DESIGN:
Delivered at the London Institution, the Royal Institution, Albemarle Street, to the University of Oxford, &c. By B. R. HAYDON, Historical Painter. With Portraits of the Author and of Sir David Wilkie, and other Illustrations, from Designs drawn on Wood by the Author. 2 vols. 8vo. 24s. cloth.

HENSLOW.—THE PRINCIPLES OF DESCRIPTIVE AND
PHYSIOLOGICAL BOTANY. By J. S. HENSLOW, M.A. F.L.S. &c. Fcp. 8vo. with Vignette Title, and nearly 70 Woodcuts, 6s. cloth.

HERSCHEL.—A TREATISE ON ASTRONOMY.
By Sir JOHN HERSCHEL. New Edition. Fcp. 8vo. with Vignette Title, 6s. cloth.

HERSCHEL.—A PRELIMINARY DISCOURSE ON THE
STUDY OF NATURAL PHILOSOPHY. By Sir JOHN HERSCHEL. New Edition. Fcp. 8vo. with vignette title, 6s. cloth.

HIGGINS.—ANACALYPSIS;
Or, an Attempt to draw aside the Veil of the Saitic Isis: an Inquiry into the Origin of Languages, Nations, and Religions. By G. HIGGINS, Esq. F.S.A. F.R. Asiatic Society, &c. 2 vols. 4to. £5 cloth.

HIGGINS.—THE CELTIC DRUIDS;
Or, an Attempt to show that the Druids were the Priests of Oriental Colonies, who emigrated from India, and were the Introducers of the First or Cadmean System of Letters, and the Builders of Stonehenge, of Carnac, and of other Cyclopean works in Asia and Europe. By G. HIGGINS, F.S.A. F.R. Asiatic Soc. &c. 4to. with numerous Illustrations, £3 cloth.

HINTS ON ETIQUETTE AND THE USAGES OF SOCIETY:
With a Glance at Bad Habits. By Αγωγός. "Manners make the man." 26th Edition, revised (with additions) by a Lady of Rank. Fcp. 8vo. 2s. 6d. cloth, gilt edges.

General Observations; Introductions—Letters of Introduction—Marriage—Dinners—Smoking; Snuff—Fashion—Dress—Music—Dancing—Conversation—Advice to Tradespeople—Visiting; Visiting Cards—Cards—Tattling—Of General Society.

HISTORICAL CHARADES.
By the Author of "Letters from Madras." Fcp. 8vo. 5s. cloth.

HISTORICAL PICTURES OF THE MIDDLE AGES,
In Black and White. Made on the spot, from Records in the Archives of Switzerland. By a WANDERING ARTIST. 2 vols. post 8vo. 18s. cloth.

HOARE.—A DESCRIPTIVE ACCOUNT OF A NEW METHOD
of PLANTING and MANAGING the ROOTS of GRAPE VINES. By CLEMENT HOARE, Author of "A Treatise on the Cultivation of the Grape Vine on Open Walls." 12mo. 5s. cloth.

HOARE.—A PRACTICAL TREATISE ON THE CULTIVATION
OF THE GRAPE VINE ON OPEN WALLS. By CLEMENT HOARE. 3d Edition. 8vo. 7s. 6d. cloth.

HOBBES.—ENGLISH WORKS OF THOMAS HOBBES,
Of Malmesbury; now first collected by Sir WILLIAM MOLESWORTH, Bart. 16 vols. 8vo. 8s. cloth.
*** Separately : the English Works, in 11 vols. £5. 10s.; the Latin Works, in 5 vols. £2. 10s.

HOLLAND.—A TREATISE ON THE MANUFACTURES IN
METAL. By J. HOLLAND, Esq. 3 vols. fcp. Vignette Titles, about 300 Woodcuts, 18s. cloth.

HOLLAND.—MEDICAL NOTES AND REFLECTIONS.
By HENRY HOLLAND, M.D. F.R.S. &c. Fellow of the Royal College of Physicians, Physician Extraordinary to the Queen, and Physician in Ordinary to His Royal Highness Prince Albert. 2d Edition. 8vo. 18s. cloth.

HOOK (DR. W. F.)—THE LAST DAYS OF OUR LORD'S
MINISTRY : a Course of Lectures on the principal Events of Passion Week. By WALTER FARQUHAR HOOK, D.D. Vicar of Leeds, Prebendary of Lincoln, and Chaplain in Ordinary to the Queen. 4th Edition. Fcp. 8vo. 6s. cloth.

HOOKER.—THE BRITISH FLORA,
In Two Vols. Vol. 1; comprising Phænogamous or Flowering Plants, and the Ferns. By Sir WILLIAM JACKSON HOOKER, K.H. LL.D. F.R.A. and L.S. &c. &c &c. Fifth Edition, with Additions and Corrections ; and 173 Figures illustrative of the Umbelliferous Plants, the Composite Plants, the Grasses, and the Ferns. 8vo. with 12 Plates, 14s. plain; with the plates coloured, 24s. cloth.

Vol. 2, in Two Parts, comprising the Cryptogamia and Fungi, completing the British Flora, and forming Vol. 5, Parts 1 and 2, of Smith's English Flora, 24s. boards.

HORNE (THE REV. T. H.)—AN INTRODUCTION TO THE
CRITICAL STUDY and KNOWLEDGE of the HOLY SCRIPTURES. By THOMAS HARTWELL HORNE, B.D. of St. John's College, Cambridge; Rector of the united Parishes of St. Edmund the King and Martyr, and St. Nicholas Acons, Lombard Street ; Prebendary of St. Paul's. A New Edition, revised and corrected. 5 vols. 8vo. with numerous Maps and Facsimilies of Biblical Manuscripts, 63s. cloth; or £5, bound in calf half-extra, by Hayday.

HORNE (THE REV. T. H.)—A COMPENDIOUS INTRODUC-
TION to the STUDY of the BIBLE. By THOMAS HARTWELL HORNE, B.D. of St. John's College, Cambridge. Being an Analysis of his "Introduction to the Critical Study and Knowledge of the Holy Scriptures." 7th Edition, corrected and enlarged. 12mo. with Maps and other Engravings, 9s. boards.

HORSLEY (BISHOP).—BIBLICAL CRITICISM
On the first Fourteen Historical Books of the Old Testament; and on the first Nine Prophetical Books. By SAMUEL HORSLEY, LL.D. F.R.S. F.S.A. Lord Bishop of St. Asaph. 2d Edition, containing Translations by the Author never before published, together with copious Indices. 2 vols. 8vo. £1. 10s. cloth.—By the same Author,

THE BOOK of PSALMS; translated from the Hebrew: with Notes, explanatory and critical Fourth Edition. 8vo. 12s. cloth.

HOWITT (MARY).—BALLADS AND OTHER POEMS. BY
Mary Howitt. Square crown 8vo. with a Portrait, from a picture by Miss Gillies, beautifully engraved by W. H. Egleton, 18s. cloth ; morocco, 36s. *(bound by Hayday.)*

HOWITT.—THE RURAL LIFE OF ENGLAND.
By WILLIAM HOWITT. 3d Edition, corrected and revised. Medium 8vo. with Engravings on wood, by Bewick and Williams, uniform with "Visits to Remarkable Places," 21s. cloth.

HOWITT.—VISITS TO REMARKABLE PLACES;
Old Halls, Battle-Fields, and Scenes illustrative of Striking Passages in English History and Poetry. By WILLIAM HOWITT. New Edition. Medium 8vo. with 40 Illustrations by S. Williams, 21s. cloth.

SECOND SERIES, chiefly in the Counties of DURHAM and NORTHUMBERLAND, with a Stroll along the BORDER. Medium 8vo. with upwards of 40 highly-finished Woodcuts, from Drawings made on the spot for this work, by Messrs. Carmichael, Richardsons, and Weld Taylor, 21s. cloth.

HOWITT.—THE RURAL AND SOCIAL LIFE OF GERMANY :
With Characteristic Sketches of its Chief Cities and Scenery. Collected in a General Tour, and during a Residence in that Country in the Years 1840-42. By WILLIAM HOWITT, Author of "The Rural Life of England," &c. Med. 8vo. with above 50 Illustrations, 21s. cloth.

HOWITT.—THE STUDENT-LIFE OF GERMANY.
From the Unpublished MSS. of Dr. Cornelius. By WILLIAM HOWITT. 8vo. with 24 Wood-Engravings, and Seven Steel Plates, 21s. cloth.

HOWITT.—COLONISATION AND CHRISTIANITY :
A Popular History of the Treatment of the Natives, in all their Colonies, by the Europeans. By WILLIAM HOWITT. Post 8vo. 10s. 6d. cloth.

HOWITT.—THE BOY'S COUNTRY BOOK :
Being the real Life of a Country Boy, written by himself; exhibiting all the Amusements, Pleasures, and Pursuits of Children in the Country. Edited by WILLIAM HOWITT, Author of "The Rural Life of England," &c. 2d Edition. Fcp. 8vo. with 40 Woodcuts, 8s. cloth.

HUDSON.—PLAIN DIRECTIONS FOR MAKING WILLS
In Conformity with the Law, and particularly with reference to the Act 7 Will. 4 and 1 Vict. c. 26. To which is added, a clear Exposition of the Law relating to the distribution of Personal Estate in the case of Intestacy ; with two Forms of Wills, and much useful information, &c. By J. C. HUDSON, Esq. New Edition, corrected. Fcp. 8vo. 2s. 6d.

HUDSON.—THE EXECUTOR'S GUIDE.
By J. C. HUDSON, Esq. of the Legacy Duty Office, London ; Author of "Plain Directions for Making Wills," and "The Parent's Hand-book." New Edition. Fcp. 8vo. 5s. cloth.

        *** These two works may be had in one volume, 7s. cloth.

HUDSON.—THE PARENT'S HAND-BOOK,
Or, Guide to the Choice of Professions, Employments, and Situations ; containing useful and practical Information on the subject of placing out Young Men, and of obtaining their Education with a view to particular occupations. By J. C. HUDSON, Esq. Author of "Plain Directions for Making Wills." Fcp. 8vo. 5s. cloth.

HUMBOLDT (BARON).—BARON HUMBOLDT'S COSMOS :
A Sketch of a Physical Description of the Universe. Translated, with the Author's Sanction and Co-operation, under the superintendence of Lieutenant-Colonel EDWARD SABINE, R.A. For. Sec. R.S. Vol. I. Post 8vo. 12s. cloth.   [*Vol. II. is in the press.*

HUNT.—RESEARCHES ON LIGHT :
An Examination of all the Phenomena connected with the Chemical and Molecular Changes produced by the Influence of the Solar Rays ; embracing all the known Photographic Processes, and new Discoveries in the Art. By ROBERT HUNT, Keeper of Mining Records, Museum of Economic Geology. 8vo. with Plate and Woodcuts, 10s. 6d. cloth.

JACKSON.—PICTORIAL FLORA ;
Or, British Botany delineated, in 1500 Lithographic Drawings of all the Species of Flowering Plants indigenous to Great Britain ; illustrating the descriptive works on English Botany of Hooker, Lindley, Smith, &c. By MISS JACKSON. 8vo. 15s. cloth.

JAENISCH & WALKER.—JAENISCH'S CHESS PRECEPTOR:
A New Analysis of the Openings of Games. By C. F. De JAENISCH, of St. Petersburgh. Translated from the French, with copious Notes, by GEORGE WALKER, Author of "Chess Studies," and various other Works on the Game of Chess. 8vo. 15s. cloth.

JAMES.—LIVES OF MOST EMINENT FOREIGN STATESMEN.
By G. P. R. JAMES, Esq., and E. E. CROWE, Esq. 5 vols. fcp. 8vo. Vignette Titles, 30s. cloth.

JAMES.—A HISTORY OF THE LIFE OF EDWARD THE
BLACK PRINCE, and of various Events connected therewith, which occurred during the Reign of Edward III. King of England. By G. P. R. JAMES, Esq. 2d Edition. 2 vols. fcp. 8vo. Map, 15s. cloth.

JEBB. — A LITERAL TRANSLATION OF THE BOOK OF

PSALMS; intended to illustrate their Poetical and Moral Structure. To which are added, Dissertations on the word "Selah," and on the Authorship, Order, Titles, and Poetical Features, of the Psalms. By the Rev. JOHN JEBB, A.M. Rector of Peterstow. 2 vols. 8vo. 21s. cloth.

JEBB (BISHOP) AND KNOX (ALEXANDER). — THIRTY

YEARS' CORRESPONDENCE between John Jebb, D.D. F.R.S. Bishop of Limerick, Ardfert, Aghadoe, and Alexander Knox, Esq. M.R.I.A. Edited by the Rev. CHARLES FORSTER, B.D. Rector of Stisted, formerly Domestic Chaplain to Bishop Jebb. 2d Edit. 2 vols. 8vo. 28s. cl.

JEFFREY. — CONTRIBUTIONS TO THE EDINBURGH

REVIEW. By FRANCIS JEFFREY, now One of the Judges of the Court of Session in Scotland. New Edition. 3 vols. 8vo. 42s. cloth.

JOHNSON.—THE FARMER'S ENCYCLOPÆDIA,

And Dictionary of Rural Affairs: embracing all the recent Discoveries in Agricultural Chemistry; adapted to the comprehension of unscientific readers. By CUTHBERT W. JOHNSON, Esq. F.R.S. Barrister-at-Law; Editor of the "Farmer's Almanack," &c. 8vo. illustrated by Wood Engravings, £2. 10s. cloth.

KATER AND LARDNER.—A TREATISE ON MECHANICS.

By Captain KATER and Dr. LARDNER. New Edition. Fcp. 8vo. with Vignette Title, and 19 Plates, comprising 224 distinct figures, 6s. cloth.

KEIGHTLEY.—OUTLINES OF HISTORY.

From the Earliest Period. By THOMAS KEIGHTLEY, Esq. New Edition, corrected and considerably improved. Fcp. 8vo. 6s. cloth; or 6s. 6d. bound.

KING (COL. J. A.) — TWENTY-FOUR YEARS IN THE

ARGENTINE REPUBLIC; embracing the Author's Personal Adventures, with the Civil and Military History of the Country, and an Account of its Political Condition before and during the Administration of Governor Rosas, his course of Policy, the Causes and Character of his Interference with the Government of Monte Video, and the circumstances which led to the Interposition of England and France. By Col. J. ANTHONY KING, an Officer in the Army of the Republic. 8vo. 14s. cloth.

KIP.—THE CHRISTMAS HOLYDAYS IN ROME.

By the Rev. W. INGRAHAM KIP, M.A. Edited by the Rev. W. SEWELL, B.D. Fellow and Tutor of Exeter College, Oxford. Fcp. 8vo. 5s. cloth.

KIRBY & SPENCE.—AN INTRODUCTION TO ENTOMOLOGY;

Or, Elements of the Natural History of Insects: comprising an account of noxious and useful Insects, of their Metamorphoses, Food, Stratagems, Habitations, Societies, Motions, Noises, Hybernation, Instinct, &c. By W. KIRBY, M.A. F.R.S. & L.S. Rector of Barham; and W. SPENCE, Esq. F.R.S. & L.S. 6th Edit. corrected and much enlarged. 2 vols. 8vo. 31s. 6d. cloth.

KNOX (ALEXANDER).—REMAINS OF ALEXANDER KNOX,

Esq. of Dublin, M.R.I.A , containing Essays, chiefly explanatory of Christian Doctrine, and Confidential Letters, with Private Papers, illustrative of the Writer's Character, Sentiments, and Life. 3d Edition, 4 vols. 8vo. £2. 8s. cloth.

LAING.—NOTES ON THE SCHISM FROM THE CHURCH OF

ROME, called the GERMAN-CATHOLIC CHURCH, instituted by J. Ronge and I. Czerski, in October 1844, on occasion of the Pilgrimage to the Holy Coat at Treves. By S. LAING, Esq. Author of "Notes of a Traveller," &c. 2d Edition. Fcp. 8vo. 5s. cloth.

LAING.—THE CHRONICLE OF THE KINGS OF NORWAY,

From the Earliest Period of the History of the Northern Sea Kings to the Middle of the Twelfth Century, commonly called *The Heimskringla*. Translated from the Icelandic of Snorro Sturleson, with Notes, and a Preliminary Discourse, by SAMUEL LAING, Author of "Notes of a Traveller," &c. 3 vols. 8vo. 36s. cloth.

LAING.—A TOUR IN SWEDEN,

In 1838; comprising observations on the Moral, Political, and Economical State of the Swedish Nation. By SAMUEL LAING, Esq. 8vo. 12s. cloth.

LANE (R. J.)—LIFE AT THE WATER-CURE;

Or, a Month at Malvern. A Diary of Facts and Fancies. To which is added, The Sequel. By RICHARD J. LANE, A.R.A. Lithographer to Her Majesty and H.R.H. Prince Albert. Post 8vo. with numerous Illustrations, 14s. cloth.

LANETON PARSONAGE:
A Tale for Children, on the Practical Use of a portion of the Church Catechism. By the Author of "Amy Herbert," and "Gertrude." Edited by the Rev. W. SEWELL, B.D. Fellow of Exeter College, Oxford. New Edition. Fcp. 8vo. 5s. cloth.

LAPLACE (THE MARQUIS DE).—THE SYSTEM OF THE
WORLD. By M. LE MARQUIS DE LAPLACE. Translated from the French, and elucidated with Explanatory Notes. By the Rev. HENRY H. HARTE, F.T.C.D. M.R.I.A. 2 vols. 8vo. 24s. boards.

LARDNER'S CABINET CYCLOPÆDIA;
Comprising a Series of Original Works on History, Biography, Literature, the Sciences, Arts, and Manufactures. Conducted and edited by Dr. LARDNER.
The Series, complete, in One Hundred and Thirty-three Volumes, £39. 18s. The works, separately, 6s. per volume.

LARDNER AND WALKER.—A TREATISE ON ELECTRICITY,
MAGNETISM, and METEOROLOGY. By D. LARDNER, LLD. F.R.S., and C. V. WALKER, Secretary of the Electrical Society. 2 vols. fcp. 8vo. with Vignette Titles, 12s. cloth.

LARDNER.—A TREATISE ON HEAT.
By D. LARDNER, LL.D., &c. Fcp. 8vo. with Woodcuts and Vignette Title, 6s. cloth.

LARDNER.—A TREATISE ON HYDROSTATICS AND PNEU-
MATICS. By Dr. LARDNER. New Edition. Fcp. 8vo. with Vignette Title, 6s. cloth.

LARDNER.—A TREATISE ON ARITHMETIC.
By D. LARDNER, LL.D. F.R.S. Fcp. 8vo. with Vignette Title, 6s. cloth.

LARDNER.—A TREATISE ON GEOMETRY,
And its Application to the Arts. By Dr. LARDNER. Fcp. 8vo. Vignette Title, and upwards of 200 figures, 6s. cloth.

L. E. L.—THE POETICAL WORKS OF LETITIA ELIZABETH
LANDON. New Edition, 4 vols. fcp. 8vo. with Illustrations by Howard, &c. 28s. cloth lettered; or handsomely bound in morocco, with gilt edges, £2. 4s.
The following Works separately:—
The IMPROVISATRICE. Fcp. 10s. 6d. cloth. | The GOLDEN VIOLET. Fcp. 8vo. 10s. 6d. cloth.
The VENETIAN BRACELET. 10s. 6d. cloth. | The TROUBADOUR. Fcp. 8vo. 10s. 6d. cloth.

LEE.—TAXIDERMY;
Or, the Art of Collecting, Preparing, and Mounting Objects of Natural History. For the use of Museums and Travellers. By Mrs. R. LEE (formerly Mrs. T. E. Bowdich), Author of "Memoirs of Cuvier," &c. 6th Edition, improved, with an account of a Visit to Walton Hall, and Mr. Waterton's Method of Preserving Animals. Fcp. 8vo. with Woodcuts, 7s. cloth.

LEE.—ELEMENTS OF NATURAL HISTORY,
For the use of Schools and Young Persons: comprising the Principles of Classification, interspersed with amusing and instructive original Accounts of the most remarkable Animals. By Mrs. R. LEE (formerly Mrs. T. E. BOWDICH), Author of "Taxidermy," "Memoirs of Cuvier," &c. 12mo. with Fifty-five Woodcuts, 7s. 6d. bound.

LEMPRIERE.—A CLASSICAL DICTIONARY;
Containing a copious Account of all the proper Names mentioned in Ancient Authors; with the Value of Coins, Weights, and Measures, used amongst the Greeks and Romans; and a Chronological Table. By T. LEMPRIERE, D.D. 20th Edition, corrected. 8vo. 9s. cloth.

LEREBOURS (N. P.)—A TREATISE ON PHOTOGRAPHY;
Containing the latest Discoveries appertaining to the Daguerréotype. Compiled from Communications by MM. Daguerre and Arago, and other eminent Men of Science. By N. P. LEREBOURS, Optician to the Observatory, Paris, &c. Translated by J. EGERTON. Post 8vo. with Plate, 7s. 6d. cloth.

LESLIE (C. R.)—MEMOIRS OF THE LIFE OF JOHN CON-
STABLE, Esq. R.A. Composed chiefly of his Letters. By C. R. LESLIE, R.A. Second Edition., with further Extracts from his Correspondence. Small 4to. with two Portraits (one from a new Sketch by Mr. Leslie), and a Plate of " Spring," engraved by Lucas. 21s. cloth.

LETTERS TO MY UNKNOWN FRIENDS.
By A LADY, Author of " Twelve Years Ago." Fcp. 8vo. 6s. 6d. cloth.
" The author is no commonplace retailer of cut and dried maxims, but a woman of strong understanding and cultivated taste, who has read much and thought more. She would have religion to be the beginning and the end of all human actions; but she is not puritanical in her pious zeal."—SPECTATOR.

LINDLEY.—INTRODUCTION TO BOTANY.

By Prof. J. LINDLEY, Ph.D. F.R.S. L.S. &c. 3d Edition with Corrections and considerable Additions. 8vo. with Six Plates and numerous Woodcuts, 18s. cloth.

LINDLEY.—FLORA MEDICA;

A Botanical Account of all the most important Plants used in Medicine, in different Parts of the World. By JOHN LINDLEY, Ph.D., F.R.S., &c. 8vo. 18s. cloth.

LINDLEY.—A SYNOPSIS OF THE BRITISH FLORA,

Arranged according to the Natural Orders. By Professor JOHN LINDLEY, Ph.D., F.R.S., &c. 3d Edition, with numerous additions, corrections, and improvements, 12mo. 10s. 6d. cloth.

LINDLEY.—THE THEORY OF HORTICULTURE;

Or, an Attempt to explain the Principal Operations of Gardening upon Physiological Principles. By JOHN LINDLEY, Ph.D., F.R.S. 8vo. with illustrations on Wood, 12s. cloth.

LINDLEY.—GUIDE TO ORCHARD AND KITCHEN GARDEN;

Or, an Account of the most valuable Fruits and Vegetables cultivated in Great Britain : with Kalendars of the Work required in the Orchard and Kitchen Garden during every month in the year. By G. LINDLEY, C.M.H.S. Edited by Prof. LINDLEY. 8vo. 16s. bds.

LINWOOD (W.)—ANTHOLOGIA OXONIENSIS,

Sive Florilegium e lusibus poeticis diversorum Oxoniensium Græcis et Latinis decerptum. Curante GULIELMO LINWOOD, M.A. Ædis Christi Alummo. 8vo. 14s. cloth.

LOUDON (MRS.)—THE AMATEUR GARDENER'S CALENDAR;

Being a Monthly Guide as to what should be avoided, as well as what should be done in a Garden in each Month, with plain Rules *how to do* what is requisite. By Mrs. LOUDON, Author of " The Lady's Country Companion," " Gardening for Ladies," &c. Fcp. 8vo. with numerous Illustrations.   [*In a few days.*

LOUDON (MRS.)—THE LADY'S COUNTRY COMPANION;

Or, How to Enjoy a Country Life Rationally. By Mrs. LOUDON, Author of " Gardening for Ladies," &c. New Edition. Fcp. 8vo. with a Steel Plate and Wood Engravings, 7s. 6d. cloth.

LOUDON.—SELF-INSTRUCTION

For Young Gardeners, Foresters, Bailiffs, Land Stewards, and Farmers; in Arithmetic, Book-keeping, Geometry, Mensuration, Practical Trigonometry, Mechanics, Land-Surveying, Levelling, Planning and Mapping, Architectural Drawing, and Isometrical Projection and Perspective; with Examples shewing their applications to Horticulture and Agricultural Purposes. By the late J. C. LOUDON, F.L.S. H.S. &c. With a Portrait of Mr. Loudon, and a Memoir by Mrs. Loudon. 8vo. with Wood Engravings, 7s. 6d. cloth.

LOUDON.—AN ENCYCLOPÆDIA OF GARDENING;

Presenting, in one systematic view, the History and Present State of Gardening in all Countries, and its Theory and Practice in Great Britain: with the Management of the Kitchen Garden, the Flower Garden, Laying-out Grounds, &c. By J. C. LOUDON, F.L.S. &c. A New Edition, enlarged and improved. 8vo. with nearly 1,000 Engravings on Wood, 50s. cloth.

LOUDON.—AN ENCYCLOPÆDIA OF TREES AND SHRUBS;

being the " Arboretum et Fruticetum Britannicum" abridged : containing the Hardy Trees and Shrubs of Great Britain, Native and Foreign, Scientifically and Popularly Described; with their Propagation, Culture, and Uses in the Arts; and with Engravings of nearly all the Species. Adapted for the use of Nurserymen, Gardeners, and Foresters. By J. C. LOUDON, F.L.S. &c. 8vo. with 2,000 Engravings on Wood, £2. 10s. cloth.

The Original Work may be had in 8 vols. 8vo. with above 400 Octavo Plates of Trees, and upwards of 2,500 Woodcuts, £10, cloth.

LOUDON.—AN ENCYCLOPÆDIA OF AGRICULTURE;

Comprising the Theory and Practice of the Valuation, Transfer, Laying-out, Improvement, and Management of Landed Property, and of the Cultivation and Economy of the Animal and Vegetable productions of Agriculture: including all the latest Improvements, a general History of Agriculture in all Countries, a Statistical View of its present State, with Suggestions for its future progress in the British Isles; and Supplement, bringing down the work to the year 1844. By J. C. LOUDON, F.L.G.Z. and H.S. &c. 5th Edition. 8vo. with upwards of 1,100 Engravings on Wood, by Branston, £2. 10s. cloth.

The SUPPLEMENT may be had *separately*, 5s. sewed.

LOUDON.—AN ENCYCLOPÆDIA OF PLANTS;

Including all the Plants which are now found in, or have been introduced into, Great Britain ; giving their Natural History, accompanied by such descriptions, engraved figures, and elementary details, as may enable a beginner, who is a mere English reader, to discover the name of every Plant which he may find in flower, and acquire all the information respecting it which is useful and interesting. By J. C. LOUDON, F.L.S. &c. The Specific Characters by an Eminent Botanist; the Drawings by J. D. C. Sowerby, F L.S. A New Edition with Supplement, and a new General Index. 8vo. with nearly 10,000 Wood Engravings, £3. 13s. 6d. cloth.—The Supplement, *separately*, 8vo. 15s. cloth.

LOUDON.—AN ENCYCLOPÆDIA OF COTTAGE, FARM, AND

VILLA ARCHITECTURE and FURNITURE; containing numerous Designs, from the Villa to the Cottage and the Farm, including Farm Houses, Farmeries, and other Agricultural Buildings; Country Inns, Public Houses, and Parochial Schools; with the requisite Fittings-up, Fixtures, and Furniture, and appropriate Offices, Gardens, and Garden Scenery: each Design accompanied by Analytical and Critical Remarks. By J. C. LOUDON, F.L.S. &c. New Edition, edited by Mrs. LOUDON. 8vo. with more than 2,000 Engravings on Wood, £3. 3s. cloth.—The Supplement, *separately*, 8vo. 7s. 6d. sewed.

LOUDON.—HORTUS BRITANNICUS:

A Catalogue of all the Plants indigenous to or introduced into Britain. The 3d Edition, with a NEW SUPPLEMENT, prepared, under the direct on of J. C. LOUDON, by W. H. BAXTER, and revised by GEORGE DON, F.L.S. 8vo. 31s. 6d. cloth.

The SUPPLEMENT *separately*, 8vo. 2s. 6d. sewed.
The LATER SUPPLEMENT *separately*, 8s.

LOUDON.—HORTUS LIGNOSIS LONDINENSIS;

Or, a Catalogue of all the Ligneous Plants cultivated in the neighbourhood of London. To which are added, their usual prices in Nurseries. By J. C. LOUDON, F.L.S. &c. 8vo. 7s. 6d. cl.

LOUDON. — THE SUBURBAN GARDENER AND VILLA

COMPANION; comprising the Choice of a Villa or Suburban Residence, or of a situation on which to form one; the Arrangement and Furnishing of the House; and the Laying-out, Planting, and general Management of the Garden and Grounds; the whole adapted for grounds from one perch to fifty acres and upwards in extent; intended for the instruction of those who know little of Gardening or Rural Affairs, and more particularly for the use of Ladies. By J. C. LOUDON, F.L.S. &c. 8vo. with above 300 Wood Engravings, 20s. cloth.

LOW.—ON THE DOMESTICATED ANIMALS OF GREAT

BRITAIN; comprehending the Natural and Economical History of the Species and Breeds; Illustrations of the Properties of External Form; and Observations on the Principles and Practice of Breeding. By DAVID LOW, Esq. F.R.S.E. Professor of Agriculture in the University of Edinburgh, &c.; Author of "Elements of Practical Agriculture," &c. 8vo. with Engravings on Wood, 25s. cloth.

LOW.—THE BREEDS OF THE DOMESTICATED ANIMALS

Of Great Britain Described. By DAVID LOW, Esq. F.R.S.E. Professor of Agriculture in the University of Edinburgh, &c. The Plates from Drawings by W. Nicholson, R.S.A. reduced from a Series of Oil Paintings, executed for the Agricultural Museum of the University of Edinburgh, by W. Shiels, R.S.A. 2 vols. atlas quarto, with 56 plates of animals, beautifully col'd after Nature, £16. 16s. half-bound in morocco.—Or in four separate portions, as follows:

The OX.   1 vol. atlas quarto, with 22 plates, £6. 16s. 6d. half-bound in morocco.
The SHEEP. 1 vol. atlas quarto, with 21 plates, £6. 16s. 6d. half-bound in morocco.
The HORSE. 1 vol. atlas quarto, with 8 plates, £3, half-bound in morocco.
The HOG.   1 vol. atlas quarto, with 5 plates, £2. 2s. half-bound in morocco.

LOW.—ELEMENTS OF PRACTICAL AGRICULTURE;

Comprehending the Cultivation of Plants, the Husbandry of the Domestic Animals, and the Economy of the Farm. By D. Low, Esq. F.R.S.E., Prof of Agriculture in University of Edinburgh. 4th Edit. with Alterations and Additions, and above 200 Woodcuts. 8vo. 21s. cloth.

LOW (PROFESSOR).—ON LANDED PROPERTY

And the ECONOMY of ESTATES; comprehending the Relation of Landlord and Tenant, and the Principles and Forms of Leases; Farm-Buildings, Enclosures, Drains, Embankments, and other Rural Works; Minerals; and Woods. By DAVID Low, Esq. F.R.S.E. Professor of Agriculture in the University of Edinburgh, &c.; Author of "Elements of Practical Agriculture," &c. 8vo. with numerous Wood Engravings, 21s. cloth.

MACAULAY.—CRITICAL AND HISTORICAL ESSAYS CON-

TRIBUTED to The EDINBURGH REVIEW. By the Right Hon. THOMAS BABINGTON MACAULAY. 4th Edition. 3 vols. 8vo. 36s. cloth.

MACAULAY.—LAYS OF ANCIENT ROME.

By the Right Hon. THOMAS BABINGTON MACAULAY. 8th Edition. Crown 8vo. 10s. 6d. cloth.

MACAULAY.—MR. MACAULAY'S LAYS OF ANCIENT ROME.

A New Edition. With numerous Illustrations, Original and from the Antique, drawn on Wood by George Scharf, Jun. and engraved by Samuel Williams. Fcp. 4to. 21s. boards; morocco, 42s. *(bound by Hayday.)*

MACKAY (CHARLES)—THE SCENERY AND POETRY OF

THE ENGLISH LAKES; a Summer Ramble. By CHARLES MACKAY, Esq. LL.D. Author of "Legends of the Isles," "The Salamandrine," "The Thames and its Tributaries," &c. 8vo. with beautiful Wood Engravings from Original Sketches, 14s. cloth.

MACKINNON. — THE HISTORY OF CIVILISATION.
By Wm. Alexander Mackinnon, F.R.S., M.P. for Lymington. 2 vols. 8vo. 24s. cloth.

MACKINTOSH (SIR JAMES).—SIR JAMES MACKINTOSH'S
MISCELLANEOUS WORKS; including his Contributions to The Edinburgh Review. Edited by Robert James Mackintosh, Esq. 3 vols. 8vo. 42s. cloth.

MACKINTOSH, &c.—THE HISTORY OF ENGLAND.
By Sir James Mackintosh; W. Wallace, Esq.; and Robert Bell, Esq. 10 vols. fcp. 8vo. with Vignette Titles, £3. cloth.

MACKINTOSH (SIR JAMES).—THE LIFE OF SIR THOMAS
MORE. By the Right Hon. Sir James Mackintosh. Reprinted from the Cabinet Cyclopædia; and intended as a Present Book or School Prize. Fcp. 8vo. with Portrait, 5s. cloth; or bound in vellum gilt (old style), 8s.

M'LEOD. — THE GEOGRAPHY OF PALESTINE OR THE
HOLY LAND, including Phœnicia and Philistia. By W. M'Leod, Head Master of the Model School, Royal Military Asylum, Chelsea; late Master of the Model School, Battersea. 12mo. [In the press.

M'CULLOCH (J. R.)—AN ACCOUNT, DESCRIPTIVE AND
STATISTICAL, of the BRITISH EMPIRE; exhibiting its Extent, Physical Capacities, Population, Industry, and Civil and Religious Institutions. By J. R. M'Culloch, Esq. 3d Edit. corrected, enlarged, and greatly improved. 2 thick vols. 8vo. £2. 2s. cloth.

M'CULLOCH.—A DICTIONARY, PRACTICAL, THEORETI-
CAL, AND HISTORICAL, OF COMMERCE AND COMMERCIAL NAVIGATION. Illustrated with Maps and Plans. By J. R. M'Culloch, Esq. An entirely New Edition, corrected to March 1847; with a Supplement. 8vo. 50s. cloth; or 55s. half-bound russia.

The Supplement to the Editions published in 1844 and 1846, may be had separately, price 4s. 6d. sewed.

M'CULLOCH.—A DICTIONARY, GEOGRAPHICAL, STATIS-
TICAL, AND HISTORICAL, of the various Countries, Places, and Principal Natural Objects in the WORLD. By J. R. M'Culloch, Esq. A New Edition. 2 vols. 8vo. with Six large Maps, £4. cloth.

₊ The new Articles have been printed separately, as a Supplement to the former Edition. They comprise a full Account of the Present State of the United Kingdom, the Oregon Territory, &c. 8vo. 5s. sewed.

M'CULLOCH. — THE LITERATURE OF POLITICAL ECO-
NOMY; being a Classified Catalogue of the principal Works in the different departments of Political Economy, with Historical, Critical, and Biographical Notices. By J. R. M'Culloch, Esq. 8vo. 14s. cloth.

M'CULLOCH. — A TREATISE ON THE PRINCIPLES AND
PRACTICAL INFLUENCE of TAXATION and the FUNDING SYSTEM. By J. R. M'Culloch, Esq. 8vo. 15s. cloth.

MAITLAND (DR. CHARLES). — THE CHURCH IN THE
CATACOMBS: a Description of the Primitive Church of Rome. Illustrated by its Sepulchral Remains. By Charles Maitland, M.D. 8vo. with numerous Wood Engravings, 14s. cloth.

MARCET.—CONVERSATIONS ON CHEMISTRY;
In which the Elements of that Science are familiarly Explained and Illustrated by Experiments. By Mrs. Marcet. New Edition, enlarged and improved. 2 vols. fcp. 8vo. 14s. cloth.

MARCET.—CONVERSATIONS ON NATURAL PHILOSOPHY;
In which the Elements of that Science are familiarly explained. By Mrs. Marcet. New Edition, enlarged and corrected. Fcp. 8vo. with 23 Plates, 10s. 6d. cloth.

MARCET.—CONVERSATIONS ON POLITICAL ECONOMY;
In which the Elements of that Science are familiarly explained. By Mrs. Marcet. New Edition revised and enlarged. Fcp. 8vo. 7s. 6d. cloth.

MARCET. — CONVERSATIONS ON VEGETABLE PHYSIO-
LOGY; comprehending the Elements of Botany, with their application to Agriculture. By Mrs. Marcet. New Edition. Fcp. 8vo. with 4 Plates, 9s. cloth.

MARCET.—CONVERSATIONS ON LAND AND WATER.
By Mrs. MARCET. New Edition, revised and corrected. Fcp. 8vo. with coloured Map, shewing the comparative altitude of Mountains, 5s. 6d. cloth.

MARCET.—CONVERSATIONS ON LANGUAGE,
For the use of Children. By Mrs. MARCET. 18mo. 4s. 6d. cloth.

MARCET.—CONVERSATIONS ON THE HISTORY OF ENG-
LAND, for the use of Children. By Mrs. MARCET. 2d Edition, with Additions. 18mo. 5s. cl.

MARGARET PERCIVAL.
By the Author of "Amy Herbert," "Gertrude," and "Laneton Parsonage." Edited by the Rev. W. SEWELL, B.D. Fellow and Tutor of Exeter College, Oxford. New Edition. 2 vols. fcp. 8vo. 12s. cloth.

MARRYAT.—MASTERMAN READY;
Or, the Wreck of the Pacific. Written for Young People. By Captain F. MARRYAT, C.B. Author of "Peter Simple," &c. 3 vols. fcp. 8vo. with Wood Engravings, 22s. 6d. cloth.

MARRYAT.—THE PRIVATEER'S-MAN ONE HUNDRED
YEARS AGO. By Captain F. MARRYAT, C.B. Author of "Masterman Ready," &c. 2 vols. fcp. 8vo. 12s. cloth.

MARRYAT.—THE SETTLERS IN CANADA.
Written for Young People. By Captain F. MARRYAT, C.B. Author of "The Privateers-man One Hundred Years Ago," &c. New Edition. Fcp. 8vo. with 2 Illustrations, 7s. 6d. cloth.

MARRYAT (CAPT.)—THE MISSION;
Or, Scenes in Africa. Written for Young People. By Captain F. MARRYAT, C.B. Author of "The Settlers in Canada," &c. 2 vols. fcp. 8vo. 12s. cloth.

MAUNDER.—THE SCIENTIFIC & LITERARY TREASURY;
A new and popular Encyclopædia of Science and the Belles-Lettres; including all Branches of Science, and every Subject connected with Literature and Art. The whole written in a familiar style, adapted to the comprehension of all persons desirous of acquiring information on the subjects comprised in the work, and also adapted for a Manual of convenient Reference to the more instructed. By SAMUEL MAUNDER. New Edition. Fcp. 8vo. 10s. cloth; bound in roan, 12s.

MAUNDER.—THE TREASURY OF HISTORY;
Comprising a General Introductory Outline of Universal History, Ancient and Modern, and a Series of separate Histories of every principal Nation that exists; their Rise, Progress, and Present Condition, the Moral and Social Character of their respective inhabitants, their Religion, Manners, and Customs, &c. By SAMUEL MAUNDER. New Edition. Fcp. 8vo. 10s. cloth; bound in roan, 12s.

MAUNDER.—THE BIOGRAPHICAL TREASURY;
Consisting of Memoirs, Sketches, and brief Notices of above 12,000 Eminent Persons of all Age. and Nations, from the Earliest Period of History; forming a new and complete Dictionary of Universal Biography. By SAMUEL MAUNDER. New Edition, revised throughout, and containing a copious Supplement, brought down to December, 1844. Fcp. 8vo. 10s. cloth; bound in roan, 12s.

MAUNDER.—THE TREASURY OF KNOWLEDGE,
And LIBRARY of REFERENCE: in Two Parts. New Edition, thoroughly revised and enlarged. Fcp. 8vo. 10s. cloth; bound in roan, 12s.

*** The principal contents of the present new and thoroughly revised edition of "The Treasury of Knowledge are—a new and enlarged English Dictionary, with a Grammar, Verbal Distinctions, and Exercises; a new Universal Gazetteer; a compendious Classical Dictionary; an Analysis of History and Chronology; a Dictionary of Law Terms; a new Synopsis of the British Peerage; and various useful Tabular Addenda.

MAURY.—THE STATESMEN OF AMERICA IN 1846;
With a Sketch of the President and People of the United States, and Notes on the Mexican War. By SARAH MYTTON MAURY. 8vo. 7s. 6d. cloth.

MEMOIRS OF THE GEOLOGICAL SURVEY OF GREAT
BRITAIN, and of the Museum of Economic Geology in London. Published by order of the Lords Commissioners of Her Majesty's Treasury. Royal 8vo. with Woodcuts and 9 large Plates (seven coloured), 21s. cloth.

MICHELET (J.)—PRIESTS, WOMEN, AND FAMILIES.

By J. MICHELET. Translated from the French (Third Edition, which contains Michelet's Preface, in reply to the attacks of the Jesuits), with the Author's approbation, by C. COCKS, B.L. New Editions. Post 8vo. 9s. cloth ; 16mo. 1s. 4d. sewed.

MICHELET (J.)—THE PEOPLE.

By M. MICHELET, Member of the Institute of France, &c. Translated, with the approbation of the Author, by C. COCKS, B.L. New Edition. Post 8vo. 9s. cloth ; 16mo. 1s. 6d. sewed.

*** Mr. Cocks's authorised translations of Michelet's " Priests, Women, and Families," and " The People," in one vol. 16mo. 3s. 6d. cloth.

MICHELET AND QUINET.—THE JESUITS, BY MM.

MICHELET and QUINET. Translated from the Seventh Edition, with the approbation of the Authors, by C. COCKS, B.L., Author of " Bordeaux, its Wines, and the Claret Country." New Edition. 16mo. 1s. 6d. sewed.

*** Mr. Cocks's Authorised Translations of MM. Michelet and Quinet's " The Jesuits," and M. Quinet's " Christianity," in one vol. 16mo. 4s. cloth.

MILES (WILLIAM).—THE HORSE'S FOOT, AND HOW TO

KEEP IT SOUND. By WILLIAM MILES, Esq. New Edit. Royal 8vo. with Engravings, 7s. cl.

MILNER (REVS. J. & I.)—THE HISTORY OF THE CHURCH

of CHRIST. By the Rev. JOSEPH MILNER, A.M. With Additions and Corrections by the late Rev. ISAAC MILNER, D.D. F.R.S. A New Edition, revised and corrected throughout, by the Rev. T. GRANTHAM, B.D. Rector of Bramber, and Chaplain to the Lord Bishop of Kildare. 4 vols. 8vo. £2. 12s. cloth.

A Continuation of the above.

THE HISTORY of the CHURCH of CHRIST, from the Diet of Augsburg, 1530, to the Eighteenth Century; originally designed as a Continuation of Milner's " History of the Church of Christ." By the Rev. HENRY STEBBING, D.D. 3 vols. 8vo. 36s. cloth.

MOHAN LAL.—LIFE OF THE AMIR DOST MOHAMMED

KHAN, of CABUL : with his Political Proceedings towards the English, Russian, and Persian Governments, including the Victory and Disasters of the British Army in Afghanistan. By MOHAL LAL, Esq. Knight of the Persian Order of the Lion and Sun ; lately attached to the Mission in Kabul. 2 vols. 8vo. with numerous Portraits, 30s. cloth.

MONTAUBAN.—A YEAR AND A DAY IN THE EAST ;

Or, Wanderings over Land and Sea. By Mrs. ELIOT MONTAUBAN. Post 8vo. 7s. cloth.

MONTGOMERY'S (JAMES) POETICAL WORKS.

New and only Complete Edition. With some additional Poems, and Autobiographical Prefaces. Collected and Edited by Mr. MONTGOMERY. 4 vols. fcp. 8vo. with Portrait, and Seven other Plates, 20s. cloth ; or bound in morocco, 36s.

MOORE'S POETICAL WORKS ;

Containing the Author's recent Introduction and Notes. Complete in one volume, uniform with Lord Byron's and Southey's Poems. 8vo. with a New Portrait, by George Richmond, and a View of the Residence of the Poet, 21s. cloth ; or 42s. bound in morocco, by Hayday.

*** Also, an Edition in 10 vols. fcp. 8vo. with Portrait, and 19 Plates, £2. 10s. cloth ; bound in morocco, £4. 10s.

MOORE'S LALLA ROOKH : AN ORIENTAL ROMANCE.

New Edition. 8vo. illustrated with 13 Engravings finished in the highest style of the Art, 21s. cloth ; morocco, 35s ; or, with India Proof Plates, 42s. cloth.

MOORE'S LALLA ROOKH : AN ORIENTAL ROMANCE.

New Edition. Fcp. 8vo. with Four Engravings, from Paintings by Westall, 10s. 6d. cloth ; or, bound in morocco, 14s.

MOORE'S IRISH MELODIES.

Illustrated by D. MACLISE, R.A. Imp. 8vo. with 161 Designs engraved on Steel, £3. 3s. bds. ; or £4. 14s. 6d. bound in morocco, by Hayday. Proof Impressions (only 200 copies printed, of which a few remain), £6. 6s boards.

*** India Proofs before Letters of the 161 Designs, on Quarter Colombier, in Portfolio (only 25 copies printed, of which a few remain), £31. 10s.

India Proofs before Letters of the 51 Large Designs, on Quarter Colombier, in Portfolio (only 25 copies printed, of which a few remain), £18. 18s.

MOORE'S IRISH MELODIES.

New Edition. Fcp. 8vo. with Engraved Title and Vignette, 10s. cloth ; or, bound in morocco, 13s. 6d.

MOORE.—THE HISTORY OF IRELAND,

From the Earliest Kings of that Realm down to its Last Chief. By THOMAS MOORE, Esq. 4 vols. fcp. 8vo., with Vignette Titles, 24s. cloth.

MOORE.—THE POWER OF THE SOUL OVER THE BODY,

Considered in relation to Health and Morals. By GEORGE MOORE, M.D. Member of the Royal College of Physicians, London. &c. New Edition. Post 8vo. 7s. 6d. cloth.

MOORE.—THE USE OF THE BODY IN RELATION TO THE

MIND. By GEORGE MOORE, M.D. Member of the Royal College of Physicians, London, &c. Post 8vo. 9s. cloth.

MORAL OF FLOWERS (THE).

3d Edition. Royal 8vo. with 24 beautifully-coloured Engravings, £1. 10s. half-bound.

MOSELEY.–THE MECHANICAL PRINCIPLES OF ENGI-

NEERING AND ARCHITECTURE. By the Rev. H. MOSELEY, M.A. F.R.S., Professor of Natural Philosophy and Astronomy in King's College, London ; and Author of "Illustrations of Mechanics," &c. 8vo. with Woodcuts and Diagrams, 24s. cloth.

MOSELEY.—ILLUSTRATIONS OF PRACTICAL MECHANICS.

By the Rev. H. MOSELEY, M.A., Professor of Natural Philosophy and Astronomy in King's College, London; being the First Volume of the Illustrations of Science by the Professors of King's College. New Edition. Fcp. 8vo. with numerous Woodcuts, 8s. cloth.

MOSHEIM'S ECCLESIASTICAL HISTORY,

Ancient and Modern. Translated, with copious Notes, by JAMES MURDOCK, D.D. Edited, with Additions, by HENRY SOAMES, M.A. Rector of Stapleford-Tawney, Essex. New Edition, revised, and continued to the present time. 4 vols. 8vo. 48s. cloth.

MURRAY.—ENCYCLOPÆDIA OF GEOGRAPHY ;

Comprising a complete Description of the Earth: exhibiting its Relation to the Heavenly Bodies, its Physical Structure, the Natural History of each Country, and the Industry, Commerce, Political Institutions, and Civil and Social State of all Nations. By HUGH MURRAY, F.R.S.E.: assisted by other Writers of eminence. New Edition. 8vo. with 82 Maps, and upwards of 1000 other Woodcuts, £3, cloth.

MY YOUTHFUL COMPANIONS.

By the Author of "My School-boy Days." 18mo. with Frontispiece, 2s. 6d. cloth.

NECKER DE SAUSSURE.—PROGRESSIVE EDUCATION ;

Or, Considerations on the Course of Life. Translated and abridged from the French of Madame NECKER DE SAUSSURE, by Miss HOLLAND. 3 vols. fcp. 8vo. 19s. 6d. cloth.

₊ Separately, Vols. I. and II. 12s. ; Vol. III. 7s. 6d.

NESBIT (A.)—A TREATISE ON PRACTICAL MENSURATION;

Containing the most approved Methods of drawing Geometrical Figures ; Mensuration of Superficies ; Land-Surveying; Mensuration of Solids ; the use of the Carpenter's Rule; Timber Measure, &c. By A. NESBIT. 12th Edition. 12mo. with nearly 300 Woodcuts, 6s. bd.

KEY. 7th Edition. 12mo. 5s. bound.

NEWELL (REV. R. H.)—THE ZOOLOGY OF THE ENGLISH

POETS, corrected by the Writings of Modern Naturalists. By the Rev. R. H. NEWELL, Rector of Little Hormead. Fcp. 8vo. with Engravings on Wood, 5s. 6d. cloth.

NICOLAS.–THE CHRONOLOGY OF HISTORY.

Containing Tables, Calculations, and Statements indispensable for ascertaining the Dates of Historical Events, and of Public and Private Documents, from the Earliest Period to the Present Time. By Sir HARRIS NICOLAS, K.C.M.G. Second Edition. Fcp. 8vo. 6s. cloth.

ORDNANCE MAPS (THE), AND PUBLICATIONS OF THE

GEOLOGICAL SURVEY OF THE UNITED KINGDOM.—Messrs. LONGMAN and Co. have been appointed by the Board of Ordnance Agents for the sale of the Maps of the Ordnance Survey of Great Britain. Also, sole Agents for the sale of the Maps, Sections, and Books of the Geological Survey of the United Kingdom, and of the Museum of Economic Geology, under the Chief Commissioner of Her Majesty's Woods, Works, and Land Revenues.

₊ Complete detailed Catalogues of both Series may be had on application.

OWEN. — LECTURES ON THE COMPARATIVE ANATOMY
and PHYSIOLOGY of the INVERTEBRATE ANIMALS, delivered at the Royal College of Surgeons in 1843. By RICHARD OWEN, F.R.S. Hunterian Professor to the College. From Notes taken by William White Cooper, M.R.C.S. and revised by Professor Owen. With Glossary and Index. 8vo. with nearly 140 Illustrations on Wood, 14s. cloth.

OWEN.—LECTURES ON THE COMPARATIVE ANATOMY
and PHYSIOLOGY of the VERTEBRATE ANIMALS, delivered at the Royal College of Surgeons in 1844 and 1846. By RICHARD OWEN, F.R.S. Hunterian Professor to the College. In 2 vols. Vol. I. 8vo. with numerous Woodcuts, 14s. cloth.   [*Vol. II. is in the press.*

PARABLES OF OUR LORD (ILLUMINATED).
PARABLES of OUR LORD, richly illuminated, with appropriate Borders, printed in Colours and in Black and Gold; with a Design from one of the early German Engravers. Square fcp. 8vo. uniform in size with the " Sermon on the Mount," 21s. in a massive carved binding in the style of the beginning of the Sixteenth Century; or 30s. bound in morocco in the Missal style, by Hayday.

PARKES.—DOMESTIC DUTIES ;
Or, Instructions to Young Married Ladies on the Management of their Households, and the Regulation of their Conduct in the various Relations and Duties of Married Life. By Mrs. W. PARKES. 5th Edition. Fcp. 8vo. 9s. cloth.

PARNELL.—A TREATISE ON ROADS,
Wherein the Principles on which Roads should be made are explained and illustrated by the Plans, Specifications, and Contracts, made use of by Thomas Telford, Esq. on the Holyhead Road. By the Right Hon. SIR HENRY PARNELL, Bart. 2d Edition, greatly enlarged. 8vo. with 9 large Plates, 21s. cloth.

PATON (A. A.)—SERVIA, THE YOUNGEST MEMBER OF THE
EUROPEAN FAMILY ; or, a Residence in Belgrade, and Travels through the Highlands and Woodlands of the Interior, during the years 1843 and 1844. By ANDREW ARCHIBALD PATON, Esq. Post 8vo. with Portrait and Plate, 12s. cloth.

PATON (A. A.)—THE MODERN SYRIANS ;
Or, Native Society in Damascus, Aleppo, and the Mountains of the Druses.   Post 8vo. 10s. 6d. cloth.

PEARSON.—PRAYERS FOR FAMILIES :
Consisting of a short but comprehensive Form for the Morning and Evening of every Day in the Week. Collected by the late EDWARD PEARSON, D.D. With a Biographical Memoir of the Author. New Edition. 18mo. 2s. 6d. cloth.

PEARSON.—AN INTRODUCTION TO PRACTICAL ASTRO-
NOMY. By the Rev. W. PEARSON, LL.D. F.R.S., &c., Rector of South Killworth, Leicestershire, and Treasurer to the Astronomical Society of London. 2 vols. 4to. with Plates, £7. 7s. boards.

PEDESTRIAN AND OTHER REMINISCENCES, AT HOME
AND ABROAD. With Sketches of Country Life. By SYLVANUS. Post 8vo. with Frontis-piece and Vignette, 10s. 6d. cloth.

PEREIRA.—A TREATISE ON FOOD AND DIET :
With Observations on the Dietetical Regimen suited for Disordered States of the Digestive Organs ; and an Account of the Dietaries of some of the principal Metropolitan and other Establishments for Paupers, Lunatics, Criminals, Children, the Sick, &c. By JON. PEREIRA, M.D. F.R.S. & L.S. Author of " Elements of Materia Medica." 8vo. 16s. cloth.

PERICLES.
A Tale of Athens in the 83d Olympiad. By the Author of " A Brief Sketch of Greek Philosophy." 2 vols. post 8vo. 18s. cloth.

PERRY (DR. W. C.)—GERMAN UNIVERSITY EDUCATION ;
Or, the Professors and Students of Germany. To which is added, a brief Account of the Public Schools of Prussia ; with Observations on the Influence of Philosophy on the Studies of the German Universities. By WALTER C. PERRY, Phil. D. of the University of Göttingen. 2d Edition. 12mo. 4s. 6d. cloth.

PESCHEL (C. F.)—ELEMENTS OF PHYSICS.
By C. F. Peschel, Principal of the Royal Military College, Dresden. Translated from the German, with Notes, by E. West. 3 vols. fcp. 8vo. with Diagrams and Woodcuts, 21s. cloth.

Separately { Part 1. The Physics of Ponderable Bodies. Fcp. 8vo. 7s. 6d. cloth.
Part 2. Imponderable Bodies (Light, Heat, Magnetism, Electricity, and Electro-Dynamics). 2 vols. fcp. 8vo 13s. 6d. cloth.

PHILLIPS.—FIGURES AND DESCRIPTIONS OF THE
PALÆOZOIC FOSSILS of CORNWALL, DEVON, and WEST SOMERSET; observed in the course of the Ordnance Geological Survey of that District. By John Phillips, F.R.S. F.G.S. &c. Published by Order of the Lords Commissioners of H.M. Treasury. 8vo. with 60 Plates, comprising very numerous figures, 9s. cloth.

PHILLIPS.—A GUIDE TO GEOLOGY.
By John Phillips, F.R.S.G.S., &c. Fcp. 8vo. with Plates, 6s. cloth.

PHILLIPS.—A TREATISE ON GEOLOGY.
By John Phillips, F.R.S.G.S., &c. 2 vols. fcp. 8vo. with Vignette Titles and Woodcuts, 12s. cloth.

PITMAN (REV. J. R.)—A COURSE OF SERMONS
On some of the chief Subjects in the Book of Psalms ; containing Three or more for each Day of the Month: abridged from Eminent Divines of the Established Church. By the Rev. J. R. Pitman, A.M. Domestic Chaplain to Her Royal Highness the Duchess of Kent. 8vo. 14s. cl.

PLUNKETT.—THE PAST AND FUTURE OF THE BRITISH
NAVY. By Captain the Hon. E. Plunkett, R.N. A New Edition, corrected and enlarged, with Notes, and new information communicated by several Officers of Distinction. Post 8vo.
[Nearly ready.

PLYMLEY (PETER).—LETTERS ON THE SUBJECT OF THE
CATHOLICS TO MY BROTHER ABRAHAM, WHO LIVES IN THE COUNTRY. By Peter Plymley. 21st Edition. Post 8vo. 7s. cloth.

POETS' PLEASAUNCE (THE) ;
Or, Garden of all Sorts of Pleasant Flowers, which our Pleasant Poets have in past time for Pastime planted: with the right ordering of them. By Eden Warwick. Square crown 8vo. with very numerous Illustrations on Wood, engraved in the best manner. [Just ready.

POISSON (S. D.)—A TREATISE ON MECHANICS.
By S. D. Poisson. 2d Edition. Translated from the French, and illustrated with Explanatory Notes, by the Rev. Henry H. Harte, late Fellow of Trinity College, Dublin. 2 vols. 8vo. £1. 8s. cloth.

POPE (ALEXANDER).—THE WORKS OF ALEXANDER POPE.
Edited by Thomas Roscoe, Esq. With the Author's Life. A New Edition. 8 vols. 8vo. £4. 4s. cloth.

PORTER.—A TREATISE ON THE MANUFACTURE OF SILK.
By G. R. Porter, Esq. F.R.S. Author of " The Progress of the Nation," &c. 1 vol. 8vo. with Vignette Title, and 39 Engravings on Wood, 6s. cloth.

PORTER.—A TREATISE ON THE MANUFACTURES OF
PORCELAIN AND GLASS. By G. R. Porter, Esq. F.R.S. Fcp. 8vo. with Vignette Title and 50 Woodcuts, 6s. cloth.

PORTLOCK.—REPORT ON THE GEOLOGY OF THE COUNTY
of LONDONDERRY, and of Parts of Tyrone and Fermanagh, examined and described under the Authority of the Master-General and Board of Ordnance. By J. E. Portlock, F.R.S. &c. 8vo. with 48 Plates, 24s. cloth.

POWELL.—THE HISTORY OF NATURAL PHILOSOPHY,
From the Earliest Periods to the Present Time. By Baden Powell, M.A., Savilian Professor of Mathematics in the University of Oxford. Fcp. 8vo. Vignette Title, 6s. cloth.

PYCROFT (REV. J.)—A COURSE OF ENGLISH READING,
adapted to every Taste and Capacity: with Anecdotes of Men of Letters. By the Rev. James Pycroft, B.A. Editor of " Virgil, with Marginal References"; Author of " Latin Grammar Practice," and " Greek Grammar Practice." Fcp. 8vo. 6s. 6d. cloth.

QUARTERLY JOURNAL OF THE GEOLOGICAL SOCIETY
of LONDON. Edited by David Thomas Ansted, M.A. F.R.S. Fellow of Jesus College, Cambridge; Professor of Geology in King's College, London ; Vice-Secretary of the Geological Society. 8vo. 4s. each number, sewed.

QUINET.—CHRISTIANITY IN ITS VARIOUS ASPECTS,
From the Birth of Christ to the French Revolution. By E. QUINET, of the College of France.
Translated, with the Author's approbation, by C. COCKS, B.L. 16mo. 2s. sewed.

RANKE'S HISTORY OF THE REFORMATION.
Translated by SARAH AUSTIN, Translator of Ranke's " History of the Popes." Vols. I. and II.
8vo. 30s., Vol. III. 18s., cloth.

READER (THOMAS).—TIME TABLES
On a New and Simplified Plan ; to facilitate the Operation of Discounting Bills, and the
Calculation of Interest on Banking and Current Accounts, &c. : shewing, WITHOUT CALCU-
LATION, the Number of Days from every Day in the Year to any other Day, for any period
not exceeding 365 Days. By THOMAS READER. Post 8vo. 14s. cloth ; or 17s. calf lettered.

REGISTRAR-GENERAL.—THE SEVENTH ANNUAL REPORT
of the REGISTRAR-GENERAL of BIRTHS, DEATHS, and MARRIAGES, in ENGLAND,
1845. 8vo. 5s. cloth.—Also,

First Report (1839), 8vo. 3s.	Third Report (1841), 8vo. 4s.	Fifth Report (1843), 8vo. 5s.
Second Report (1840), 8vo. 4s.	Fourth Report (1842), 8vo. 4s.	Sixth Report (1844), 8vo. 5s.

REECE.—THE MEDICAL GUIDE,
For the use of the Clergy, Heads of Families, Seminaries, and Junior Practitioners in Medicine ; comprising a complete Modern Dispensatory, and a Practical Treatise on the Distinguishing Symptoms, Causes, Prevention, Cure and Palliation, of the Diseases incident to the
Human Frame. By R. REECE, M.D. 16th Edition. 8vo. 12s. boards.

REID (DR.)—ILLUSTRATIONS OF THE PRINCIPLES AND
PRACTICE of WARMING and VENTILATING, with Preliminary Remarks on Health and
Length of Life. By D. B. REID, M.D. F.R.S.E. 8vo. with Diagrams and Woodcuts, 16s. cloth.

REPTON.—THE LANDSCAPE GARDENING & LANDSCAPE
ARCHITECTURE of the late HUMPHRY REPTON, Esq. ; being his entire works on these
subjects. New Edition, with an historical and scientific Introduction, a systematic Analysis,
a Biographical Notice, Notes, and a copious alphabetical Index. By J. C. LOUDON, F.L.S. &c.
8vo. with 250 Engravings, and Portrait, 30s. cloth ; with coloured plates, £3. 6s. cloth.

REYNARD THE FOX :
A renowned Apologue of the Middle Age. Reproduced in Rhyme. Embellished throughout
with Scroll Capitals, in Colours, from Wood-block Letters made expressly for this work, after
Designs of the 12th and 13th Centuries. With an Introduction, by SAMUEL NAYLOR, late
of Queen's College, Oxford. Large square 8vo. 18s. cloth.

RIDDLE.—A COMPLETE ENGLISH-LATIN AND LATIN-
ENGLISH DICTIONARY, compiled from the best sources, chiefly German. By the Rev.
J. E. RIDDLE, M.A. 6th Edition. 8vo. 31s. 6d. cloth.

Separately { The English-Latin Dictionary, 10s. 6d. cloth.
{ The Latin-English Dictionary, 21s. cloth.

RIDDLE.—A DIAMOND LATIN-ENGLISH DICTIONARY.
For the Waistcoat-pocket. A Guide to the Meaning, Quality, and right Accentuation of Latin
Classical Words. By the Rev. J. E. RIDDLE, M.A. New Edition. Royal 32mo. 4s. bound.

RIDDLE.—ECCLESIASTICAL CHRONOLOGY;
Or, Annals of the Christian Church, from its Foundation to the present Time. Containing a
View of General Church History, and the Course of Secular Events ; the Limits of the
Church and its Relations to the State ; Controversies ; Sects and Parties ; Rites,
Institutions, and Discipline ; Ecclesiastical Writers, &c. By the Rev. J. E. RIDDLE, M.A.,
Author of " A Complete Latin Dictionary." 8vo. 15s. cloth.

RIDDLE.—LETTERS FROM AN ABSENT GODFATHER;
Or, a Compendium of Religious Instruction for Young Persons. By the Rev. J. E. RIDDLE,
M.A.; Author of " A Complete Latin Dictionary." Fcp. 8vo. 6s. cloth.

RITCHIE (ROBERT.)—RAILWAYS: THEIR RISE AND
PROGRESS, and CONSTRUCTION. With Remarks on Railway Accidents, and Proposals
for their Prevention. By ROBERT RITCHIE, Esq. F.R.S. S.A. Civil Engineer, Associate of
the Institute of Civil Engineers. Fcp. 8vo. with Woodcuts and Diagrams, 9s. cloth.

RIVERS.—THE ROSE AMATEUR'S GUIDE;
Containing ample Descriptions of all the fine leading varieties of Roses, regularly classed in
their respective Families ; their History and mode of Culture. By T. RIVERS, Jun. 4th Edition,
corrected and improved. Fcp. 8vo. 6s. cloth.
  _ In this edition only the most select varieties are described, both old and new ; those of inferior interest have
been omitted ; and several pages of new matter have been added.

ROBERTS.—A COMPREHENSIVE VIEW OF THE CULTURE
of the VINE under GLASS. By JAMES ROBERTS, Gardener to Matthew Wilson, Esq. Eshton Hall, Skipton, Yorkshire. 12mo. 5s. 6d. cloth.

ROBINSON (JAMES). — THE WHOLE ART OF CURING,
PICKLING, AND SMOKING MEAT AND FISH, both in the British and Foreign Modes. With many useful Miscellaneous Receipts, and full Directions for the Construction of an economical Drying Chimney and Apparatus, on an entirely New Plan. By JAMES ROBINSON, Eighteen Years a Practical Curer. Fcp. 8vo. 4s. 6d. cloth.

ROGERS.—THE VEGETABLE CULTIVATOR;
Containing a plain and accurate Description of all the different Species of Culinary Vegetables, with the most approved Method of Cultivating them by Natural and Artificial Means and the best Modes of Cooking them. Together with a Description of the Physical Herbs in general Use. By J. ROGERS, Author of "The Fruit Cultivator." 2d Edition. Fcp. 8vo. 7s. cloth.

ROGET (P. M.)—THE ECONOMIC CHESS-BOARD;
Being a Chess-Board, provided with a complete set of Chess-Men, for playing Games in Carriages, or Out of Doors, and for folding up, and carrying in the pocket, without disturbing the Game. Invented by P. M. ROGET, M.D. and Registered according to Act of Parliament. New Edition. In a neat foolscap 8vo. case, price 2s. 6d.

. This Chess-Board is peculiarly adapted for working out Chess Problems, and for the study of published Games and Positions.

ROME.—THE HISTORY OF ROME.
(In the Cabinet Cyclopædia.) 2 vols. fcp. 8vo. with Vignette Titles, 12s. cloth.

ROSCOE.—LIVES OF EMINENT BRITISH LAWYERS.
By HENRY ROSCOE, Esq. Fcp. 8vo. with Vignette Title, 6s. cloth.

ROWTON (F.)—THE DEBATER;
Being a Series of complete Debates, Outlines of Debates, and Questions for Discussion; with ample References to the best Sources of Information on each particular Topic. By FREDERIC ROWTON, Lecturer on General Literature. Fcp. 8vo. 6s. cloth.

SANDFORD (REV. JOHN).—PAROCHIALIA.
Or, Church, School, and Parish. By JOHN SANDFORD, B.D. Vicar of Dunchurch, Chaplain to the Lord Bishop of Worcester, and Rural Dean. 8vo. with Woodcuts, 16s. cloth.

SANDFORD.—WOMAN IN HER SOCIAL AND DOMESTIC
CHARACTER. By Mrs. JOHN SANDFORD. 6th Edition. Fcp. 8vo. 6s. cloth.

SANDFORD.—FEMALE IMPROVEMENT.
By Mrs. JOHN SANDFORD. 2d Edition. Fcp. 8vo. 7s. 6d. cloth.

SCHLEIDEN (PROFESSOR).—PRINCIPLES OF SCIENTIFIC
BOTANY. By M. J. SCHLEIDEN, Professor of Botany at Jena. Translated by E. LANKESTER, M.D. F.L.S. 8vo. with numerous Wood Engravings. [*Preparing for publication.*

SCHOPENHAUER.—YOUTHFUL LIFE AND PICTURES OF
TRAVEL : being the Autobiography of JOANNA SCHOPENHAUER. 2 vols. post 8vo.
[*In the press.*

" This lady's life was a varied and eventful one. It was her lot to live through, and partly to witness, some of the greatest events of modern times. She has left a circumstantial and lively account of the scenes of which she was an eye-witness. At Weimar she lived in the closest intimacy with Goethe ; and her house was the resort of the eminent persons who were attracted to that remarkable court."—EDINBURGH REVIEW.

SCOTT.—THE HISTORY OF SCOTLAND.
By Sir WALTER SCOTT, Bart. New edition. 2 vols. fcp. 8vo. with Vignette Titles, 12s. cloth.

SEAWARD.— SIR EDWARD SEAWARD'S NARRATIVE OF
HIS SHIPWRECK, and consequent Discovery of certain Islands in the Caribbean Sea : with a detail of many extraordinary and highly interesting Events in his Life, from 1733 to 1749, as written in his own Diary. Edited by Miss JANE PORTER. 3d Edition, with a New Nautical and Geographical Introduction. 2 vols. post 8vo. 21s. cloth.

SERMON ON THE MOUNT (THE).
Intended for a Birth-day Present, or Gift Book for all Seasons. Printed in Gold and Colours, in the Missal style, with Ornamental Borders by OWEN JONES, Architect, and an illuminated Frontispiece by W. BOXALL, Esq. A New Edition. Fcp. 4to. in a rich brocaded silk cover, 21s.; or bound in morocco, by Hayday, 25s.

SELECT WORKS OF THE BRITISH POETS,

From Ben Jonson to Beattie. With Biographical and Critical Prefaces, by Dr. AIKIN. A New Edition, with Supplement, by LUCY AIKIN ; consisting of additional Selections from more recent Poets. 8vo. 18s. cloth.

SELECT WORKS OF THE BRITISH POETS,

From Chaucer to Withers. With Biographical Sketches, by R. SOUTHEY, LL.D. 8vo. 30s. cloth ; with gilt edges, 31s. 6d.

. The peculiar feature of these two works is, that the Poems are printed entire, without mutilation or abridgment—a feature not possessed by any similar work, and adding obviously to their interest and utility.

SHAKSPEARE, BY BOWDLER.

THE FAMILY SHAKSPEARE; in which nothing is *added* to the Original Text ; but those words and expressions are *omitted* which cannot with propriety be read aloud. By T BOWDLER, Esq. F.R.S. 9th Edition. 8vo. with 36 Engravings on Wood, from designs by Smirke, Howard, and other Artists, 21s. cloth ; or, in 8 vols. 8vo. without Illustrations, £4. 14s. 6d. boards.

SHELDON (F.)—THE MINSTRELSY OF THE ENGLISH

BORDER: being a Collection of Ballads, Ancient, Remodelled, and Original, founded on well-known Border-Legends: with illustrative Notes. By FREDERICK SHELDON. Square post 8vo. 15s. cloth ; morocco, 30s. *(bound by Hayday.)*

SHELLEY, &c.—LIVES OF THE MOST EMINENT LITERARY

MEN OF ITALY, SPAIN, and PORTUGAL. By Mrs. SHELLEY, Sir D. BREWSTER, J. MONTGOMERY, &c. 3 vols. fcp. 8vo. with Vignette Titles, 18s. cloth.

SHELLEY.—LIVES OF MOST EMINENT FRENCH WRITERS.

By Mrs. SHELLEY, and others. 2 vols. fcp. 8vo. with Vignette Titles, 12s. cloth.

SHEPHERD (THE REV. W.)—HORÆ APOSTOLICÆ ;

Or, a Digested Narrative of the Acts and Writings of the Apostles of Jesus Christ. Arranged according to Townsend. By the Rev. WILLIAM SHEPHERD, B.D. Fcp. 8vo. 5s. 6d. cloth.

SHORT WHIST :

Its Rise, Progress, and Laws; with Observations to make any one a Whist Player; containing also the Laws of Piquet, Cassino, Ecarté, Cribbage, Backgammon. By Major A * * * * *. 9th Edition. To which are added, Precepts for Tyros. By Mrs. B****. Fcp. 8vo. 3s cloth.

SINNETT.—THE BYWAYS OF HISTORY.

By Mrs. PERCY SINNETT. 2 vols. post 8vo.   [*In the press.*

SMITH (GEORGE).—PERILOUS TIMES ;

Or, the Aggressions of Antichristian Error on Scriptural Christianity, considered in reference to the Dangers and Duties of Protestants. By GEO. SMITH, F.A.S. &c. Fcp. 8vo. 6s. cloth.

SMITH (GEORGE). — THE RELIGION OF ANCIENT

BRITAIN HISTORICALLY CONSIDERED: or, a Succinct Account of the several Religious Systems which have obtained in this Island from the Earliest Times to the Norman Conquest : including an Investigation into the Early Progress of Error in the Christian Church, the Introduction of the Gospel into Britain, and the State of Religion in England till Popery had gained the ascendancy. By GEORGE SMITH, F.A.S. &c. 2d Edition. 8vo. 7s. 6d. cloth.

SMITH.—THE ENGLISH FLORA.

By Sir JAMES EDWARD SMITH, M.D. F.R.S., late President of the Linnæan Society, &c. 6 vols. 8vo. £3. 12s. boards.
Contents :—Vols. I. to IV. The FLOWERING PLANTS and the FERNS, £2. 8s.
Vol. V. Part 1, 12s.—CRYPTOGAMIA ; comprising the Mosses, Hepaticæ, Lichens, Characeæ, and Algæ. By Sir W. J. HOOKER.
Vol. V. Part 2, 12s.—The FUNGI—completing the work, by Sir J. W. HOOKER, and the Rev. M. J. BERKELEY, F.L.S. &c.

SMITH (S. H.)—THE FEMALE DISCIPLE OF THE FIRST

THREE CENTURIES of the CHRISTIAN ERA : her Trials and her Mission. By Mrs. HENRY SMITH. Fcp. 8vo. 6s. cloth.

SMITH.—COMPENDIUM OF THE ENGLISH FLORA.

By Sir J. E. SMITH. 2d Edit. with Additions, &c. By Sir W. J. HOOKER. 12mo. 7s. 6d. cl.
THE SAME IN LATIN. 5th Edition, 12mo. 7s. 6d.

SMITH.—AN INTRODUCTION TO THE STUDY OF BOTANY.

By Sir J. E. Smith, late President of the Linnean Society. 7th Edition, corrected; in which the object of Smith's "Grammar of Botany" is combined with that of the "Introduction." By Sir William Jackson Hooker, K.H., LL.D., &c. 8vo. with 36 Steel Plates, 16s. cloth; with the Plates coloured, £2. 12s. 6d. cloth.

SMITH (SYDNEY).—SERMONS PREACHED AT ST. PAUL'S

Cathedral, the Foundling Hospital, and several Churches in London; together with others addressed to a Country Congregation. By the late Rev. Sydney Smith, Canon Residentiary of St. Paul's Cathedral. 8vo. 12s. cloth.

SMITH.—THE WORKS OF THE REV. SYDNEY SMITH.

3d Edition, with Additions. 3 vols. 8vo. with Portrait, 36s. cloth.
   •‗• This collection consists of the author's contributions to the Edinburgh Review, Peter Plymley's Letters on the Catholics, and other miscellaneous works.

SOPHOCLES, BY LINWOOD.

SOPHOCLIS TRAGŒDIÆ SUPERSTITES. Recensuit, et brevi adnotatione instruxit Gulielmus Linwood, A.M. Ædis Christi apud Oxonienses Alumnus. 8vo. 16s. cloth.

SOUTHEY'S (ROBERT) COMPLETE POETICAL WORKS;

Containing all the Author's last Introductions and Notes. Complete in one volume, with Portrait and View of the Poet's Residence at Keswick, uniform with Byron's and Moore's Poems. 8vo. 21s. cloth; or 42s. bound in morocco, by Hayday.
Also, an Edition in 10 vols. fcp. 8vo. with Portrait and 19 Plates, £2. 10s. cloth; morocco, £4.10s.

SOUTHEY (ROBERT).—THE DOCTOR, &c.

Vol. VI. From the Papers of the late Robert Southey, LL.D. Edited by his Son-in-Law, the Rev. John Wood Warter. Post 8vo. 10s. 6d. cloth.

SOUTHEY (ROBERT). — THE LATE MR. SOUTHEY'S

COMMON-PLACE BOOK; comprising his Readings and Collections in History, Biography, Manners and Literature, Voyages and Travels, &c. &c.; systematically arranged.
                                             [In the press.

SOUTHEY.—THE LIFE OF WESLEY;

And Rise and Progress of Methodism. By Robert Southey, Esq. LL.D. 3d Edition, with Notes by the late Samuel Taylor Coleridge, Esq., and Remarks on the Life and Character of John Wesley, by the late Alexander Knox, Esq. Edited by the Rev. Charles Cuthbert Southey, A.M. Curate of Cockermouth. 2 vols. 8vo. with 2 Portraits, 28s. cloth.

SOUTHEY, &c.—LIVES OF THE BRITISH ADMIRALS;

With an Introductory View of the Naval History of England. By R. Southey, Esq. and R. Bell, Esq. 5 vols. fcp. 8vo. with Vignette Titles, £1. 10s. cloth.

SPIRIT OF THE WOODS (THE).

By the Author of "The Moral of Flowers." 2d Edition. Royal 8vo. with 23 beautifully-coloured Engravings of the Forest Trees of Great Britain, £1. 11s. 6d. cloth.

STABLE TALK AND TABLE TALK;

or, SPECTACLES for YOUNG SPORTSMEN. By Harry Hieover. 2 vols. 8vo. with Portrait, 24s. cloth.
    "This work will become a great favourite with all persons who are connected with the turf, the chase, and the world of manly sports. It is written in a pleasant, off-hand, dashing manner, and contains an immense variety of information and entertaining matter."—Weekly Dispatch.

STEBBING.—THE HISTORY OF THE CHRISTIAN CHURCH,

from its Foundation to A.D. 1492. By the Rev. H. Stebbing, M.A. &c. 2 vols. fcp. 8vo. with Vignette Titles, 12s. cloth.

STEBBING.—THE HISTORY OF THE REFORMATION.

By the Rev. H. Stebbing. 2 vols. fcp. 8vo. with Vignette Titles, 12s. cloth.

STEEL'S SHIPMASTER'S ASSISTANT:

Compiled for the use of Merchants, Owners and Masters of Ships, Officers of Customs, and all Persons connected with Shipping or Commerce: containing the Law and Local Regulations affecting the Ownership, Charge, and Management of Ships and their Cargoes; together with Notices of other Matters, and all necessary Information for Mariners. New Edition, rewritten throughout. Edited by Graham Willmore, Esq. M.A. Barrister-at-Law;—The Customs and Shipping Department, by George Clements, of the Customs, London, Compiler of "The Customs Guide;—The Exchanges, &c. and Naval Book-keeping, by William Tate, Author of "The Modern Cambist." 8vo. 28s. cloth; or, 29s. bound.

STEEPLETON;

Or, High Church and Low Church. Being the present Tendencies of Parties in the Church, exhibited in the History of Frank Faithful. By a Clergyman. New Edition. Fcp. 8vo. 6s. cloth.

STEPHENS.—A MANUAL OF BRITISH COLEOPTERA;

or, BEETLES: containing a Description of all the Species of Beetles hitherto ascertained to inhabit Great Britain and Ireland, &c. With a Complete Index of the Genera. By J. F. STEPHENS, F.L.S. Author of "Illustrations of Entomology." Post 8vo. 14s. cloth.

SWAINSON.—A PRELIMINARY DISCOURSE ON THE

STUDY OF NATURAL HISTORY. By W. SWAINSON, Esq. Fcp. 8vo. 6s. cloth.

A TREATISE ON THE NATURAL HISTORY AND CLASSIFICATION OF ANIMALS. By W. Swainson, Esq. Fcp. 8vo. 6s.

NATURAL HISTORY AND CLASSIFICATION OF QUADRUPEDS. By W. Swainson, Esq. Fcp. 8vo. with Woodcuts, 6s. cloth.

NATURAL HISTORY AND CLASSIFICATION OF BIRDS. By W. Swainson, Esq. 2 vols. fcp. 8vo. with 300 Woodcuts, 12s. cloth.

HISTORY AND NATURAL ARRANGEMENT OF INSECTS. By W. Swainson, Esq., and W. E. Shuckard, Esq. Fcp. 8vo. 6s. cloth.

ANIMALS IN MENAGERIES. By W. Swainson, Esq. Fcp. 8vo. Vignette Title and numerous Woodcuts, 6s. cloth.

NATURAL HISTORY AND CLASSIFICATION OF FISH, AMPHIBIANS, AND REPTILES. By W. Swainson, Esq. 2 vols. fcp. 8vo. 12s.

HABITS AND INSTINCTS OF ANIMALS. By W. Swainson, Esq. Fcp. 8vo. with Vignette and numerous Woodcuts, 6s. cloth.

A TREATISE ON MALACOLOGY; or, the Natural Classification of Shells and Shell-fish. By W. Swainson, Esq. Fcp. 8vo. 6s. cloth.

A TREATISE ON TAXIDERMY; with the Biography of Zoologists, and Notices of their Works. By W. Swainson, Esq. Fcp. 8vo. 6s.

SWITZERLAND.—THE HISTORY OF SWITZERLAND.

(In the Cabinet Cyclopædia.) Fcp. 8vo. with Vignette Title, 6s. cloth.

SYMONDS.—THE LAW RELATING TO MERCHANT SEAMEN,

Arranged chiefly for the Use of Masters and Officers in the Merchant Service. With an Appendix, containing the Act 7 and 8 Vic. c. 112 ; the Regulations under which Lascars may be employed; and some forms of Proceedings before Magistrates. By E. W. SYMONDS, Esq. Chief Clerk to the Thames Police Court. 3d Edition. 12mo. 5s. cloth.

TATE.—HORATIUS RESTITUTUS;

Or, the Books of Horace arranged in Chronological Order, according to the Scheme of Dr. Bentley, from the Text of Gesner, corrected a.... ..proved. With a Preliminary Dissertation, very much enlarged, on the Chronology of the Works, on the Localities, and on the Life and Character of that Poet. By the Rev. JAMES TATE, M.A. 2d Edition. 8vo. 12s. cloth.

TATE.—THE CONTINUOUS HISTORY OF THE LIFE AND

WRITINGS OF ST. PAUL, on the basis of the Acts; with Intercalary Matter of Sacred Narrative, supplied from the Epistles, and elucidated in occasional Dissertations: with the Horæ Paulinæ of Dr. Paley, in a more correct edition, subjoined. By JAMES TATE, M.A. Canon Residentiary of St. Paul's. 8vo. with Map, 13s. cloth.

TAYLER (REV. CHARLES B.)—MARGARET;

Or, the Pearl. By the Rev. CHARLES B. TAYLER, M.A. Rector of St. Peter's, Chester, Author of "May You Like It," "Records of a Good Man's Life," &c. 2d Edition. Fcp. 8vo. 6s. cloth.

TAYLER (REV. CHARLES B.)—LADY MARY;

Or, Not of the World. By the Rev. CHARLES B. TAYLER, Rector of St. Peter's, Chester; Author of "Margaret, or the Pearl," &c. Fcp. 8vo. 6s. 6d. cloth.

TAYLER (REV. C. B.)—TRACTARIANISM NOT OF GOD:

Sermons. By the Rev. C. B. TAYLER, M.A. Rector of St. Peter's, and Evening Lecturer of St. Mary's, Chester; Author of "Records of a Good Man's Life," &c. Fcp. 8vo. 6s. cloth.

TAYLER (REV. C. B.)—DORA MELDER;

A Story of Alsace. By META SANDER. A Translation. Edited by the Rev. C. B. Tayler, Author of "Records of a Good Man's Life," &c. Fcp. 8vo. with two Illustrations, 7s. cloth.

TAYLOR (JEREMY).—BISHOP JEREMY TAYLOR'S WORKS.

With the References verified. A New and thoroughly-revised Edition.

*** This Work is in the hands of a competent Editor at Oxford, and will be published in volumes, price 10s. 6d. each ; to be completed in 12 volumes, each of 600 closely-printed pages, published at intervals of two months. The first volume will probably be published in May, 1847. Subscribers' Names received by the Proprietors, and all Booksellers.

THIRLWALL.—THE HISTORY OF GREECE.

By the Right Rev. the LORD BISHOP OF ST. DAVID'S (the Rev. Connop Thirlwall). A New Edition, revised ; with Notes. Vols. I. to III. 8vo. with Maps, 36s. cloth. To be completed in 8 volumes, price 12s. each. [Vol. IV. is nearly ready.

*** Also, an Edition in 8 vols. fcp. 8vo. with Vignette Titles, £2. 8s. cloth.

THOMSON'S SEASONS.

Edited by BOLTON CORNEY, Esq. Illustrated with Seventy-seven Designs drawn on Wood, by Members of the Etching Club. Engraved by Thompson and other eminent Engravers. Square crown 8vo. uniform with "Goldsmith's Poems," 21s. cloth; or, bound in morocco, by Hayday, 36s.

THOMSON.—THE DOMESTIC MANAGEMENT OF THE SICK

ROOM, necessary, in Aid of Medical Treatment, for the Cure of Diseases. By ANTHONY TODD THOMSON, M.D. F.L.S. &c. 2d Edition. Post 8vo. 10s. 6d. cloth.

THOMSON (JOHN).—TABLES OF INTEREST,

At Three, Four, Four-and-a-Half, and Five per Cent., from One Pound to Ten Thousand, and from One to Three Hundred and Sixty-five Days, in a regular progression of single Days; with Interest at all the above Rates, from One to Twelve Months, and from One to Ten Years. Also, numerous other Tables of Exchanges, Time, and Discounts. By JOHN THOMSON, Accountant in Edinburgh. 12mo. 8s. bound.

THOMSON.—EXPERIMENTAL RESEARCHES ON THE FOOD

of ANIMALS and the FATTENING of CATTLE: with Remarks on the Food of Man. By ROBERT DUNDAS THOMSON, M.D. of the University of Glasgow. Fcp. 8vo. 5s. cloth.

THORNTON (W.T.)—OVER-POPULATION AND ITS REMEDY;

Or, an Enquiry into the Extent and Causes of the Distress prevailing among the Labouring Classes of the British Islands, and into the Means of Remedying it. By WILLIAM THOMAS THORNTON. 8vo. 10s. 6d. cloth.

"We look upon this as one of the most important books that has appeared for many years. It is the work of an acute and comprehensive thinker, who speaks not only out of the abundance of the heart, but out of the fulness of the understanding."—MORNING CHRONICLE.

TISCHENDORF.—CONSTANTINE TISCHENDORF'S TRA-

VELS in the EAST. Translated from the German. 16mo. uniform with the cheap authorised English Translations of the Works of Michelet and Quinet. [In the press.

TOMLINE (BISHOP).—AN INTRODUCTION TO THE STUDY

of the BIBLE: containing Proofs of the Authenticity and Inspiration of the Holy Scriptures; a Summary of the History of the Jews; an Account of the Jewish Sects; and a brief Statement of the Contents of the several Books of the Old and New Testaments. By GEORGE TOMLINE, D.D. F.R.S. 20th Edition Fcp. 8vo. 4s. 6d. cloth.

TOMLINS.—A POPULAR LAW DICTIONARY;

Familiarly explaining the Terms and Nature of English Law; adapted to the comprehension of persons not educated for the legal profession, and affording information peculiarly useful to Magistrates, Merchants, Parochial Officers, and others. By THOMAS EDLYNE TOMLINS, Attorney and Solicitor. Post 8vo. 18s. cloth.

TOOKE.—A HISTORY OF PRICES;

With reference to the Causes of their principal Variations, from 1792 to the Present Time Preceded by a Sketch of the History of the Corn Trade in the last Two Centuries. By THOMAS TOOKE, Esq. F.R.S. 3 vols. 8vo. £2. 8s. cloth.

*** Separately, Vols. 1 and 2, 36s.; Vol. 3, 12s.

TOPHAM.—CHEMISTRY MADE EASY,

For the Use of Agriculturists. By JOHN TOPHAM, A.M. Rector of St. Andrew, St. Mary Witton, and St. Nicholas, Droitwich. 3d Edition. 16mo. 2s. sewed.

TOWNSEND (CHARLES). — THE LIVES OF TWELVE

EMINENT JUDGES of the LAST and of the PRESENT CENTURY. By W. CHARLES TOWNSEND, Esq. A.M. Recorder of Macclesfield; Author of "Memoirs of the House of Commons." 2 vols. 8vo. 28s. cloth.

TREVOR; OR, THE NEW SAINT FRANCIS.

A Tale for the Times. Fcp. 8vo. 6s. cloth.

TROLLOPE (REV. W.)—ANALECTA THEOLOGICA:

A Critical, Philological, and Exegetical Commentary on the New Testament, adapted to the Greek Text: compiled and digested from the most approved sources, British and Foreign, and so arranged as to exhibit the comparative weight of the different Opinions on Disputed Texts. By the Rev. WILLIAM TROLLOPE, M.A. New Edition. 2 vols. 8vo. £1. 12s. cloth.

TURNER.—THE HISTORY OF ENGLAND,

From the Earliest Period to the Death of Elizabeth. By SHARON TURNER, Esq. F.A.S. R.A.S.L. New Editions. 12 vols. 8vo. £8. 3s. cloth.—Or, separately,

THE HISTORY of the ANGLO-SAXONS. 3 vols. 8vo. £2. 5s. boards.
THE HISTORY of ENGLAND during the MIDDLE AGES. 5 vols. 8vo. £3, bds.
THE HISTORY of the REIGN of HENRY VIII. 2 vols. 8vo. 26s. boards.
THE REIGNS of EDWARD VI., MARY, and ELIZABETH. 2 vols. 8vo. 32s. bds.

TURNER.—THE SACRED HISTORY OF THE WORLD,

Philosophically considered. By SHARON TURNER, F.S.A. R.A.S.L. New Edit. 3 vls. 8vo. 42s. cl.

TURNER.—A TREATISE ON THE FOOT OF THE HORSE,

And a New System of Shoeing, by one-sided nailing; and on the Nature, Origin, and Symptoms of the Navicular Joint Lameness, with Preventive and Curative Treatment. By JAMES TURNER, M.R.V.C. Royal 8vo. 7s. 6d. boards.

TURTON'S (DR.) MANUAL OF THE LAND AND FRESH-

WATER SHELLS of the BRITISH ISLANDS. A New Edition, thoroughly revised and with considerable Additions. By JOHN EDWARD GRAY, Keeper of the Zoological Collection in the British Museum. Post 8vo. with Woodcuts, and 12 Coloured Plates 15s. cloth.

TWELVE YEARS AGO.

By the Author of "Letters to my Unknown Friends." Fcp. 8vo. [*Nearly ready*.

TYTLER (PROF.) — PROFESSOR TYTLER'S ELEMENTS

OF GENERAL HISTORY, Ancient and Modern, with Dr. NARES' Continuation. A New Edition, revised and continued to the Death of William IV. 8vo. with 7 Maps, 14s. cloth.

URE.—DICTIONARY OF ARTS, MANUFACTURES, & MINES;

Containing a clear Exposition of their Principles and Practice. By ANDREW URE, M.D. F.R.S. M.G.S. M.A.S. Lond.; M. Acad. N.L. Philad.; S. Ph. Soc. N. Germ. Hanov.; Mulii. &c. &c. 3d Edition, corrected. 8vo. with 1,240 Engravings on Wood, 50s. cloth.—Also, SUPPLEMENT of RECENT IMPROVEMENTS. 2d Edition. 8vo. with Woodcuts, 14s. cloth.

VON ORLICH (CAPT.)—TRAVELS IN INDIA;

Including Scinde and the Punjab, in 1842 and 1843. By Capt. LEOPOLD VON ORLICH. Translated from the German, by H. EVANS LLOYD, Esq. 2 vols. 8vo. with coloured Frontispieces, and numerous Illustrations on Wood, 25s. cloth.

WALFORD (J. E.)—THE LAWS OF THE CUSTOMS,

Compiled by Direction of the Lords Commissioners of Her Majesty's Treasury, and published under the Sanction of the Commissioners of Her Majesty's Customs; with Notes and a General Index. Edited by J. G. WALFORD, Esq. Solicitor for the Customs. 8vo. 10s. 6d. cloth.

WALKER'S PRONOUNCING DICTIONARY OF THE ENGLISH

LANGUAGE, adapted to the present State of Literature and Science. By B. H. SMART, Author of "Theory and Practice of Elocution," &c. 2d Edition. To which are now added, an enlarged Etymological Index; and a Supplement, containing nearly 3000 Words not included in the previous edition of the Dictionary. 8vo. 15s. cloth.

** The Supplement, with the Etymological Index, may be had separately. 8vo. 3s. 6d. swd.

☞ Walker's Pronouncing Dictionary Epitomised, by Smart. New Edition. 16mo. 7s. 6d. cl.

WALKER (GEO.)—CHESS STUDIES;

Comprising One Thousand Games of Chess, as really played by the first Chess Players; forming a complete Encyclopædia of Reference, and presenting the greatest Collection extant of fine specimens of strategy in every stage of the Game. Selected and arranged by GEORGE WALKER, Author of "Chess made Easy," &c. 8vo. 10s. 6d. sewed.

WARDLAW.—DISCOURSES ON THE PRINCIPAL POINTS

OF THE SOCINIAN CONTROVERSY—the Unity of God, and the Trinity of Persons in the Godhead; the Supreme Divinity of Jesus Christ; the Doctrine of the Atonement; the Christian Character, &c. By RALPH WARDLAW, D.D. 5th Edition, 8vo. 15s. cloth.

WATERTON.—ESSAYS ON NATURAL HISTORY,

Chiefly Ornithology. By CHARLES WATERTON, Esq., Author of "Wanderings in South America." With an Autobiography of the Author, and a View of Walton Hall. New Edition. Fcp. 8vo. 8s. cloth.

SECOND SERIES. With Continuation of Mr. WATERTON's Autobiography. New Edition. Fcp. 8vo. with Vignette by T. Creswick, A.R.A. 6s. 6d. cloth.

WATTS (A. A.)—ALARIC WATTS' POETRY AND PAINTING.

LYRICS OF THE HEART; with other Poems. By ALARIC A. WATTS. Illustrated by Forty highly finished Line-Engravings, from the Designs of many of the most celebrated modern Painters, by some of the most eminent Engravers of the age. Square crown 8vo. printed and embellished uniformly with Rogers's "Italy" and "Poems," 31s. 6d. boards; or proof impressions, 63s. boards; proofs before letters, on quarto colombier, India paper, (only 50 copies printed), £5. 5s. [*In the press.*

WEBSTER.—AN ENCYCLOPÆDIA OF DOMESTIC ECONOMY;
Comprising such subjects as are most immediately connected with Housekeeping: as, The Construction of Domestic Edifices, with the modes of Warming, Ventilating, and Lighting them—A description of the various articles of Furniture, with the nature of their Materials—Duties of Servants, &c. &c. &c. By Thomas Webster, F.G.S. &c.; assisted by the late Mrs. Parkes, Author of "Domestic Duties." 8vo. with nearly 1,000 Woodcuts, 50s. cloth.

WEIL (DR. G.)—THE BIBLE, THE KORAN, AND THE
TALMUD; or, Biblical Legends of the Mussulmans, compiled from Arabic Sources, and compared with Jewish Traditions. By Dr. G. Weil, Librarian of the University of Heidelberg, Fellow of the Asiatic Society of Paris, &c. Translated from the German, with Occasional Notes. Post 8vo. 7s. 6d. cloth.

WESTWOOD (J. O.)—AN INTRODUCTION TO THE MODERN
CLASSIFICATION OF INSECTS; founded on the Natural Habits and compounding Organisation of the different Families. By J. O. Westwood, F.L.S. &c. &c. &c. 2 vols. 8vo. with numerous Illustrations, £2. 7s. cloth.

WHITLEY.—THE APPLICATION OF GEOLOGY TO AGRI-
CULTURE, and to the Improvement and Valuation of Land: with the Nature and Properties of Soils, and the Principles of Cultivation. By Nicholas Whitley, Land-Surveyor. 8vo. 7s. 6d. cloth.

WILBERFORCE (W.)—A PRACTICAL VIEW OF THE PRE-
VAILING RELIGIOUS SYSTEMS of PROFESSED CHRISTIANS, in the Higher and Middle Classes in this Country, contrasted with Real Christianity. By Wm. Wilberforce, Esq. M.P. 17th Edition. 8vo. 8s. boards.—20th Edition. Fcp. 8vo. 4s. 6d. cloth.

WILKINSON.—A CATECHISM OF CHURCH HISTORY IN
GENERAL, from the Apostolic Age to the Present Time. To which is added, a Catechism of English Church History; with a Summary of principal Events, in Chronological Order. By the Rev. W. F. Wilkinson, A.M. Theological Tutor of Cheltenham College. Fcp. 8vo. 6s. cloth.

WILLIS (N. P.)—DASHES AT LIFE WITH A FREE PENCIL.
By N. P. Willis, Esq. Author of "Pencillings by the Way," &c. 3 vols. post 8vo. 31s. 6d.

WILLOUGHBY (LADY).—A DIARY,
Purporting to be by the LADY WILLOUGHBY, of the Reign of Charles I.; embracing some Passages of her Domestic History from 1635 to 1648. Produced in the style of the period to which the Diary refers. 5th Edit. Square fcp. 8vo. 8s. boards; or 18s. in morocco by Hayday.

WINTER (J. W.)—THE HORSE IN HEALTH AND DISEASE:
Or, Suggestions on his Natural and General History, Varieties, Conformation, Paces, Age, Soundness, Stabling, Condition, Training, and Shoeing. With a Digest of Veterinary Practice. By James W. Winter. M.R.C.V.S.L. Member of the Association Littéraire d'Egypte, late Veterinary Surgeon to Mehemet Ali and Ibrahim Pasha. 8vo. 10s. 6d. cloth.

WOOD.—A PRACTICAL TREATISE ON RAILROADS,
And Interior Communication in General; containing numerous Experiments on the Powers of the Improved Locomotive Engines, and Tables of the comparative Cost of Conveyance on Canals, Railways, and Turnpike Roads. By Nicholas Wood, Memb. Inst. Civ. Eng. &c. 3d Edition. 8vo. with Plates and Woodcuts, 31s. 6d. cloth.

WOODWARD.—ESSAYS, SERMONS, ETC.
By the Rev. Henry Woodward, A.M. formerly of Corpus Christi College, Oxford; Rector of Fethard, in the Diocese of Cashel. 4th Edition. 2 vols. 12mo. 14s. cloth.
By the same Author,
THE SHUNAMMITE: a Series of Lectures and Reflections on 2 Kings, iv. 2 vols. 12mo. 12s. cloth. Vol. II. separately, 6s. cloth.

ZOOLOGY OF THE VOYAGE OF H.M.SS. EREBUS AND
TERROR. Under the Command of Capt. Sir James Clark Ross, R.N. F.R.S. during the years 1839, 40, 41, 42, 43. Published by Authority of the Lord's Commissioners of the Admiralty. Edited by John Richardson, M.D. F.R.S. &c.; and John Edward Gray, Esq. F.R.S. Parts I. to X. royal 4to. with numerous coloured and plain Plates, 10s. each.

ZUMPT (PROF.)—A GRAMMAR OF THE LATIN LANGUAGE.
By C. G. Zumpt, Ph. D. Professor in the University of Berlin, and Member of the Royal Academy of Berlin. Translated from the Ninth Edition of the original, and adapted for the use of English Students, by L. Schmitz, Ph. D., Rector of the High School of Edinburgh; with many Additions and Corrections communicated by the Author. 8vo. 14s. cloth.

WILSON AND OGILVY, SKINNER STREET, SNOWHILL, LONDON.

CLASSIC TEXTS IN MUSIC EDUCATION

In recent years the social history of music has begun to receive wider attention. In particular, the role of music in educational thought and practice now forms an accepted field for both graduate and post-graduate studies. But original research is often seriously handicapped by a scarcity of source material.

With *Classic Texts in Music Education*, under the authorship and general editorship of Bernarr Rainbow, some of the most seminal and important titles will now be available in facsimile reprint. The addition of an extended Introduction to each volume enables modern scholarship to place the work of earlier teachers and reformers in historical perspective. Those works not in English will normally have page-by-page translations.

First Series: Popular Education

The books in this first series have been chosen to represent important stages in the development of popular music teaching. Thus, Rhau summarises medieval practice; Agricola and Bourgeois record post-Reformation methods; Bathe rejects medieval pedantry. *English Psalmody Prefaces* traces the development of indigenous sol-fa. Rousseau urges simplification; Pestalozzi's disciples synthesise instruction. Glover introduces child-centred music teaching; Curwen perfects Glover's work. Galin and de Berneval represent innovation in France in the first half of the nineteenth century; Turner, Hickson and Mainzer hold an equivalent place in Britain. Hullah defines the first state-sponsored system temporarily eclipsing the work of other teachers in England. Fétis presents the first widely adopted treatise of the Appreciation movement; Langdale and Macpherson herald the spread of the movement to English schools. Hullah and J. S. Curwen each report on visits to observe music teaching in continental schools. Kretzschmar demands and outlines reform in Germany. Borland describes the achievements and aspirations of the widening field of school music in Britain, early in the present century.

At a time when the range and scope of music teaching in schools has increased to present a bewildering array of traditional and experimental techniques, first hand acquaintance with the work of earlier music educators appears valuable in helping to achieve perspective. That such an investigation is interesting in its own right adds considerably to its attraction. The first series of *Classic Texts in Music Education* has been prepared in that joint belief. A second series dealing with Specialist Education is planned.

The following titles are in preparation.
All have introductions by Bernarr Rainbow
and translations where necessary

Georg Rhau *Complete Manual of Practical Music* (*Enchiridion utrisque Musicae practicae*, 1518)

Martin Agricola *First Steps in Music* (*Rudimentum musicae*, 1539)

H. G. Naegeli *The Pestalozzi Method for Instruction in Song* (*Die Pestalozzische Gesangbildunglehre*, 1809)

H. G. Naegeli *Method for Instruction in Song* (*Gesangbildunglehre*, 1810)

E. Jue de Berneval *Music Simplified* (1832)

H. Kretzschmar *Musical Questions of the Day* (*Musikalische Zeitfragen*, 1903)

OTHER BOETHIUS PRESS PUBLICATIONS

Musical Sources

A Fifteenth-Century Song Book
The Turpyn Book of Lute Songs
The Burwell Lute Tutor
The Sampson Lute Book
John Dowland *Lachrimae* (1604)
The Mynshall Lute Book
The Maske of Flowers (1614)
Tallis & Byrd *Cantiones Sacrae* (1575)
The Board Lute Book
Narcissus Marsh's Lyra Viol Book
The Robarts Lute Book
The Brogyntyn Lute Book
The Willoughby Lute Book
Mozart-C minor Piano Concerto K.491
The Harpsicord Master II and III
Use of Sarum 1-Processionale
Anne Brontë's Song Book
Branwell Brontë's Flute Book
The Trumbull Lute Book
The Marsh Lute Book
The Hirsch Lute Book
Tho. Ravenscroft *A Briefe Discourse*
Jane Pickeringe's Lute Book
Thomas Weelkes: Keyboard Music

Boethius Editions

Richard Charteris *A Catalogue of the Printed Books on Music, Printed Music and Music Manuscripts in Archbishop Marsh's Library, Dublin*

Thomas Lupo: The Complete Vocal Music

John Coprario: The Six-part Consorts and Madrigals

Thomas Lupo: The Four-part Consort Music

Mozart/Wilby: Allegro in F, KV Anh. 90 (580b)

Mahler: Serenade for Voice and Wind Instruments

Ramsey: Two Six-part Latin Motets